Beginning C# 5.0 Databases

Second Edition

Vidya Vrat Agarwal

Apress®

Beginning C# 5.0 Databases, Second Edition

Copyright © 2012 by Vidya Vrat Agarwal

This work is subject to copyright. All rights are reserved by the Publisher, whether the whole or part of the material is concerned, specifically the rights of translation, reprinting, reuse o f illustrations, recitation, broadcasti ng, reproduction on microfilms or i n any other physical way, and transmission or i nformation storage and retrieval, electronic adaptation, computer sof tware, or by si milar or d issimilar methodology now known or hereaf ter developed. Exempted from this legal reservation are brief excerpts in connection with reviews or scholarly analysis or material supplied specifically for the purpose of being entered and executed on a computer system, for exclusive use by the purchaser of the work. Duplication of this publication or parts thereof is permitted only under the provisions of the Copyright Law of the Publisher's location, in its current version, and permission for use must always be obtained from Springer. Permissions for use may be obtained through RightsLink at the Copyright Clearance Center. Violations are liable to prosecution under the respective Copyright Law.

ISBN-13 (pbk): 978-1-4302-4260-4

ISBN-13 (electronic): 978-1-4302-4261-1

Trademarked names, logos, an d images may app ear in this book. Rather than us e a trademark s ymbol with every occurrence of a trademarked name, logo, or image we use the names, logos, and images only in an editorial fashion and to the benefit of the trademark owner, with no intention of infringement of the trademark.

The use in this publication of trade names, tr ademarks, service marks, and similar terms, ev en if th ey are not identified as such, is not to be ta ken as an expression of opinion as to whether or not they are subject to proprietary rights.

While the advice and information in this book are believed to be true and accurate at the date of publication, neither the authors nor the editors nor the publisher can accept any legal responsibility for any errors or omissions that may be made. The publisher makes no warranty, express or implied, with respect to the material contained herein.

President and Publisher: Paul Manning
Lead Editor: Jonathan Hassell
Development Editor: Douglas Pundick
Technical Reviewer: Michael Mayberry
Editorial Board: Steve Anglin, Ewan Buckingham, Gary Cornell, Louise Corrigan, Morgan Ertel, Jonathan Gennick, Jonathan Hassell, Robert Hutchinson, Michelle Lowman, James Markham, Matthew Moodie, Jeff Olson, Jeffrey Pepper, Douglas Pundick, Ben Renow-Clarke, Dominic Shakeshaft, Gwenan Spearing, Matt Wade, Tom Welsh
Coordinating Editors: Jessica Belanger, Christine Ricketts
Copy Editor: Kim Wimpsett
Compositor: Bytheway Publishing Services
Indexer: SPi Global
Artist: SPi Global
Cover Designer: Anna Ishchenko

Distributed to the book trade worldwide by Springer Scie nce+Business Media New York, 233 Spring Street, 6th Floor, New York, NY 10013. Phone 1-800-SPRINGER, fax (201) 348-4505, e-mail orders-ny@springer-sbm.com, or visit www.springeronline.com.

For information on translations, please e-mail rights@apress.com, or visit www.apress.com.

Apress and friends of ED book s may be purchased in bulk f or academic, corporate, or promo tional use. eBoo k versions and licenses are also available for most titles. For more information, reference our Special Bulk Sales–eBook Licensing web page at www.apress.com/bulk-sales.

Any source code or other supplementary materials referenced by the author i n this text is av ailable to re aders at www.apress.com. For detailed information about how to locate your book's source code, go to www.apress.com/source-code.

To my sweet daughters, Arshika ("Sparkly") and Vamika ("Pearly"),
and my beautiful beloved and supportive wife, Rupali.
You are all precious in my eyes and honoured and I love you.
—Vidya Vrat Agarwal

Contents at a Glance

iv

Contents

About the Author

Vidya Vrat Agarwal, a Microsoft .NET purist and an MCT, MCPD, MCTS, MCSD.NET, MCAD.NET, and MCSD, works with Lionbridge Technologies (NASDAQ: LIOX), and his business card reads Technical Architect. He is also a lifetime member of the Computer Society of India (CSI). He started working on Microsoft .NET with its beta release. He has contributed as an author and technical reviewer to many books published by Apress.

He lives with his beloved wife, Rupali, and lovely daughters, Vamika ("Pearly") and Arshika ("Sparkly"). He believes that nothing will turn into a reality without them. He is the follower of the concept "No pain, no gain." He blogs at http://Dotnetpassion.blogspot.com. You can reach him at vidya_mct@yahoo.com.

About the Technical Reviewer

 **Michael Mayberry** has been developing software with Microsoft technologies for more than 13 years. Over those years he has consistently adopted new solutions and tools to solve increasingly larger problems.

Michael currently serves as a software architect for a large nonprofit organization in the Dallas–Fort Worth area. He has become an expert in integration, providing solutions that allow new software to interact with existing systems. His experiences range from content management systems to data warehouses to CRM systems.

Michael has always valued team building and sharing his knowledge with others. Recently, he expanded his focus to include writing and reviewing. He has been a technical reviewer for many projects and has coauthored a book.

When he is not working, Michael enjoys spending time with his beautiful wife and four children.

Acknowledgments

I would like to thank my wife, Rupali, for being so understanding, patient, and helpful. I also would like to thank my two little angels, my daughters Arshika ("Sparkly") and Vamika ("Pearly"); you are great kids.

Like my previously authored books, this book is also an outcome of the sacrifices my wife and kids made on daily basis so that I could remain focused.

Rupali, you are an amazing person who is an entrepreneur in the professional world and also managed the home and kids; all my successes are dedicated to you. I am so thankful to God for having the three of you in my life.

I also would like to thank my technical reviewer, Michael Mayberry, who comes with great experience in database programming and helped me refine this work for a better reader experience.

I also would like to thank Christine, Apress project manager, and Douglas, Apress editor, for helping me throughout this book with schedule and editing.

Introduction

Welcome to this book. You have in your hands a book of ready-made solutions to common problems encountered while writing SQL to run against an Oracle database. I've written this book for the person in a hurry who needs to solve a specific problem and then get on with the job. Each recipe addresses a specific problem and presents a solid, working solution to that problem. For those who are interested, each recipe also provides an extended discussion of the solution and sometimes alternative solutions.

Who This Book Is For

If you are an application developer who likes to interact with databases using C#, this book is for you, because it covers programming SQL Server 2012 using C# 5.0. This book does not require or even assume that you have sound knowledge of C# 2.0 or SQL Server 2000 and database concepts. I have covered all the fundamentals that other books assume a reader must have before moving on with the chapters.

This book is a must for any application developer who intends to interact with databases using C# 2012 as the development tool; if this is you, then this book is a must.

How This Book Is Structured

I've split the book into four parts, each covering one broad aspect of building database applications using C# 5.0 and SQL Server 2012 database.

Part 1 deals with understanding the fundamentals of databases.

Part 2 covers the concepts of working with databases and XML.

Part 3 discusses working with data using ADO.NET.

Part 4 is a compendium of special topics and ranges from advanced ADO.NET features to SQL CLR.

Conventions

Throughout the book, I've kept a consistent style for presenting SQL and results. Where a piece of code, a SQL reserved word, or a fragment of SQL appears in the text, it is presented in fixed-width Courier font, such as this (working) example:

```
select * from dual;
```

Where I discuss the syntax and options of SQL commands, I've used a conversational style so you can quickly reach an understanding of the command or technique. This means I haven't duplicated large syntax diagrams that better suit a reference manual.

Downloading the Code

The code for the examples shown in this book is available on the Apress web site, www.apress.com. A link can be found on the book's information page under the Source Code/Downloads tab. This tab is located underneath the Related Titles section of the page.

Contacting the Author

Should you have any questions or comments—or even spot a mistake you think I should know about— you can contact the author at vidya_mct@yahoo.com.

PART I

Understanding Tools and Fundamentals Databases

CHAPTER 1

Getting and Understanding Your Tools

This book is designed to help you learn how to build database-oriented applications with the C# 2012 programming language and the SQL Server 2012 database server application. The development tools used in this book are Microsoft Visual Studio 2012 and Microsoft SQL Server 2012 (code name Denali) Express edition, both of which work with Microsoft .NET Framework 4.5.

Note For the purposes of this book, I'm using the free versions of Visual Studio and SQL Server that are available for download from `http://msdn.microsoft.com`. If you are using the more full-featured versions of these tools, you can still follow along with the examples in this book.

Visual Studio 2012 targets multiple .NET Framework versions by allowing you to build and maintain applications for earlier versions of the .NET Framework, namely, .NET 2.0, .NET 3.0, .NET 3.5, and .NET 4.0, in addition to its native and default support for .NET 4.5. The Visual Studio integrated development environment (IDE) helps developers be productive, and it offers various types of application templates and tools to perform most of the application development activities.

SQL Server is one of the most advanced relational database management systems (RDBMSs) available. SQL Server continues to provide and support the integration of the .NET common language runtime (CLR) into the SQL Server database engine, making it possible to implement database objects using managed code written in a .NET language such as Visual C# .NET or Visual Basic .NET. Besides this, just like previous releases, SQL Server comes with multiple services such as analysis services, data transformation services, reporting services, notification services, Service Broker, Database Mail, PowerShell support, and so on. SQL Server offers one common environment, SQL Server Management Studio (SSMS), for both database developers and database administrators (DBAs).

SQL Server 2012 Express edition is the relational database subset of SQL Server 2012 that provides virtually all the online transaction processing (OLTP) capabilities of SQL Server 2012 Express, that supports databases up to 10GB in size (and up to 32,767 databases per SQL Server 2012 Express instance), and that can handle hundreds of concurrent users.

Now that you know a little about these development tools, you'll learn how to obtain and install them, and you'll learn about the sample databases you'll need to work through the example in this book. This chapter will cover the following:

- Obtaining Visual Studio 2012

- Installing SQL Server 2012 Express

- Troubleshooting the SQL Server service

- Installing the AdventureWorks sample database

Obtaining Visual Studio 2012

This book requires Visual Studio 2012 to be installed on your computer. At the time of this writing, the available version of Visual Studio is Visual Studio 2012 Developer Preview. To find download information about Visual Studio 2012, go to http://msdn.microsoft.com/vstudio.

You can also directly download the installer ISO image files from the MSDN Subscriptions site at http://msdn.microsoft.com. Access the downloadable setup files by clicking the Visual Studio link in the Developer Center; then extract the downloaded file and run Setup.exe.

If you have a setup DVD or CDs of Visual Studio 2012, just put the DVD or CD1 into your computer's disk drive and complete the setup by following the instructions, making sure you have enough disk space on your C drive.

Visual Studio 2012 has various software components, so you need to decide whether you want to install them when installing Visual Studio. The examples in this book require only the C# language component, but you may want to install other languages such as VB .NET, VC++, and F#, and so on, for your future programming needs.

Installing SQL Server 2012 Express

To install SQL Server 2012 Express for the purposes of working through the examples in this book, follow these steps:

1. Go to www.microsoft.com/betaexperience/pd/SQLEXPCTAV2/enus/default.aspx. Decide which version you need based on your CPU architecture, 32-bit or 64-bit, and in the Select Product drop-down, select Express with Tools. Then click Download.

2. The Download Manager will begin. If the Download Manager is not already installed on your computer, then it will prompt you to install it. Click Install.

3. Based on whether you chose the 32-bit or 64-bit version, you will be prompted to save the file SQLEXPRWT_x86_ENU.exe or SQLEXPRWT_x64_ENU.exe, which is the SQL Server 2012 Express setup utility.

4. Save this file to a location on your host computer (such as on your desktop). When the download of the file is complete, click Close.

5. Run the file to begin the installation, and follow the steps to install it.

6. When the Completing the SQL Server Management Setup window appears, click the Finish button.

7. After a successful installation, you will see all the SQL Server components installed in your Start All Programs Microsoft SQL Server 2012 menu. It is important to make sure your SQL Server service is running, so to verify that, you need to invoke the Services list. Go to Start, Run, Services.msc or Control Panel Administrative Tools Services. A Services window will load; scroll down until you see SQL Server service listed, as shown in Figure 1-1.

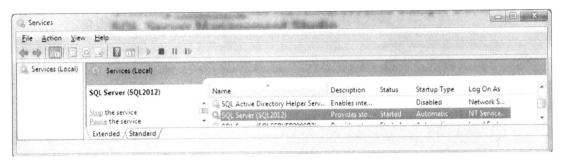

Figure 1-1. Services window showing SQL Server service running

8. Please note the name in the parentheses (your SQL instance name). This might be different from machine to machine; hence, it is important to know the SQL instance name before you connect with it to continue working with SQL Server. If you have multiple versions of SQL Server, then multiple SQL Server Services will be listed, and you will be required to know your SQL Server 2012 instance name that you want to use.

9. If the SQL Server service is not running, then you can manually start it by right-clicking and choosing Start. Your service should be then listed as Started under Status. You must have this service running before you perform any database-related operation.

Again, you need to remember the SQL Server instance name you used during this installation so you can smoothly connect to and build database applications.

Because SQL Server 2012 doesn't come with a sample database, you need to install and configure the sample databases separately. The next section talks about installing and configuring the AdventureWorks databases in SQL Server Management Studio.

Installing and Attaching the AdventureWorks Sample Database

For your database query purposes and in order to build a database application with C#, you need a database. For these purposes, this book will use AdventureWorks for the SQL Server 2012 release.

Installing the AdventureWorks Database

To install the database, follow these steps:

1. Go to http://msftdbprodsamples.codeplex.com/releases/view/4004, and click the link AdventureWorksDB.msi.

2. Click I Agree for the license agreement; you will be prompted to run or save the AdventureWorksDB.msi file to your system.

3. Change the location to save the file; you can keep it anywhere on your computer system, but it is recommended you keep it with the other database files under your SQL Server instance, which will be located at C:\Program Files\Microsoft SQL Server\MSSQL11.<your SQL Server 2012 instance name>\MSSQL\DATA. You can verify the folder name of your SQL instance by

viewing the name in your machine; as shown in Figure 1-1, the name you see in parentheses on your system will be the folder name where you may want to save the database files.

4. If you are not able to find the folder location that maps to the SQL Server instance, you can choose to save the files at any location on your system.

5. After choosing the file location, the setup wizard will bring the AdventureWorks_Data.mdf and AdventureWorks_Log.ldf files to your specified location. Click Finish to close the wizard after the successful installation of the files.

Attaching the AdventureWorks Sample Database

Attach is the process used to associate the .mdf file to the database server so that you can start working with the database objects and data associated with tables.

You need to access SQL Server Management Studio to attach the AdventureWorks2008 database. To do so, follow these steps:

1. Make sure you know your SQL Server instance name through which your SQL Server is running; in my case, it's SQL2012, as you saw in Figure 1-1 earlier. You can check your instance name as described earlier.

2. Open SQL Server Management Studio from your installed SQL Server 2012 application, and in the Connect to Server dialog box, enter **localhost\<your server name >** as the server name (see Figure 1-2). In some cases, you may see *localhost* being replaced by just a dot (.) or real machine name. (You can view the machine name from your computer properties.)

Figure 1-2. Connect to Server dialog

3. As shown in Figure 1-2, set the following options:

   a. Set "Server type" to Database Engine.

   b. Set "Server name" to localhost\<your server name>. For me, as shown in Figure 1-1, the name is SQL2012, so the server name will be localhost\SQL2012. Also note that the server name is not case-sensitive; you can type in any case (lower or upper) you want.

   c. Set Authentication to Windows Authentication. This is the default authentication type SQL Server gets installed with. This indicates that the machine's logged-in user name will be carried over to connect to SQL Server.

   d. Set "User name" to the user credentials by which you want to connect to SQL Server. Many SQL Server databases are installed with Windows Authentication, and hence you will see the same machine's logged-in user name by default added here. In many cases, it might be Administrator or a unique name like you see in Figure 1-2, which is Redmond\v-vidyag.

4. Click the Connect button, and you will be taken to SQL Server Management Studio, which will look something like Figure 1-3.

Figure 1-3. *SQL Server Management Studio after successful connection to SQL Server database engine*

5. If instead of having a window as shown in Figure 1-3 you get an error after clicking the Connect button in the Connect to Server dialog, it will look like Figure 1-4.

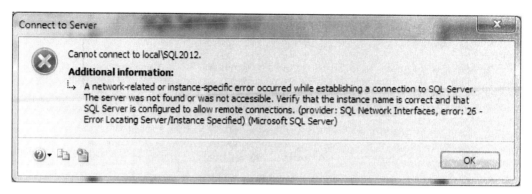

Figure 1-4. Error while connecting to server

You may receive this error for a few reasons:

- The SQL Server service instance name (in this example it is SQL2012) you provided is not running.

- The machine name you used to specify the SQL instance is not correct. The error shown in Figure 1-3 says I used "local\SQ2012" as "machine name\instance name," which is incorrect unless that machine name is really local (in which case the SQL Server instance name is not correct).

1. To fix the error, specify the correct parameter, check that the SQL Server service is started, or pass the correct machine name.

2. Once you have successfully loaded SSMS, the next step is to attach the sample database AdventureWorks2008R2, which you have already downloaded. To do so, right-click the Databases node and select Attach, as shown in Figure 1-5.

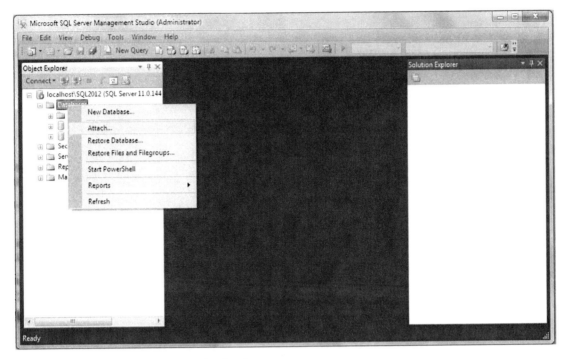

Figure 1-5. Preparing for attaching the databasse

3.   Click the Attach option, and the Attach Databases dialog will appear, as shown in Figure 1-6.

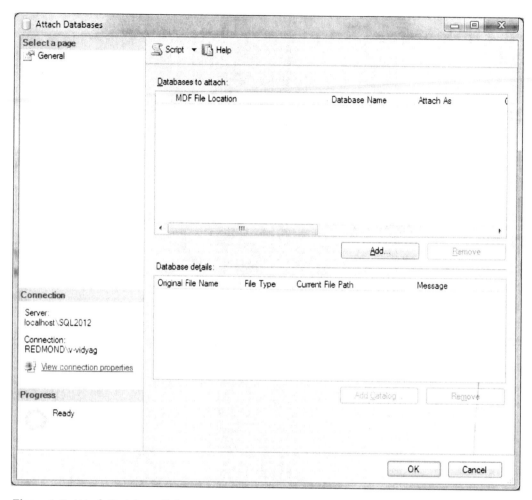

Figure 1-6. Attach Database dialog

4. Click Add, which will open a window to provide the `.mdf` file for the database, as shown in Figure 1-7.

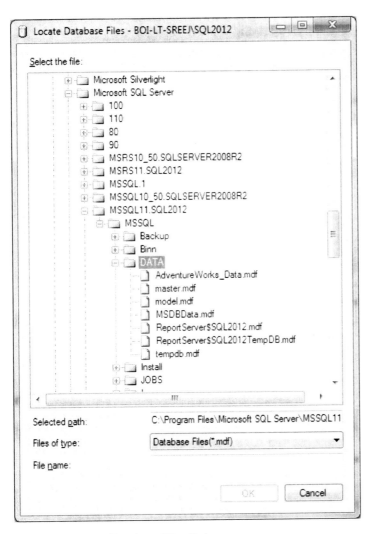

Figure 1-7. Locate Database Files dialog

5. As you can see, I am taken to the DATA folder of the SQL2012 instance of SQL Server 2012, because this is what I connected with. You can also see the AdventureWorks2008_Data.mdf file listed under DATA, because I saved it at this location.

6. Select AdventureWorks2008_Data.mdf, and click OK; you will see a screen like the one shown in Figure 1-8.

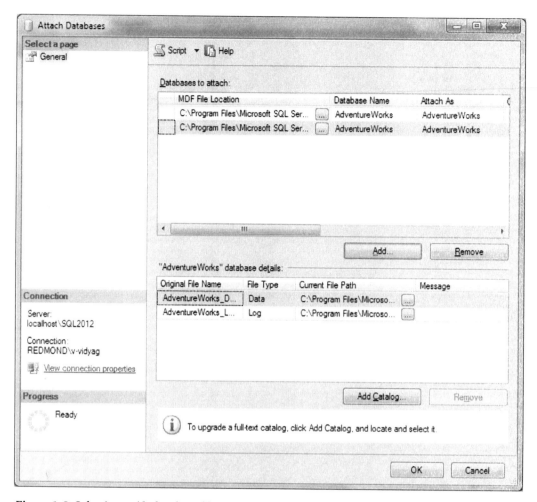

Figure 1-8. Selecting .mdf database files to attach the database

7. As you can see, both the files data and log are selected; click OK. If you're asked
    to confirm that you have added full-text catalogs, click OK; this will let you
    proceed with the database-attaching process, and a window will open that
    says "Executing," as shown on the bottom left of Figure 1-9.

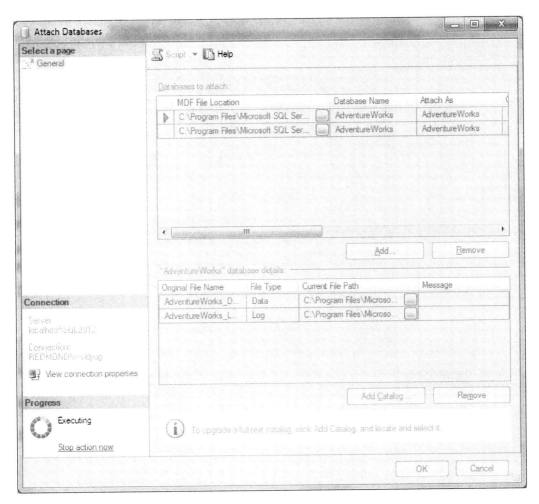

Figure 1-9. Attaching database in progress

8. Once this process of execution is complete, you will be able to see AdventureWorks listed under the Databases node in SQL Server Management Studio, as shown in Figure 1-10.

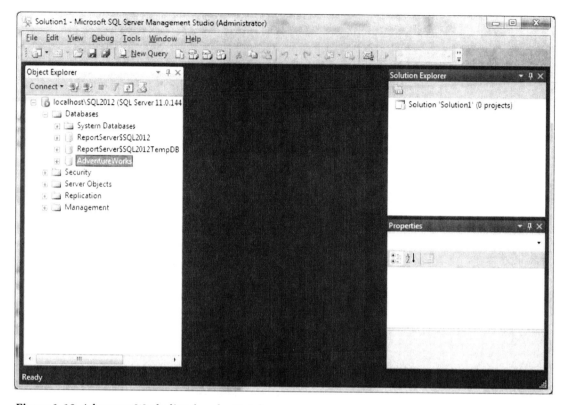

Figure 1-10. AdventureWorks listed under Databases

Summary

In this chapter, you prepared your development environment by installing Visual Studio 2012, SQL Server 2012, and the sample AdventureWorks database. You also used SQL Server Management Studio to attach the AdventureWorks database in SQL Server 2012.

Now that you have your tools, it's time to get acquainted with them.

CHAPTER 2

Understanding Relational Databases

Now that you have gotten to know the tools you'll use in this book, I'll step back a bit and briefly introduce the important fundamental concepts of the database world.

In this chapter, I'll cover the following:

- What is a database?

- Choosing between a spreadsheet and a database

- Why use a database?

- Benefits of using a relational database management system

- Comparing desktop and server RDBMS systems

- The database life cycle

- Mapping cardinalities

- Understanding keys

- Understanding data integrity

- Normalization concepts

- Drawbacks of normalization

What Is a Database?

In very simple terms, a *database* is a collection of structured information. Databases are designed specifically to manage large bodies of information, and they store data in an organized and structured manner that makes it easy for users to manage and retrieve that data when required.

A *database management system* (DBMS) is a software program that enables users to create and maintain databases. A DBMS also allows users to write queries for an individual database to perform required actions such as retrieving data, modifying data, deleting data, and so forth.

DBMSs support *tables* (aka *relations* or *entities)* to store data in *rows* (aka *records* or *tuples)* and *columns* (aka *fields* or *attributes*), similar to how data appears in a spreadsheet application.

A *relational database management system* (RDBMS) is a type of DBMS that stores information in the form of related tables. RDBMS is based on the *relational model.*

Choosing Between a Spreadsheet and a Database

If databases are much like spreadsheets, why do people still use database applications? A database is designed to perform the following actions in an easier and more productive manner than a spreadsheet application would require:

- Retrieve all records that match particular criteria

- Update or modify a complete set of records at one time

- Extract values from records distributed among multiple tables

Why Use a Database?

The following are some of the reasons why you would use databases:

- *Compactness*: Databases help you maintain large amounts of data and thus completely replace voluminous paper files.

- *Speed*: Searches for a particular piece of data or information in a database are much faster than sorting through piles of paper.

- *Less drudgery*: It is a dull work to maintain files by hand; using a database completely eliminates such maintenance.

- *Currency*: Database systems can easily be updated and so provide accurate information all the time and on demand.

Benefits of Using a Relational Database Management System

RDBMSs offer various benefits by controlling the following:

- *Redundancy*: RDBMSs prevent you from having duplicate copies of the same data, which takes up disk space unnecessarily.

- *Inconsistency*: Each redundant set of data may no longer agree with other sets of the same data. When an RDBMS removes redundancy, inconsistency cannot occur.

- *Data integrity*: Data values stored in the database must satisfy certain types of consistency constraints. (I'll discuss this benefit in more detail in the section "Understanding Data Integrity" later in this chapter.)

- *Data atomicity*: In event of a failure, data is restored to the consistent state it existed in prior to the failure. For example, fund transfer activity must be atomic. (I'll cover the fund transfer activity and atomicity in more detail in Chapter 6.)

- *Access anomalies*: RDBMSs prevent more than one user from updating the same data simultaneously; such concurrent updates may result in inconsistent data.

- *Data security*: Not every user of the database system should be able to access all the data. Security refers to the protection of data against any unauthorized access.

- *Transaction processing*: A transaction is a sequence of database operations that represents a logical unit of work. In RDBMSs, a transaction either commits all the changes or rolls back all the actions performed until the point at which the failure occurred.

- *Recovery*: Recovery features ensure that data is reorganized into a consistent state after a transaction fails.

- *Storage management*: RDBMSs provide a mechanism for data storage management. The internal schema defines how data should be stored.

Comparing Desktop and Server RDBMS Systems

In the industry today, you'll mainly work with two types of databases: desktop databases and server databases. Here, I'll give you a brief look at each of them.

Desktop Databases

Desktop databases are designed to serve a limited number of users and run on desktop PCs, and they offer a less-expansive solution wherever a database is required. Chances are you have worked with a desktop database program; Microsoft SQL Server Express, Microsoft Access, Microsoft FoxPro, FileMaker Pro, Paradox, and Lotus are all desktop database solutions.

Desktop databases differ from server databases in the following ways:

- *Less expensive*: Most desktop solutions are available for just a few hundred dollars. In fact, if you own a licensed version of Microsoft Office Professional, you're already a licensed owner of Microsoft Access, which is one of the most commonly and widely used desktop database programs around.

- *User friendly*: Desktop databases are quite user friendly and easy to work with, because they do not require complex SQL queries to perform database operations (although some desktop databases also support SQL syntax if you want to write code). Desktop databases generally offer an easy-to-use graphical user interface.

Server Databases

Server databases are specifically designed to serve multiple users at a time and offer features that allow you to manage large amounts of data very efficiently by serving multiple user requests simultaneously. Well-known examples of server databases include Microsoft SQL Server, Oracle, Sybase, and DB2. For the purpose of building database applications in this book, we will use SQL Server 2012 as the database application. Once you have learned how to build an application with a certain database, it is not difficult to build your application against other databases as well.

The following are some other characteristics that differentiate server databases from their desktop counterparts:

- *Flexibility*: Server databases are designed to be very flexible and support multiple platforms, respond to requests coming from multiple database users, and perform any database management task with optimum speed.

- *Availability*: Server databases are intended for enterprises, so they need to be available 24/7. To be available all the time, server databases come with some high-availability features, such as mirroring and log shipping.

- *Performance*: Server databases usually have huge hardware support, so servers running these databases have large amounts of RAM and multiple CPUs. This is why server databases support rich infrastructure and give optimum performance.

- *Scalability*: This property allows a server database to expand its ability to process and store records even if it has grown tremendously.

The Database Life Cycle

The database life cycle defines the complete process from conception to implementation. The development and implementation processes of this cycle can be divided into small phases; only after completing each phase can you move on to the next.

Before getting into the development of any system, you need to have strong a life-cycle model to follow. The model must have all the phases defined in the proper sequence, which will help the development team build the system with fewer problems and full functionality as expected.

The database life cycle consists of the following stages, from the basic steps involved in designing a global schema of the database to database implementation and maintenance:

- *Requirements analysis*: Requirements need to be determined before you can begin design and implementation. The requirements can be gathered by interviewing both the producer and the user of the data; this process helps in creating a formal requirement specification.

- *Logical design*: After requirements gathering, data and relationships need to be defined using a conceptual data modeling technique such as an entity-relationship (ER) diagram. This diagram shows how one object will connect to the other one and by what relationship (one-one or one-many). Relationships are explained later in this chapter.

- *Physical design*: Once the logical design is in place, the next step is to produce the physical structure for the database. The physical design phase involves creating tables and selecting indexes. An introduction to indexes is out of this book's scope, but an index is basically like an index of a book, which allows you to jump to a particular page based on the topic of your choice and helps you avoid shuffling all the pages of the book to reach the page of interest. Database indexes do something similar; they manage and maintain the order of rows when inserted into the table, which helps SQL queries pull data fast based on a provided value for the index column.

  Database implementation: Once the design is completed, the database can be created through the implementation of formal schema using the data definition language (DDL) of the RDBMS. The DDL consists of the statements that play key roles in creating, modifying, and deleting the database or database objects. CREATE, ALTER, and DROP are prime examples of a DDL.

- *Data modification*: A data modification language (DML) can be used to query and update the database as well as set up indexes and establish constraints such as referential integrity. A DML consists of the statements that play key roles in inserting, updating and deleting the data from database tables. INSERT, UPDATE, and DELETE are prime examples of a DDL.

- *Database monitoring*: As the database begins operation, monitoring indicates whether performance requirements are being met; if they are not, modifications should be made to improve database performance. Thus, the database life cycle continues with monitoring, redesign, and modification.

Mapping Cardinalities

Tables are the fundamental components of a relational database. In fact, both data and relationships are stored simply as data in tables. Tables are composed of rows and columns. Each column represents a piece of information.

Mapping cardinalities, or *cardinality ratios*, express the number of entities to which another entity can be associated via a relationship set. *Cardinality* refers to the uniqueness of data values contained in a particular column of a database table. The term *relational database* refers to the fact that different tables quite often contain related data. For example, one sales rep in a company may take many orders, which were placed by many customers. The products ordered may come from different suppliers, and chances are that each supplier can supply more than one product. All of these relationships exist in almost every database and can be classified as follows:

One-to-one (1:1): For each row in Table A, there is at most only one related row in Table B, and vice versa. This relationship is typically used to separate data by frequency of use to optimally organize data physically. For example, one department can have only one department head.

One-to-many (1:M): For each row in Table A, there can be zero or more related rows in Table B; but for each row in Table B, there is at most one row in Table A. This is the most common relationship. Figure 2-1 shows an example of a one-to-many relationship of tables in Northwind. Note the Customers table has a CustomerID field as the *primary key* (indicated by the key symbol on the left), which has a relation with the CustomerID field of the Orders table; CustomerID is considered *a foreign key* in the Orders table. The link shown between the Customers and Orders tables indicates a one-to-many relationship, because many orders can belong to one customer. Here, Customers is referred to as the *parent* table, and Orders is the *child* table in the relationship.

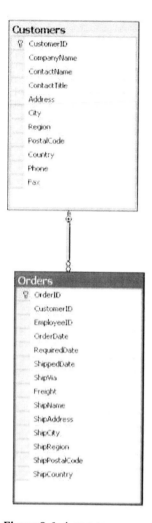

Figure 2-1. *A one-to-many relationship*

> *Many-to-many (M:M)*: For each row in Table A, there are zero or more related rows in Table B, and vice versa. Many-to-many relationships are not so easy to achieve, and they require a special technique to implement them. This relationship is actually implemented in a one-many-one format, so it requires a third table (often referred to as a *junction table)* to be introduced in between that serves as the path between the related tables.

This is a very common relationship. Figure 2-2 shows an example from Northwind: an order can have many products, and a product can belong to many orders. The Order Details table not only represents the M:M relationship but also contains data about each particular order-product combination.

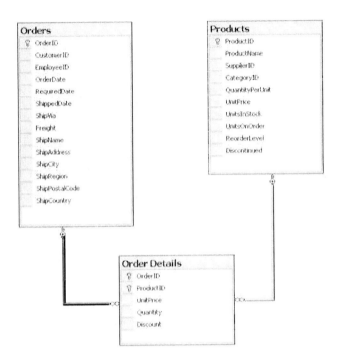

Figure 2-2. *A many-to-many relationship*

▪ **Note** Though relationships among tables are extremely important, the term *relational database* has nothing to do with them. Relational databases are (to varying extents) based on the *relational model of data* invented by Dr. Edgar F. Codd at IBM in the 1970s. Codd based his model on the mathematical (set-theoretic) concept of a *relation.* Relations are sets of tuples that can be manipulated with a well-defined and well-behaved set of mathematical operations—in fact, two sets: *relational algebra* and *relational calculus.* You don't have to know or understand the mathematics to work with relational databases, but if you hear it said that a database is relational because it "relates data," you'll know that whoever said it doesn't understand relational databases.

Understanding Keys

The key, the whole key, and nothing but the key, so help me Codd.

Relationships are represented by data in tables. To establish a relationship between two tables, you need to have data in one table that enables you to find related rows in another table. That's where *keys* come in, and an RDBMS mainly works with two types of keys, as mentioned earlier: primary keys and foreign keys.

A key is one or more columns of a relation that is used to identify a row.

Primary Keys

A primary key is an attribute (column) or combination of attributes (columns) whose values uniquely identify records in an entity.

Before you choose a primary key for an entity, an attribute must have the following properties:

- Each record of the entity must have a not-null value.

- The value must be unique for each record entered into the entity.

- The values must not change or become null during the life of each entity instance.

- There can be only one primary key defined for an entity.

Besides helping in uniquely identifying a record, the primary key also helps in searching records because an index automatically gets generated as you assign a primary key to an attribute.

An entity will have more than one attribute that can serve as a primary key. Any key or minimum set of keys that could be a primary key is called a *candidate key*. Once candidate keys are identified, choose one, and only one, primary key for each entity.

Sometimes it requires more than one attribute to uniquely identify an entity. A *primary key* that consists of more than one attribute is known as a *composite key*. There can be only one *primary key* in an entity, but a *composite key* can have multiple attributes (in other words, a *primary key* will be defined only once, but it can have up to 16 attributes). The primary key represents the parent entity. Primary keys are usually defined with the IDENTITY property, which allows insertion of an auto-incremented integer value into the table when you insert a row into the table.

When an extra attribute is an identity property and it is added to a column, it is called as *surrogate key*. The value of such columns is generated at runtime right before the record is inserted and then stored into a table.

Foreign Keys

A *foreign key* is an attribute that completes a relationship by identifying the parent entity. Foreign keys provide a method for maintaining integrity in the data (called *referential integrity)* and for navigating between different instances of an entity. Every relationship in the model must be supported by a foreign key. For example, in Figure 2-1 earlier, the Customers and Orders tables have a primary key and foreign key relationship, where the Orders table's CustomerID field is the foreign key having a reference to the CustomerID field, which is the primary key of the Customers table.

Understanding Data Integrity

Data integrity means that data values in a database are correct and consistent. There are two aspects to data integrity: *entity integrity* and *referential integrity.*

Entity Integrity

We mentioned previously in "Primary Keys" that no part of a primary key can be null. This is to guarantee that primary key values exist for all rows. The requirement that primary key values exist and that they are unique is known as *entity integrity* (EI). The DBMS enforces *entity integrity* by not allowing operations (INSERT, UPDATE) to produce an invalid primary key. Any operation that creates a duplicate primary key or one containing nulls is rejected. That is, to establish entity integrity, you need to define primary keys so the DBMS can enforce their uniqueness.

Referential Integrity

Once a relationship is defined between tables with foreign keys, the key data must be managed to maintain the correct relationships, that is, to enforce *referential integrity* (RI). RI requires that all foreign key values in a child table either match primary key values in a parent table or (if permitted) be null. This is also known as satisfying *a foreign key constraint.*

Normalization Concepts

Normalization is a technique for avoiding potential update anomalies, basically by minimizing redundant data in a logical database design. Normalized designs are in a sense "better" designs because they (ideally) keep each data item in only one place. Normalized database designs usually reduce update processing costs but can make query processing more complicated. These trade-offs must be carefully evaluated in terms of the required performance profile of a database. Often, a database design needs to be *denormalized* to adequately meet operational needs.

Normalizing a logical database design involves a set of formal processes to separate the data into multiple, related tables. The result of each process is referred to as a *normal form*. Five normal forms have been identified in theory, but most of the time third normal form (3NF) is as far as you need to go in practice. To be in 3NF, a *relation* (the formal term for what SQL calls a table and the precise concept on which the mathematical theory of normalization rests) must already be in second normal form (2NF), and 2NF requires a relation to be in first normal form (1NF). Let's look briefly at what these normal forms mean:

> *First normal form (1NF)*: In first normal form, all column values are *scalar*, in other words, they have a single value that can't be further decomposed in terms of the data model. For example, although individual characters of a string can be accessed through a procedure that decomposes the string, only the full string is accessible *by name* in SQL, so as far as the data model is concerned, they aren't part of the model. Likewise, for a Managers table with a manager column and a column containing a list of employees in the Employees table who work for a given manager, the manager and the list would be accessible by name, but the individual employees in the list wouldn't be. All relations—and SQL tables—are by definition in 1NF since the lowest level of accessibility (known as the table's *granularity)* is the column level, and column values are scalars in SQL.

> *Second normal form (2NF)*: Second normal form requires that *attributes* (the formal term for SQL columns) that aren't parts of keys *be functionally dependent* on a key that uniquely identifies them. Functional dependence basically means that for a given key value, only one value exists in a table for a column or set of columns. For example, if a table contained employees and their titles and more than one employee could have the same title (very likely), a key that uniquely identified employees wouldn't uniquely identify titles, so the titles wouldn't be functionally dependent on a key of the table. To put the table into 2NF, you'd create a separate table for titles—with its own unique key—and replace the title in the original table with a foreign key to the new table. Note how this reduces data redundancy. The titles themselves now

appear only once in the database. Only their keys appear in other tables, and key data isn't considered redundant (though, of course, it requires columns in other tables and data storage).

Third normal form (3NF): Third normal form extends the concept of functional dependence to *full functional dependence*. Essentially, this means that all nonkey columns in a table are uniquely identified by the whole, not just part of, the primary key. For example, if you revised the hypothetical 1NF Managers-Employees table to have three columns (ManagerName, EmployeeId, and EmployeeName) instead of two and you defined the composite primary key as ManagerName + EmployeeId, the table would be in 2NF (since EmployeeName, the nonkey column, is dependent on the primary key), but it wouldn't be in 3NF (since EmployeeName is uniquely identified by part of the primary key defined as the column named EmployeeId). Creating a separate table for employees and removing EmployeeName from Managers-Employees would put the table into 3NF. Note that even though this table is now normalized to 3NF, the database design is still not as normalized as it should be. Creating another table for managers using an ID shorter than the manager's name, though not required for normalization here, is definitely a better approach and is probably advisable for a real-world database.

Drawbacks of Normalization

Database design is an art more than a technology, and applying normalization wisely is always important. On the other hand, normalization inherently increases the number of tables and therefore the number of operations (called *joins*) required to retrieve data. Because data is not in one table, queries that have a complex join can slow things down. This can cost in the form of CPU usage: the more complex the queries, the more CPU time is required.

Denormalizing one or more tables, by intentionally providing redundant data to reduce the number or complexity of joins to get quicker query response times, may be necessary. With either normalization or denormalization, the goal is to control redundancy so that the database design adequately (and ideally, optimally) supports the actual use of the database.

Summary

This chapter has explained fundamental database concepts. You also learned about desktop and server databases, the stages of the database life cycle, and the types of keys and how they define relationships. You also looked at normalization forms for designing a better database.

In the next chapter, you'll start creating databases and manipulating data and objects.

CHAPTER 3

Creating Database and Tables

When developing applications, you'll often be required to create a database and add tables to it, rather than just using an existing database and table objects. This chapter is about creating a fresh database and then creating the tables that it contains.

In this chapter, I'll cover the following:

- Launching SQL Server Management Studio

- Types of SQL Server databases

- The architecture of a SQL Server database

- Creating a database in a simple way

- Creating a database with your own settings

- Creating tables

Launching SQL Server Management Studio

SQL Server Management Studio (SSMS) has been the main development tool for SQL Server since 2005. You can use SSMS to implement, develop, and administer databases. Of course, because this book is for application developers, our focus will be on development.

As mentioned in Chapter 1, it is important to have your SQL Server services up and running (in other words, started) before you can successfully connect with Database Engine in SSMS and begin creating your own database and tables.

To launch SSMS, select All Programs   Microsoft SQL Server 2012   SQL Server Management Studio. Make sure that the Connect to Server dialog has the correct vales, and then click Connect. This should launch SQL Server Management Studio.

Types of SQL Server Databases

SQL Server has two types of databases: system databases and user databases.

- System databases are those that come preinstalled with all SQL Server versions and support the SQL Server database system when you're performing tasks such as creating, maintaining, and administering databases. They are located under the System Databases folder and are named master, model, msdb, and tempdb, as shown in Figure 3-1.

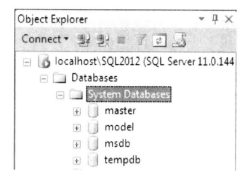

Figure 3-1. SQL Server system databases

Table 3-1 describes each of SQL Server's system databases, as shown in Figure-3-1.

Table 3-1. SQL Server System Databases

Database	Description
master	This is a main controlling database that stores system-level information about users, various configuration settings, and even information about every other database in SQL Server.
model	This is a template database; hence, it has default settings that get applied to all other databases you create.
msdb	SQL Server administration most of the time requires you to perform scheduled jobs. SQL Server Agent (which is also listed in Services.msc below the SQL Server service) is a main consumer of this database.
tempdb	This is a temporary storage dedicated to SQL Server, and it can contain all the temporary objects such as tables, stored procedures, and so on. This can also serve the needs of any other temporary storage requirements that SQL Server might have.

- User databases are those that are either available as sample databases like AdventureWorks (which you downloaded and attached in Chapter 1) or any SQL Server database that has ever been created, anywhere in any SQL Server system, including one you or your organization is building an application upon. Some Microsoft-provided sample databases are pubs, northwind, and AdventureWorks. Since you have already attached AdventureWorks to your SQL Server 2012, it will be listed in Object Explorer, as shown in Figure 3-2.

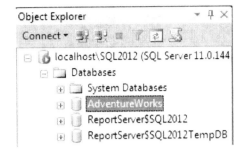

Figure 3-2. SQL Server user databases

Moving onward, the databases you create will be user databases and listed after the System Databases folder. It is worth mentioning here that there is no way you can create your own system database or create a database and put it in the System Databases folder.

The Architecture of a SQL Server Database

SQL Server 2012 databases consist of data and log information. This data and log information is stored in individual files.

- *Primary data file*: This is the main file that constructs a SQL Server database, because it points to other files in the database. The required file extension for this file is .mdf, and a SQL Server database can have only one primary data file.

- *Log data files*: This is the recovery file, which stores all the log information that is used to recover a database in case of failure. The required file extension for this file is .ldf. Any database must consist of at least one log file, but there can be more than one log file in a database.

Note There is a third type of file as well, known as the *secondary data file*, that is also used to store data information, pointed to by primary data file. A database can have multiple data files, and the required extension for a data file is .ndf. Because most of the industrial databases are made of primary and log files, I am not including more details about the secondary one and instead will focus on primary and log files. You may want to learn more about it at http://msdn.microsoft.com.

The fact that each database consists of .mdf and .ldf files applies to system databases as well as user databases. To see this, go to your SQL Server folder under Program Files (see Chapter 1 for information about how to find your SQL Server folder path); once you are at your SQL Server location, you will see the database file. In my case, my SQL folder path shows me the files in Figure 3-3.

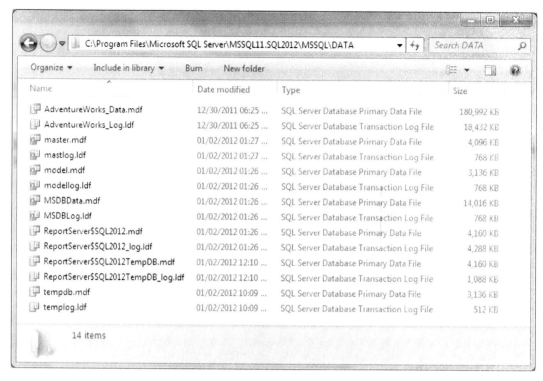

Figure 3-3. *SQL Server database files*

The folder lists all the .mdf and .ldf file names that comprise a SQL Server database, including system and user databases. For example, refer to master.mdf and master.ldf and see these files' description under the Type column to the right. Also, you can see the AdventureWorks database that you attached in Chapter 1 is also listed here with its associated .mdf and .ldf files. Now if you continue to work with this particular instance of SQL Server, all your databases will be under the same location.

■ **Note** Compare the folder structure shown in Figure 3-3 with your folder. It will probably show a different set of databases files, especially for user databases and some SQL Server features like Reporting Services. Hence, the view of your SQL Server system may differ from the figure.

Creating a Database in a Simple Way

To begin creating a database, you need to open SSMS if it's not already open.

Then click New Query, and you should see a window like in Figure 3-4.

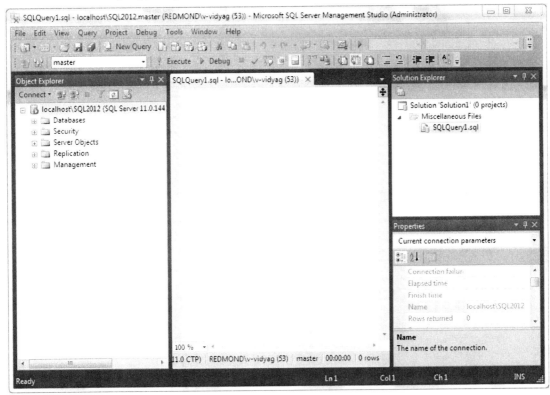

Figure 3-4. *SQL Server Management Studio: New Query pane*

SSMS has a new look and feel in the release of SQL Server 2012; actually, Microsoft has utilized the Visual Studio IDE for SQL Server 2012, so if you have used Visual Studio 2010 before, you will find it similar. If you have not worked with Visual Studio 2010 yet, then you will see the UIs are similar when we start coding for C# using Visual Studio 2012 later in the book.

To create a database in simple way, follow these steps:

1. Make sure your New Query pane shows the master database just below the Save icon on the toolbar.

2. Go to the query pane, and to make sure you are in the master database, type the following:

   ```
   use master
   ```

3. Select the statement, and click Execute or press F5; you should see the message "Command(s) completed successfully."

4. Now press Enter to add a new line, and type the following:

   ```
   create database MySQLDb
   ```

5. In this example, we are creating a new database named MySQLDb. Remember, SQL Server is not case-sensitive, so no matter how you type your SQL statements, they will work just fine.

6. After typing the create statement, select this newly added create statement, and press Execute or F5. When you look at the list of databases under the Databases folder in Object Explorer, you should see the MySQLDb database you just created, as shown in Figure 3-5.

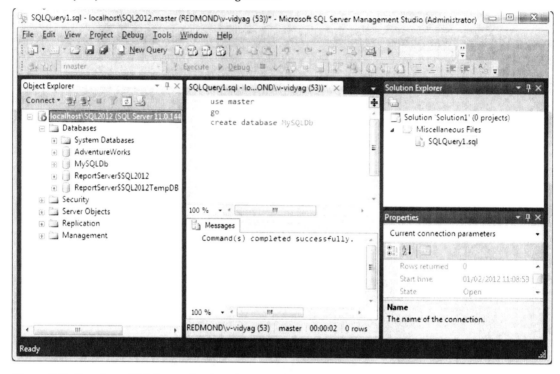

Figure 3-5. Creating a SQL Server database in a simple way

This newly created database will be no different from any other databases in that it will consist of .mdf and .ldf files. By using this one-liner SQL statement…

```
Create Database database-name
```

you have given control to SQL Server to create the files with its own predefined settings on your behalf. But this approach has limitations and restrictions:

- It stores data and log files on the same disk under Program Files\Microsoft SQL Server; what if you want to separate the log file from the data files and put one on another disk or in another folder?

- By default data and log files are given the freedom to continue growing until the disk is full; in other words, they have unrestricted access to disk space. In real-world organizations, it is critical to manage the storage, so a size limitation is given to a database.

Exploring Database Properties

After a database is created, sometimes you will want to know its properties such as its file name, path, size, and so on. Follow these steps to explore the database properties:

1. Right-click the newly created database MySqlDb in Object Explorer, and select Properties.

2. Go to the Files tab on the left side. You will see the settings that SQL Server chooses on your behalf while executing the one-liner database creation statement shown earlier. The Database Properties dialog will look Figure 3-6.

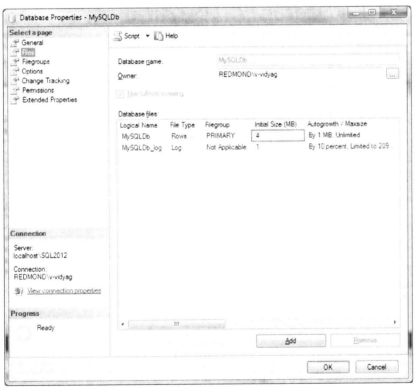

Figure 3-6. *Exploring database properties*

Creating Database with Your Own Settings

Sometimes you want to have control over creating a database so you can control things such as the maximum size a database can grow to, the amount of growth after the initial amount is consumed, or even the location/folder of your data and log files. Table 3-4 shows the arguments you can use.

Table 3-2. Create Database Arguments

Argument Name	Description
Name	This is the logical name of the database file, by which it can be referred to in your SQL Server system.
Filename	This is the physical path where the database files (`.mdf` and `.ldf`) are going to be stored.
Size	This is the initial size you want to create your database with. The size can be in kilobytes, megabytes, gigabytes, or terabytes. If you don't specify any unit by default, it is megabytes. For example, Size = 1 is the same as specifying Size= 1MB.
	One limitation of the Size argument is that it has to be a minimum of 4MB initially so it can accommodate the model database's settings. If you specify a size less than 4MB, then you will receive an error when executing the `create database` statement.
MaxSize	This is the maximum size limit that the database you are creating can grow to. Hence, if you omit this argument, then you are letting SQL Server continue growing your database as long as there is a disk space, in other words, until the disk is full. The MaxSize setting can be in kilobytes, megabytes, gigabytes, or terabytes; the default is megabytes.
FileGrowth	This is the size your database will grow to whenever new space is required to accommodate incoming data. As you recall, Size specifies only the initial allocation of space to begin with. But after that, your database grows dynamically as and when on demand. This can be specified in percentage or in kilobytes, megabytes, gigabytes, or terabytes. The default is megabytes. Also, it's worth knowing that if you don't specify this argument at all, then the default FileGrowth setting is 1MB.

Now let's try the arguments discussed in Table 3-2 in a SQL query syntax to create a database with your argument values. Follow these steps:

1. Make sure your New Query pane shows the master database just below the Save icon on the toolbar.

2. Go to the query pane, and to make sure you are in the master database, type the following:

   ```
   use master
   ```

3. Select the statement, and click Execute or press F5; you should see the message "Command(s) completed successfully."

4.   Now press Enter to add a new line, and type the create database statement, as
     shown here.

■ **Note** Please notice the bold text in the FileName argument in the following code; this represents your SQL
Server 2012 instance name. I suggest you browse to your SQL Server folder location through Windows Explorer, as
shown in Figure 3-3, and then copy and paste the path in the FileName argument.

5.
```
CREATE DATABASE SQL2012Db
ON PRIMARY
( NAME = Sql2012Data,
 FILENAME = 'C:\Program Files\Microsoft SQL
Server\MSSQL11.SQL2012\MSSQL\DATA\Sql2012Data.mdf',
 SIZE = 4MB,
 MAXSIZE = 15MB,
 FILEGROWTH = 20%
)
LOG ON
 (
 NAME = Sql2012Log,
 FILENAME =' C:\Program Files\Microsoft SQL
Server\MSSQL11.SQL2012\MSSQL\DATA\Sql2012Log.ldf',
 SIZE = 1MB,
 MAXSIZE = 5MB,
 FILEGROWTH = 1MB
 )
```

6.   Select the whole statement, and click Execute or press F5.

7.   After successful execution of the statement, select the Databases node in
     Object Explorer, right-click, and select Refresh to list the recently created
     database(s). You should see a list something similar to Figure 3-7.

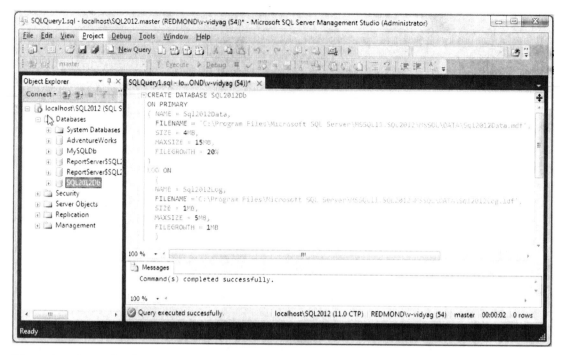

Figure 3-7. Create database statement with arguments

Now you know how to create a database using code, both by using simple techniques and by using arguments, so it's time to learn how to create tables in those databases.

Understanding Table Fundamentals

The database you created earlier will be of no use if there is no table in it, because tables provide the infrastructure for data storage.

Before you start creating a table, you should understand the basics of it. A table consists of columns, and then data is added (*inserted*) into the table as rows. (In relational database theory, a row is also known as a *record* or *tuple*, and a column is known as a *field*.) The type of data that can be entered as a row is defined by the data type of individual columns in the table. Most of the time it becomes obvious what type of data you need to enter; for example, a name will require a string or character data type, whereas an age will require an integer data type.

In addition, it is important to know which column needs a data entry. Null or Not Null keywords specify the data acceptance criteria, in other words, whether you must enter or can skip a column value.

For example, consider you are filling a form for insurance and are asked to enter your first name, followed by your address and SSN. In such a scenario, not everyone will have SSN, but a first name is a must for any individual.

Based on these two columns, you have a business scenario, and this business requirement in terms of a database can be accomplished by specifying the first name column as Not Null and the SSN column as Null while creating a table.

Null means an undefined or unknown value, which means nothing is specified. For example, consider that in the first name field someone filled in blank spaces; technically this is considered information because a blank is a space, which is a character and therefore information.

Similarly, what if a person who didn't have an SSN entered 000-00-0000 as the SSN? This is also not an undefined value because they entered zeros, which are characters and therefore information.

By default a created column allows Null, unless Not Null is specified at the time of column creation explicitly.

SQL Server Data Types for Table Columns

To support business requirements, SQL Server provides various data types (see Table 3-3).

Table 3-3. SQL Server Data Types

Type of Data	SQL Server Data Type
Character data	Char, Varchar, Text
Integer data	int, bigint, smallint, tinyint
Date and time	Datetime, Smalldatetime, Date, Time

Creating a Table in SQL Server

To create a table in SQL Server, you need to establish a context to a database. In other words, you need to get into a database where you want to create your tables. In this chapter, you created two databases: MySqlDb and Sql2012Db. You will use the Sql2012Db database to create tables.

In Object Explorer, expand the Databases node, select the Sql2012Db database, and then click New Query (either in the toolbar or from the context menu); you will see that the Sql2012Db database is selected for this New Query pane you have opened.

In this query pane, type the following code:

```
CREATE TABLE MySqlTable
(
    Name varchar(10) Not Null, --Name value is a must and can't be Null
    Age int,
    SSN varchar(11),
    Date datetime,
    Gender char(6)
)
```

Select the whole create statement, and click Execute or press F5. In Object Explorer, expand the Sql2012Db database where you created this table and then expand the Tables node; you will see the newly created table listed. This is how each database stores the tables inside it.

Also, to investigate the table you created, you can expand it. In the example case, you named it MySqlTable, so expand that, and you will see the Columns node. Expand the Columns node as well, and you will see all the columns you created in the previous create table statement. To help you recall, any field or column that explicitly doesn't include Not Null with its declaration during table creation is Null by default; therefore, except the Name column, all other fields or columns are made Null by SQL Server, which you should be able to see in Figure 3-8.

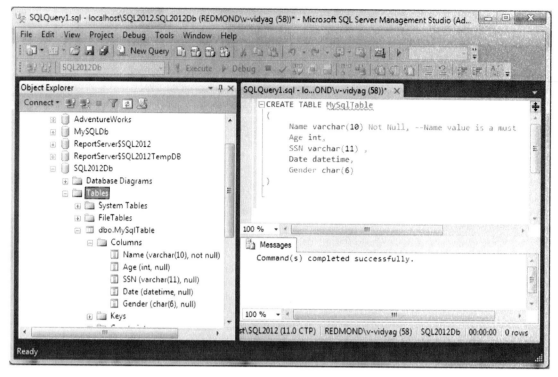

Figure 3-8. The create table statement and Column properties

Adding an IDENTITY Column in a Table

Sometimes developers and database programmers need to create a new column in an existing table. SQL Server provides an ALTER statement to modify/alter the objects that are already created.

In this case, the table you created is missing a column that can help uniquely identify each person, because a name could be common with two people; for example, both might be the same age and gender and without an SSN. In such a scenario, having a column that can uniquely identify each row is a valuable addition, and it's also how all the real-world databases are designed.

The best way to have each person identified with a distinct value or ID is to use SQL Server's IDENTITY property. IDENTITY is an auto-incremented value that is inserted by SQL Server automatically for each inserted row to a table. That is, you are not responsible for specifying the value of the IDENTITY column.

This IDENTITY property requires an Integer type column to be associated with it. The IDENTITY property is used for those columns that need automatically generated unique system values. This property can be used to generate sequential numbers. The syntax for this is IDENTITY (Seed,Increment). Seed is the starting or initial value for the IDENTITY column. Increment is the step value used to generate the next value for column.

For example, int ColumnName IDENTITY(1,1) means the first row will have the value 1, the second row will have 2, and so on. The same IDENTITY property definition can be written as int ColumnName IDENTITY. Hence, IDENTITY and IDENTITY(1,1) are the same.

There are two ways to add this ID column to a table: using the `alter table` statement and dropping and re-creating the table.

ALTER TABLE

Adding an identity key to a precreated column is based on an `alter table` statement. To try it, type the following statement in the query pane, select it, and press Execute.

```
ALTER TABLE MySqlTable
ADD Id int IDENTITY(1,1)
```

This statement will add an Id column to the table. To see this newly added column, you need to refresh the table by selecting it in Object Explorer, right-clicking, and choosing Refresh. Then expand the Table node and the Columns node, and you will see the Id column added to the table, as shown in Figure 3-9.

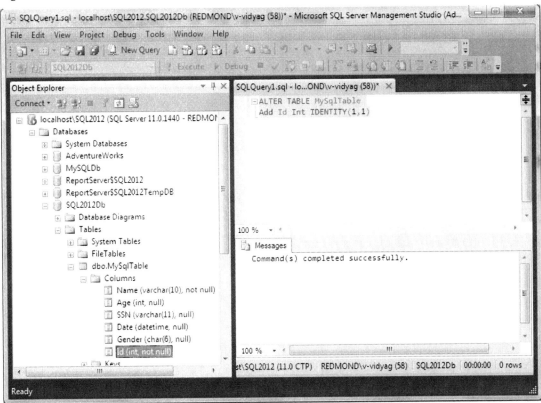

Figure 3-9. Looking at the newly added column to an existing table

So, now you have learned how to add a column to an already created column. The only problem with this approach is that any column you add using ALTER is always added at the very end of the column list, and there is no way you can move or switch its position in any way.

Considering common business situations, Id and similar columns are usually added as the first column in most tables, and if you have a similar desire, then you need to follow a different approach, as explained next.

Drop and Re-create the Table

As stated earlier, if you want to have the Id column as the first column in your table, then you have to define the table from scratch. To do so, you have to drop the table first and then re-create it.

In the query pane, enter the following statement, select it, and press Execute.

```
DROP TABLE MySqlTable
```

This will delete or remove the table permanently; if you select the Tables node in Object Explorer, right-click, and choose Refresh option, you will see that there is no table listed because you just dropped it.

Now, you will re-create the MySqlTable with an IDENTITY column added to the table definition at the time of creation itself, as shown in the following statement:

```
CREATE TABLE MySqlTable
(
    Id int IDENTITY (1,1), --Identity makes the column Not Null internally
    Name varchar(10) Not Null, --Name value is a must and can't be Null
    Age int,
    SSN varchar(11),
    Date datetime,
    Gender char(6)
)
```

Select this create table statement and press Execute; then select the MySqlDb database in Object Explorer, right-click, and choose Refresh. You will see a fresh MySqlTable created and in it is the first column, unlike it was added when you used the alter table statement.

You can also see the column list by expanding the Tables node and then the Columns node, and you will be able to see the list of columns, as shown in Figure 3-10.

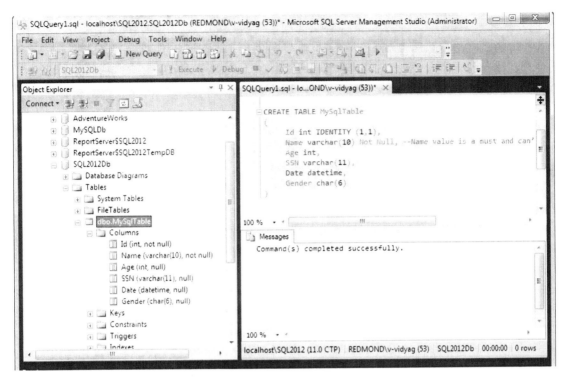

Figure 3-10. Looking at the re-created table and column list

You may want to compare Figures 3-9 and 3-10 to understand the difference, which is achieved by using ALTER and CREATE, respectively.

Summary

This chapter described how to create database and tables. You also learned about techniques to add a column to an already created table through the ALTER statement, which basically modifies a precreated table. You also learned to use the DROP statement, which removes a table object from the database.

In the next chapter, you'll start working with data manipulation concepts.

PART II

Working with Database and XML

CHAPTER 4

Manipulating Database Data

Now that you know how to create databases and tables, it's time to turn your attention to modifying data, such as inserting, updating, and deleting it.

In this chapter, we'll cover the following:

- Inserting data

- Updating data

- Deleting data

Inserting Data

After creating a table, you need to be able to add data such as rows to a table. You do this by using the INSERT statement.

A basic INSERT statement has these parts:

```
INSERT INTO <table>
(<column1>, <column2>, ..., <columnN>)
VALUES (<value1>, <value2>, ..., <valueN>)
```

Using this syntax, let's add a new row to the MySqlTable table of the newly created SQL2012Db database.

Try It: Inserting a New Row

To insert a new row into a table, open a New Query window in SQL Server Management Studio. Enter the following query, and click Execute:

```
Use SQL2012Db
Go
insert into MySqlTable ( Name, Age, SSN, Date, Gender )
   Values('Vidya Vrat',36,'111-20-3456',GetDate(),'Male')
Go
```

Executing this statement in the query pane should produce a Messages window reporting "(1 row(s) affected)," as shown in Figure 4-1.

■ **Note** GetDate() is SQL Server's built-in datetime function that returns the current date and time, so if you use this function, it enters the current date and time into the column.

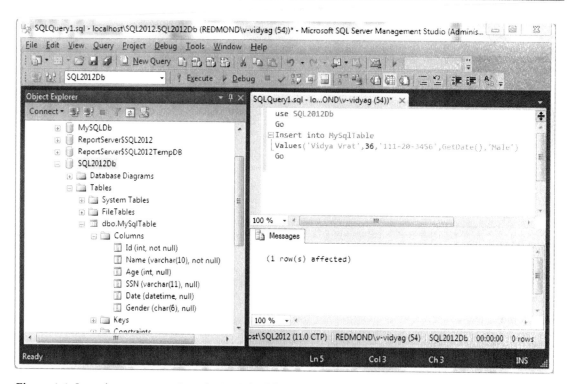

Figure 4-1. Inserting a new row into the MySqlTable table[[kim

How It Works

The first column, ID, is an identity column, and you can't insert values into it explicitly—the SQL Server database engine will make sure that a unique and SQL Server–generated value is inserted for the ID field. So, the INSERT statement needs to be written in such a way that you specify the column list you want to insert values for explicitly; though the MySqlTable contains six fields, ID is an identity column, and it does not expect any value to be inserted from the user. SQL Server can detect an identity column when executing the INSERT statement. However, it is best practice to specify the column list and then pass the respective values to these fields, as shown in the following query:

```
Insert into MySqlTable (Name,Age,SSN,Date,Gender)
Values('Rupali',31,'222-10-6789',GetDate(),'Female')
```

After inserting the row, type the following query in the query pane:

```
Select * from MySqlTable
```

Select the statement, and click Execute or press F5; you'll see that the new rows have been added, as shown in Figure 4-2.

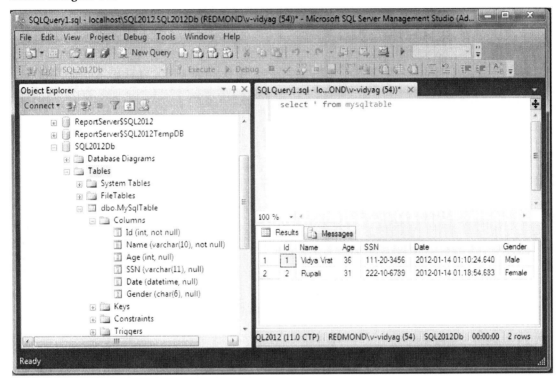

Figure 4-2. *The MySqlTable after adding rows*

Be careful to insert data of the correct data type. In this example, you have seen columns of the character, int, and datetime types.

Inserting Multiple Rows Through a Single INSERT Statement

Typically a single INSERT statement added one row to the table, but since SQL Server 2008, an INSERT statement is capable of adding multiple rows via a single INSERT statement. You just need to separate each row of data with a comma, as shown in the following statement, and then click Execute or press F5.

```
Insert into MySqlTable (Name,Age,SSN,Date,Gender)
Values('Vamika',6,'333-30-1234',GetDate(),'Female'),
       ('Arshika',1,'444-40-5678',GetDate(),'Female')
```

This should show a successful execution, as in Figure 4-3.

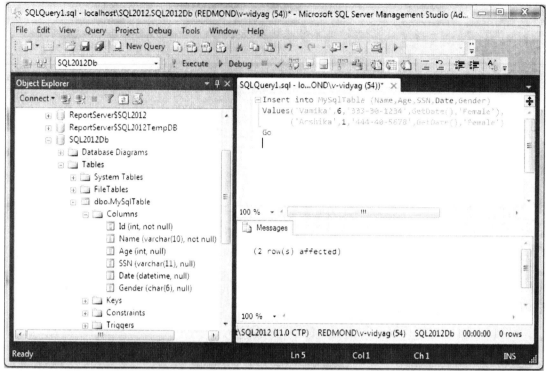

Figure 4-3. Adding multiple rows with a single INSERT statement

Now if you want to execute the following SELECT statement, you should see the four rows with an auto-incremented ID value, going from 1 to 4. In other words, the first record will be 1, and each record inserted after that will be incremented by 1. See Figure 4-4.

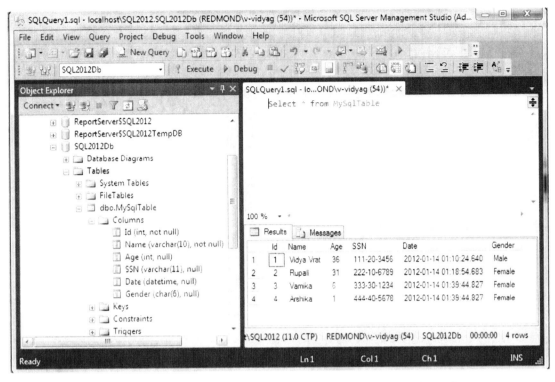

Figure 4-4. SELECT statement showing all the inserted rows with autogenerated ID value

Updating Data

You can modify data with the UPDATE statement. When coding UPDATE statements, you must be careful to include a WHERE clause, or you'll update *all* the rows in a table. So, always code an appropriate WHERE clause; if you miss a WHERE clause, as shown in the following UPDATE statement, then you will change all the records of the table, and I am sure no business case requires that!

```
UPDATE <table>
SET <columnl> = <valuel>, <column2> = <value2>, ..., <columnN> = <valueN>
```

Now that you're aware of the implications of the UPDATE statement, let's take a good look at it. In essence, it's a simple statement that allows you to update values in one or more rows and columns.

```
UPDATE <table>
SET <columnl> = <valuel>, <column2> = <value2>, ..., <columnN> = <valueN>
WHERE <predicate>
```

Try It: Updating a Row

To change a row's value, open a New Query window in SQL Server Management Studio Express. Enter the following query, and click Execute:

```
update MySqlTable
set Name = 'Pearly'
where Id = 3
```

How It Works

The ID is the SQL-generated unique identifier for rows of the MySqlTable table, so you can use it to locate the one row we want to update. Running the query should produce a Messages pane reporting "(1 row(s) affected)." Now if you execute the Select * from MySqlTable statement, you will see the modified records, as shown in Figure 4-5.

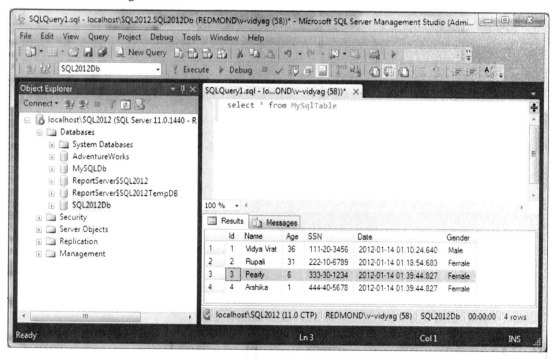

Figure 4-5. *SELECT statement showing modified row after the UPDATE statement*

When you update more than one column, you still use the SET keyword only once, and you separate the column names and their respective values that you want to set with a comma. For example, the following statement would change both the name and the Social Security number of a person we have added to the table:

```
update MySqlTable
set Name = 'Sparkly',
SSN = '444-50-9100'
where Id = 4
```

If you execute Select * from MySqlTable, you would see that the Name and SSN values for person have changed, as shown in Figure 4-6.

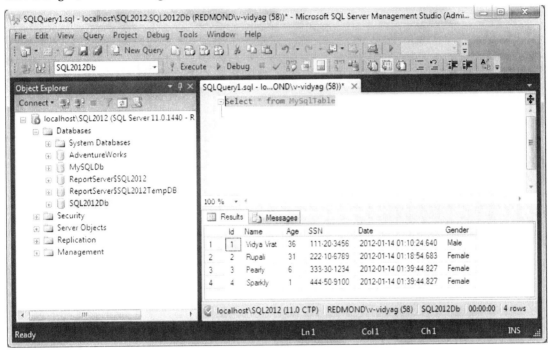

Figure 4-6. SELECT statement showing modified row after UPDATE statement for multiple columns

Deleting Data

To remove data, you use the DELETE statement. The DELETE statement has the same implications as the UPDATE statement. It's all too easy to delete every row (not just the wrong rows) in a table by forgetting the WHERE clause, so be careful. The DELETE statement removes entire rows, so it's not necessary (or possible) to specify columns. Its basic syntax is as follows (remember, the WHERE clause is optional, but without it, all rows will be deleted):

```
DELETE FROM <table>
WHERE <predicate>
```

If you need to remove a record or set of records from the MySqlTable table, then you need to determine the records you want to delete with some unique value like an identity key or primary key, and then you specify this unique value of the row you want to remove with the WHERE condition of the DELETE statement.

```
delete from MySqlTable
where Id = 2
```

This should produce a Messages pane reporting "(1 row(s) affected)." Execute the Select * from MySqlTable statement, and you'll see that the row with an ID of 2 has been removed, as shown in Figure 4-7.

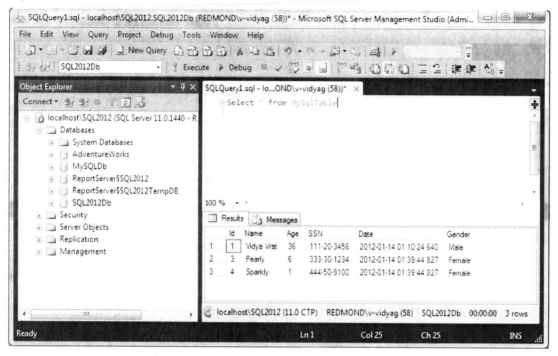

Figure 4-7. SELECT statement showing rows after the DELETE statement

Again, it's important to use the WHERE clause with the DELETE statement; if you specify a DELETE statement without it, then you will delete all the rows of the specified table.

Summary

In this chapter, you learned how to use the following T-SQL keywords to perform data manipulation tasks against a database: INSERT, UPDATE, and DELETE.

In the next chapter, you will learn how to query a database.

CHAPTER 5

Querying Databases

In this chapter, you will learn about coding queries in SQL Server 2012. SQL Server uses T-SQL as its language, and it has a wide variety of functions and constructs for querying. You will see how to use SQL Server Management Studio and the AdventureWorks database to submit queries for various scenarios of querying data. This chapter covers the following:

- Retrieving data
- Using the GROUP BY clause
- Pattern matching
- Using aggregate functions
- Using DATETIME functions
- Using the list operator
- Using the range operator
- Finding null values
- Using joins

Retrieving Data

A SQL query retrieves data from a database. Data is stored as *rows* in *tables*. Rows are composed of *columns*. In its simplest form, a query consists of two parts:

- A SELECT list, where the columns to be retrieved are specified
- A FROM clause, where the table or tables to be accessed are specified

■ **Tip** I've written SELECT and FROM in capital letters simply to indicate they're SQL keywords. SQL isn't case-sensitive, and keywords are typically written in lowercase in code. In T-SQL, queries are called SELECT statements, but the ISO/ANSI standard clearly distinguishes "queries" from "statements." The distinction is conceptually important. A *query* is an operation on a table that produces a table as a result; *statements* may (or may not) operate on tables and don't produce tables as results. Furthermore, *subqueries* can be used in both queries and statements. So, we'll typically call queries *queries* instead of SELECT statements. Call queries whatever you prefer, but keep in mind that queries are a special feature of SQL.

Using two keywords, SELECT and FROM, here's the simplest possible query that will get all the data from the specified table:

```
Select * from <table name>
```

The asterisk (*) means you want to select all the columns in the table.

You will be using an instance of SQL Server 2012 in this chapter. Open SQL Server Management Studio, and in the Connect to Server dialog box type *localhost*\\<**SQL Server 2012 instance name**> as the server name; then click Connect. SQL Server Management Studio will open. Expand the Databases node, and select the AdventureWorks database. Your screen should resemble Figure 5-1.

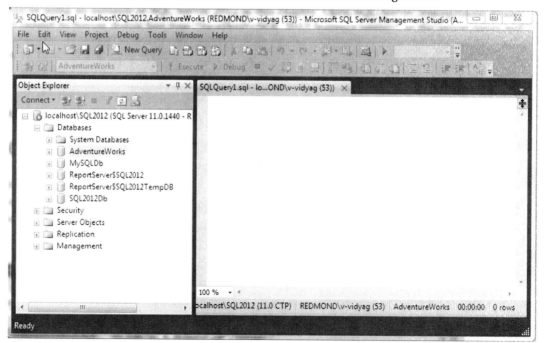

Figure 5-1. *Selecting a database to query*

Try It: Running a Simple Query

To submit a query to retrieve all employee data, open a New Query window in SQL Server Management Studio. Select the AdventureWorks in the Object Explorer, and then click the New Query button on the toolbar. This will open a New Query window. Enter the following query, and click Execute. You should see the results shown in Figure 5-2.

```
Select * from Person.Address
```

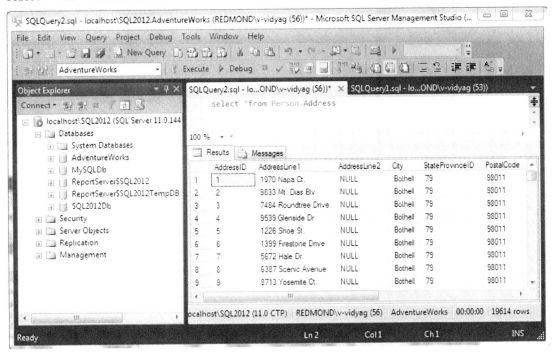

Figure 5-2. *Query results pane*

How It Works

You ask the database to return the data for all the columns, and you get exactly that. If you scroll to the right, you'll find all the columns in the Address table.

Most of the time, you should limit queries to only relevant columns. When you select columns you don't need, you waste resources. To explicitly select columns, enter the column names after the SELECT keyword, as shown in the following query, and click Execute. Figure 5-3 shows the results.

```
Select AddressID, AddressLine1, City from Person.Address
```

This query selects all the rows from the Address table but only the AddressID, AddressLine1, and City columns.

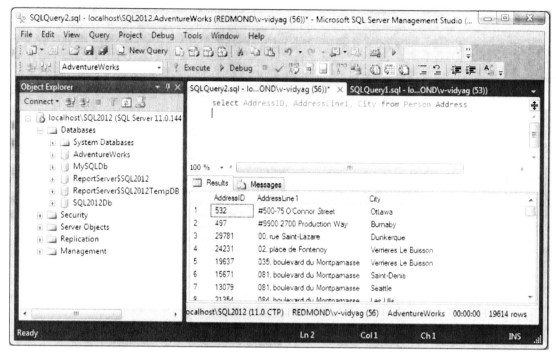

Figure 5-3. *Selecting specific columns*

Using the WHERE Clause

Queries can have WHERE clauses. The WHERE clause allows you to specify criteria for selecting rows. This clause can be complex, but we'll stick to a simple example for now. The syntax is as follows:

```
WHERE <column1> <operator> <column2 / Value>
```

Here, <operator> is a comparison operator (for example, =, <>, >, or <). (Table 5-1, later in the chapter, lists the T-SQL comparison operators.)

Try It: Refining Your Query

In this exercise, you'll see how to refine your query.

1. Add the following WHERE clause to the query in Figure 5-3:

```
Where City = 'Redmond'
```

2. Run the query by pressing F5, and you should see the results shown in Figure 5-4.

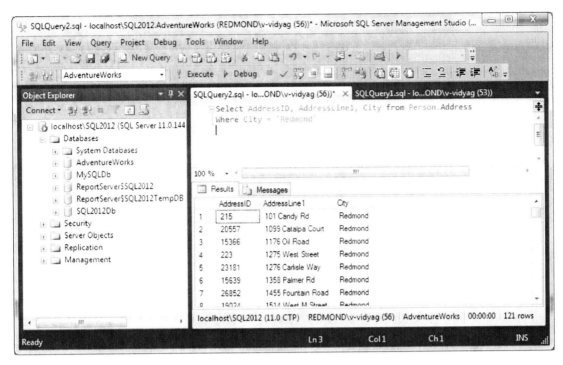

Figure 5-4. Using a WHERE clause

⬛ **Caution** SQL Server keywords are not case-sensitive. SQL Server case sensitivity depends upon the collation setting of the database. However, the default collation of the SQL Server installation, SQL_Latin1_General_CP1_CI_AS, is not case-sensitive. So, most of the time, developers will not need to worry about case sensitivity. But the AdventureWorks database is set as case-sensitive. Hence, if you try running the query shown in Figure 5-4 with *redmond*, you will not show any result rows because of case sensitivity, which will not find a city with the provided name.

Using Comparison Operators

You can use a number of different comparison operators in a WHERE clause (see Table 5-1).

Table 5-1. Comparison Operators

Operator	Description	Example
=	Equals	AddressID = 1
<	Less than	AddressID < 1
>	Greater than	AddressID > 1
<=	Less than or equal to	AddressID <= 1
>=	Greater than or equal to	AddressID >= 1
<>	Not equal to	AddressID <> 1
!=	Not equal to	AddressID != 1
!<	Not less than	AddressID !< 1
!>	Not greater than	AddressID !> 1

■ **Tip** As mentioned earlier, every database vendor has its own implementation of SQL. This discussion is specific to T-SQL; for example, standard SQL doesn't have the != operator and calls <> the *not equals operator.* In fact, standard SQL calls the expressions in a WHERE clause *predicates*; we'll use that term because predicates are either true or false, but other expressions don't have to be. If you work with another version of SQL, please refer to its documentation for specifics.

You may want to test the comparison operator like in the example, as shown in Figure 5-5.

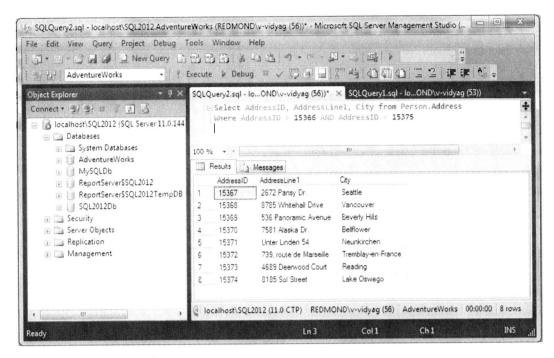

Figure 5-5. Using comparison operators

Sorting Data

After you've filtered the data you want, you can sort the data by one or more columns and in a certain direction. Since tables are by definition unsorted, the order in which rows is retrieved by a query is unpredictable. To impose an ordering, you use the ORDER BY clause.

```
ORDER BY <column> [ASC | DESC] {, n}
```

The <column> is the column that should be used to sort the result. The {, n} syntax means you can specify any number of columns separated by commas. The result will be sorted in the order in which you specify the columns.

The following are the two sort directions:

- ASC: Ascending (1, 2, 3, 4, and so on)

- DESC: Descending (10, 9, 8, 7, and so on)

If you omit the ASC or DESC keyword, the sort order defaults to ASC. The following is the basic syntax for queries:

```
SELECT <column>
FROM <table>
WHERE <predicate>
ORDER BY <column> ASC | DESC
```

Now that you've seen it, you'll put this syntax to use in an example.

Try It: Writing an Enhanced Query

In this example, you'll code a query that uses the basic syntax just shown. You want to do the following:

- Select all the addresses that are in Redmond.

- Display only AddressID, AddressLine1, City.

- Sort the addresses by the AddressID.

Open a New Query window in SQL Server Management Studio. Enter the following query, and click Execute. You should see the results shown in Figure 5-6.

```
Select AddressID, AddressLine1, City from Person.Address
Where City= 'Redmond'
Order By AddressID Asc
```

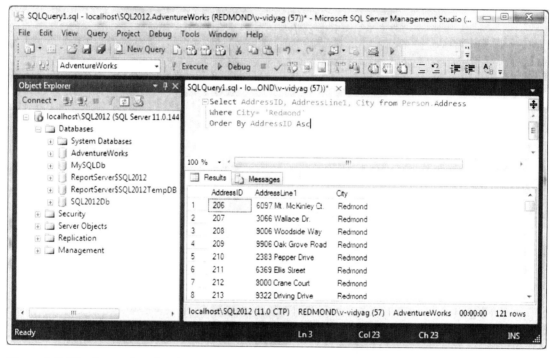

Figure 5-6. Filtering and sorting data

How It Works

Let's look at the clauses individually. The SELECT list specifies which columns you want to use.

```
select AddressID, AddressLine1, City
```

The FROM clause specifies that you want to use the Address table.

```
from Person.Address
```

The WHERE clause specifies that you want all the records for Redmond.

```
where City = 'Redmond'
```

The ORDER BY clause specifies the order in which the rows are sorted. The rows will be sorted by AddressID in ascending order.

```
order by AddressID asc
```

GROUP BY Clause

The GROUP BY clause is used to organize output rows into groups. The SELECT list can include aggregate functions and produce summary values for each group. Often you'll want to generate reports from the database with summary figures for a particular column or set of columns. For example, you may want to find out the total quantity of addresses that belong to a particular city from the Person.Address table.

Try It: Using the GROUP BY Clause

The Person.Address table contains the address details. You want to know the total of how many addresses belong to a particular city. For example, if you look at the query and number of records in Figure 5-6, you will notice that there are a total of 121 address entries for Redmond.

Open a New Query window in SQL Server Management Studio Express. Enter the following query, and click Execute. You should see the results shown in Figure 5-7.

```
Select City, Count(City) As 'Total Count'
from Person.Address
Group By City
Order By City Asc
```

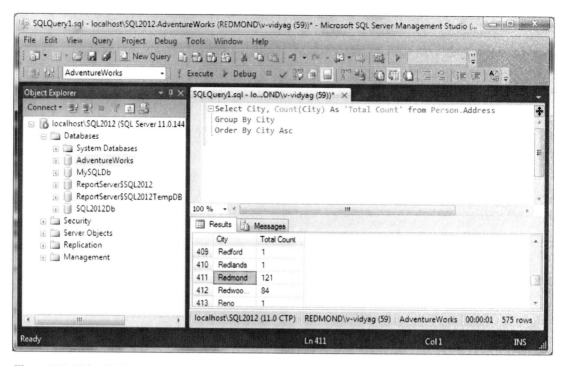

Figure 5-7. Using GROUP BY to aggregate values

If you will scroll the result set down to the Redmond, then you will see that it shows 121 rows, as you saw in Figure 5-6.

How It Works

You specify the City column and use the COUNT function to count the total number of cities listed for each address in the Address table.

```
Select City, count(City) AS 'Total Count'
from Person.Address
```

The GROUP BY clause enforces the grouping on the specified columns, and the results should be displayed in the form of groups for the City column.

```
group by City
```

The ORDER BY clause ensures that the result shown will be organized in the proper sequential order based upon city.

```
order by City Asc
```

Pattern Matching

Pattern matching is a technique that determines whether a specific character string matches a specified pattern. A pattern can be created by using a combination of regular characters and wildcard characters. During pattern matching, regular characters must exactly match as specified in the character string. `LIKE` and `NOT LIKE` (negation) are the operators are used for pattern matching. Remember that pattern matching is case-sensitive. SQL Server supports the following wildcard characters for pattern matching:

- *% (percent mark)*: This wildcard represents zero to many characters. For example, `WHERE title LIKE '%C# 5.0%'` finds all book titles containing the text *C# 5.0*, regardless of where in the title that text occurs—at the beginning, middle, or end. In this case, book titles such as *C# 5.0: An Introduction, Accelerated C#5.0*, and *Beginning C# 5.0 Databases* will be listed.

- *_ (underscore)*: A single underscore represents any single character. By using this wildcard character, you can be very specific in your search about the character length of the data you seek. For example, `WHERE au_fname LIKE '_ean'` finds all the first names that consist of four letters and that end with *ean* (Dean, Sean, and so on). `WHERE aufname LIKE 'a___n'` finds all the first names that begin with *a* and end with *n* and have any other three characters in between, for example, allan, amman, aryan, and so on.

- *[] (square brackets)*: These specify any single character within the specified range, such as `[a-f]`, or a set, such as `[abcdef]` or even `[adf]`. For example, `WHERE aulname LIKE '[C-K]arsen'` finds author last names ending with *arsen* and starting with any single character between *C* and *K*, such as Carsen, Darsen, Larsen, Karsen, and so on.

- *[^] (square brackets and caret)*: These specify any single character not within the specified range, such as `[^a-f]`, or a set, such as `[^abcdef]`. For example, `WHERE au_lname LIKE 'de[^l]%'` retrieves all author last names starting with *de*, but the following letter cannot be *l*.

Try It: Using the Percent (%) Character

To see how the % wildcard character works, open a New Query window in SQL Server Management Studio Express. Enter the following query, and click Execute. You should see the results shown in Figure 5-8.

```
Select AddressID, AddressLine1, City
from Person.Address
where City like 'R%'
```

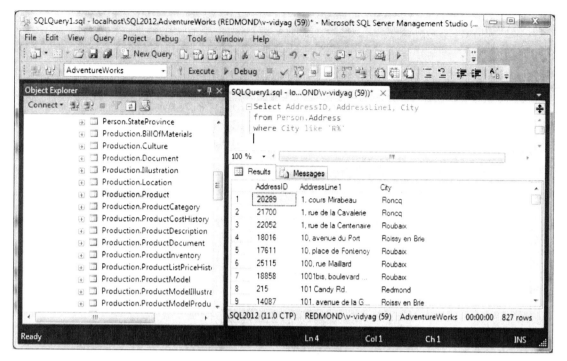

Figure 5-8. *Using the* LIKE *operator with* %

How It Works

You specify three columns of the Address table.

```
select AddressID, AddressLine1, City
from Person.Address
```

You specify the WHERE clause with a pattern using the LIKE operator to list all cities that begin with the letter *R* and that consist of any number of letters after that.

```
where City like 'R%'
```

Try It: Using the Underscore (_) Character

To see how the underscore (_) wildcard character works, open a New Query window in SQL Server Management Studio. Enter the following query, and click Execute. You should see the results shown in Figure 5-9.

```
Select AddressID, AddressLine1, City
from Person.Address
where City like 'S_____' -- S followed by 6 underscores
```

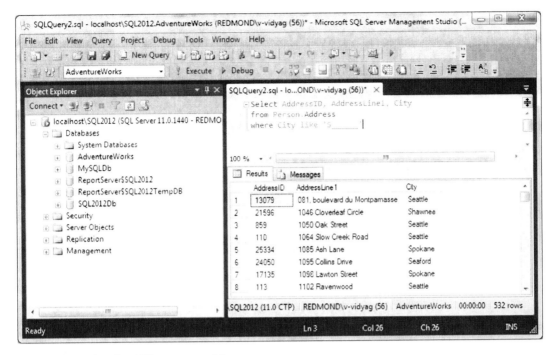

Figure 5-9. *Using the LIKE operator with _*

How It Works

You specify three columns of the Address table.

```
select AddressID, AddressLine1, City
from Person.Address
```

You specify the WHERE clause with a pattern using the LIKE operator to list all cities that begin with the letter *S* and consist of a maximum of six letters after that, for example Seattle, Spokane, Shawnee, and so on.

```
where City like 'S_____'
```

Try It: Using the Square Bracket ([]) Characters

To see how the [ ] characters work in pattern matching, open a New Query window in SQL Server Management Studio. Enter the following query, and click Execute. You should see the results shown in Figure 5-10.

```
Select AddressID, AddressLine1, City
from Person.Address
where City like '[B,R,S]%'
Order by City Asc
```

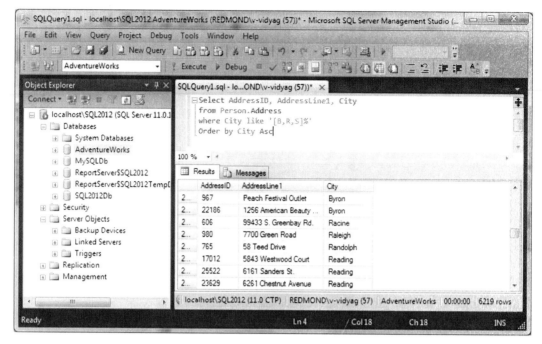

***Figure 5-10.** Using the LIKE operator with [ ]*

How It Works

You specify three columns of the Address table.

```
select AddressID, AddressLine1, City
from Person.Address
```

You specify the WHERE clause with a pattern using the LIKE operator to list all cities that begin with the letter *B* or *R* or *S* and consist of any number of letters after that, for example Bellevue, Redmond, Seattle, and so on.

```
where City like '[B,R,S]%'
Order by City Asc
```

Try It: Using the Square Bracket and Caret ([^]) Characters

To see how the [^B,R,S] characters work in pattern matching, open a New Query window in SQL Server Management Studio Express. Enter the following query, and click Execute. You should see the results shown in Figure 5-11.

```
Select AddressID, AddressLine1, City
from Person.Address
where City like '[^B,R,S]%'
Order by City Asc
```

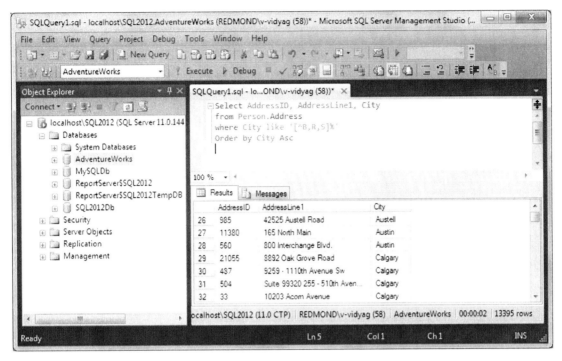

Figure 5-11. *Using the LIKE operator with [^]*

How It Works

You specify three columns of the Address table.

```
select AddressID, AddressLine1, City
from Person.Address
```

You specify the WHERE clause with a pattern using the LIKE operator to list all cities that do not begin with the letter *B* or *R* or *S* and consist of any number of letters after that; for example, Bellevue, Redmond, Seattle, and so on, are not going to be included in the result set.

```
where City like '[^B,R,S]%'
Order by City Asc
```

Aggregate Functions

SQL has several built-in functions that aggregate the values of a column. Aggregate functions are applied on sets of rows and return a single value. For example, you can use aggregate functions to calculate the average unit price of orders placed. You can find the order with the lowest price or the most expensive. MIN, MAX, SUM, AVG, and COUNT are frequently used in aggregate functions.

Try It: Using the MIN, MAX, SUM, and AVG Functions

Let's find the minimum, maximum, sum, and average of the unit price (UnitPrice) of each sales order (SalesOrderID) from the SalesOrderDetail table.

Open a New Query window in SQL Server Management Studio. Enter the following query, and click Execute. You should see the results shown in Figure 5-12.

```
select SalesOrderID,min(UnitPrice)as "Min",
max(UnitPrice) as "Max",Sum(UnitPrice) as "Sum",
Avg(UnitPrice)as "Avg"
from Sales.SalesOrderDetail
where SalesOrderID between 43659 and 43663
group by SalesOrderID
```

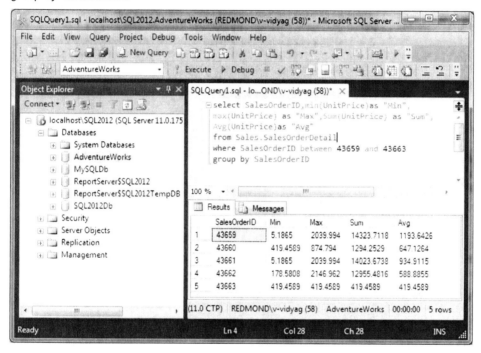

Figure 5-12. Using aggregate functions

How It Works

You use the MIN and MAX functions to find the minimum and maximum values, the SUM function to calculate the total value, and the AVG function to calculate the average value.

```
min(UnitPrice) as "Min",
max(UnitPrice) as "Max",
Sum(UnitPrice) as "Sum",
Avg(UnitPrice)as "Avg"
```

Since you want the results listed by SalesOrderID, you use the GROUP BY clause. From the result set, you see that order 1 had a minimum unit price of 5.1865, a maximum unit price of 2039.994, a total unit price of 14323.7118, and an average unit price of 1193.6426.

Try It: Using the COUNT Function

Let's find the count of records from the Person.Contact table.

Open a New Query window in SQL Server Management Studio. Enter the following query, and click Execute. You should see the results shown in Figure 5-13.

```
Select count(*) as "Total Records"
from Person.Contact

Select count(Title)as "Not Null Titles"
from Person.Contact
```

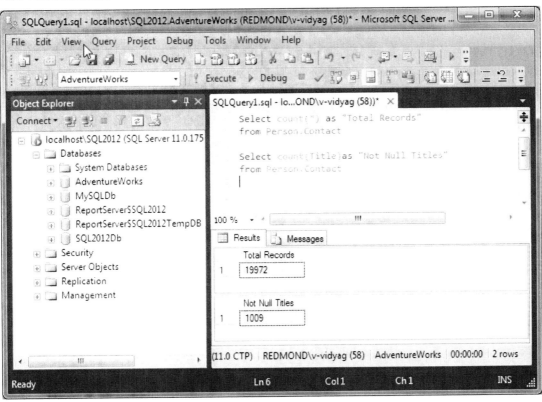

Figure 5-13. Using the COUNT aggregate function

How It Works

The COUNT function has different behavior depending upon the parameter passed to the function. If you try COUNT(*), the query will return you the number of total records available in the table, as shown in the topmost results: table Person.Contact contains a total of 19,972 records, and Count(*) counts null.

If you pass a column name to the COUNT function, it will return the total number of records again, but it will ignore all those rows that contain null values for that column. In the second query, you are querying the same table, which has listed 19,972 records, but because your second query applies to the Title column, it returns only 1,009 records, because this time it has ignored all null values. In other words, Count(ColumnName) ignores null.

DATETIME Functions

Although the SQL standard defines a DATETIME data type and its components, YEAR, MONTH, DAY, HOUR, MINUTE, and SECOND, it doesn't dictate how a DBMS makes this data available. Each DBMS offers functions that extract parts of DATETIMEs. Let's look at some examples of T-SQL DATETIME functions.

Try It: Using T-SQL Date and Time Functions

Let's practice with T-SQL date and time functions.

Open a New Query window in SQL Server Management Studio Express (database context does not affect this query). Enter the following query, and click Execute. You should see the results shown in Figure 5-14.

```
select
current_timestamp'standard datetime',
getdate()'Transact-SQL datetime',
datepart(year, getdate())'datepart year',
year(getdate())'year function',
datepart(hour, getdate())'hour'
```

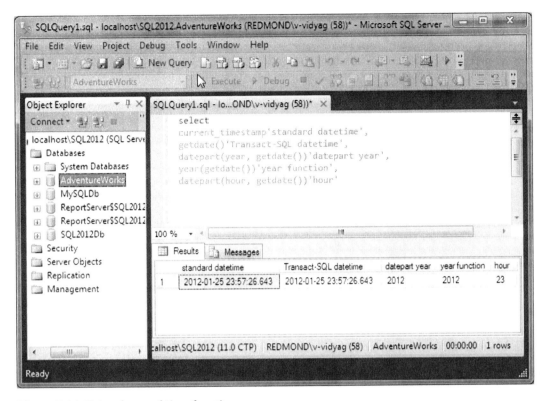

Figure 5-14. *Using date and time functions*

How It Works

You use a nonstandard version of a query, omitting the FROM clause, to display the current date and time and individual parts of them. The first two columns in the SELECT list give the complete date and time.

```
current_timestamp 'standard datetime', getdate() 'Transact-SOL datetime',
```

The first line uses the CURRENTTIMESTAMP value function of standard SQL; the second uses the GETDATE function of T-SQL. They're equivalent in effect, both returning the complete current date and time.

The next two lines each provide the current year. The first uses the T-SQL DATEPART function; the second uses the T-SQL YEAR function. Both take a DATETIME argument and return the integer year. The DATEPART function's first argument specifies what part of a DATETIME to extract. Note that T-SQL doesn't provide a date specifier for extracting a complete date, and it doesn't have a separate DATE function.

```
datepart(year, getdate()) 'datepart year', year(getdate()) 'year function',
```

The final line gets the current hour. The T-SQL DATEPART function must be used here since no HOUR function is analogous to the YEAR function. Note that T-SQL doesn't provide a time specifier for extracting a complete time, and it doesn't have a separate TIME function.

```
datepart(hour, getdate()) 'hour'
```

You can format dates and times and alternative functions for extracting and converting them in various ways. Dates and times can also be added and subtracted and incremented and decremented. How this is done is DBMS-specific, though all DBMSs comply to a reasonable extent with the SQL standard in how they do it. Whatever DBMS you use, you'll find that dates and times are the most complicated data types to employ. But, in all cases, you'll find that functions (sometimes a richer set of them than in T-SQL) are the basic tools for working with dates and times.

■ **Tip** When providing date and time input, character string values are typically expected; for example, 1/26/2012 would be the appropriate way to specify the value for a column holding the current date from the example. However, DBMSs store dates and times in system-specific encodings. When you use date and time data, read the SQL manual for your database carefully to see how to best handle it.

List Operator

IN is SQL Server's list operator; it allows you to specify the list of choices you want to base your condition upon. For example, you want to extract all the cities of your desired list. SQL Server offers its negation as well, NOT IN, so you can choose the values that you *don't* want to be included in your result set.

Try It: Using the IN Operator

Open a New Query window in SQL Server Management Studio. Enter the following query, and click Execute. You should see the results shown in Figure 5-15.

```
select AddressID, AddressLine1, City
from Person.Address
where City in ('Bellevue', 'Redmond', 'Seattle')
```

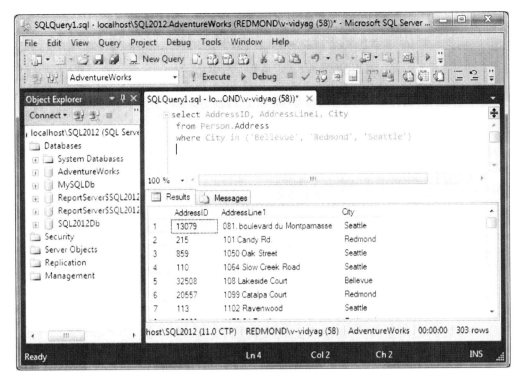

Figure 5-15. *Using IN operator*

How It Works

You specify three columns of the Address table.

```
select AddressID, AddressLine1, City
from Person.Address
```

You specify the list operator IN with the city name you want to extract records for. Hence, it filters 303 records for the provided cities only. If you scroll down, you will see that all the records will belong to the mentioned cities only.

```
where City in ('Bellevue', 'Redmond', 'Seattle')
```

Try It: Using the NOT IN Operator

Open a New Query window in SQL Server Management Studio. Enter the following query, and click Execute. You should see the results shown in Figure 5-16.

```
select AddressID, AddressLine1, City
from Person.Address
where City not in ('Bellevue', 'Redmond', 'Seattle')
```

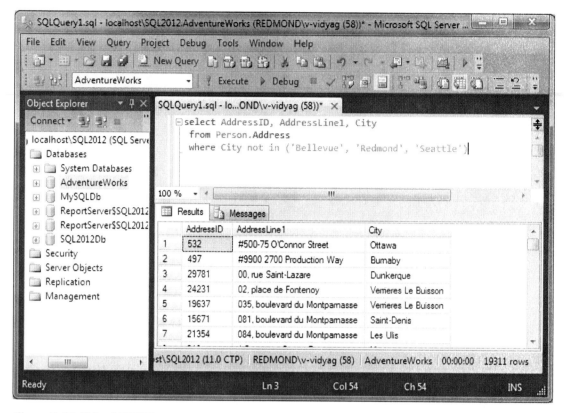

Figure 5-16. Using NOT IN operator

How It Works

You specify three columns of the Address table.

```
select AddressID, AddressLine1, City
from Person.Address
```

You specify the list operator NOT IN with the city name you do not want to include the records for. Hence, it filters 19,311 records for the cities other than what we listed in the NOT IN list. If you scroll down, you will not see any record belonging to any of the mentioned cities.

```
where City not in ('Bellevue', 'Redmond', 'Seattle')
```

Range Operator

BETWEEN is SQL Server's range operator; it allows you to specify the range of data you want to base your condition upon. For example, you want to provide the range of data you would like to see. SQL Server offers its negation as well, NOT Between, so you can choose the values that you don't want to be included in your result set.

Try It: Using the BETWEEN Operator

Open a New Query window in SQL Server Management Studio. Enter the following query, and click Execute. You should see the results shown in Figure 5-17.

```
select AddressID, AddressLine1, City
from Person.Address
where AddressID between 201 and 300
```

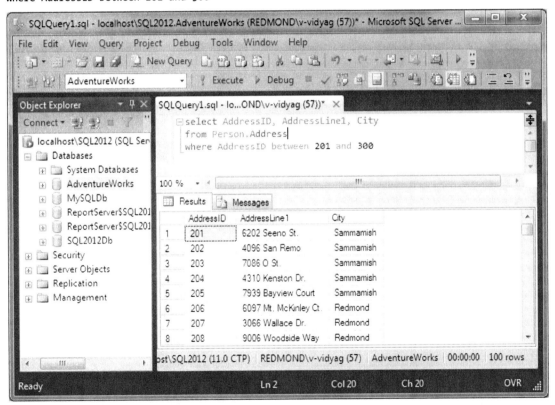

Figure 5-17. Using the Between operator

How It Works

You specify three columns of the Address table.

```
select AddressID, AddressLine1, City
from Person.Address
```

You specify the range operator BETWEEN with the range of AddressID you want to include the records for. Hence, it filters 100 records for the address, ranging between 201 and 300, in other words, a total of 100 records.

```
where AddressID between 201 and 300
```

Try It: Using the NOT BETWEEN Operator

Open a New Query window in SQL Server Management Studio. Enter the following query, and click Execute. You should see the results shown in Figure 5-18.

```
select AddressID, AddressLine1, City
from Person.Address
where AddressID between 201 and 32521
```

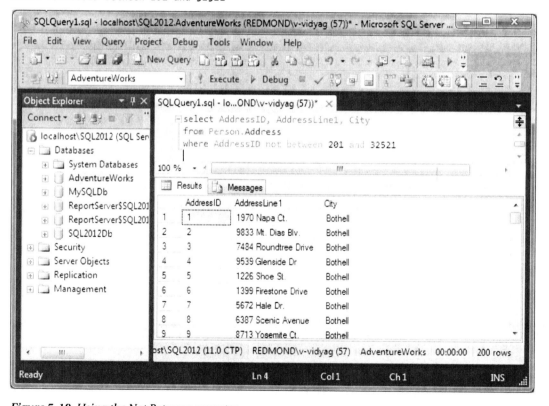

Figure 5-18. Using the Not Between operator

How It Works

You specify three columns of the Address table.

```
select AddressID, AddressLine1, City
from Person.Address
```

You specify the range operator BETWEEN with the range of AddressID you want to include the records for. Hence, it filters 200 records for the address, ranging *not* between 201 and 32521, in other words, a total of 200 records.

```
where AddressID between 201 and 32521
```

Finding NULL Values

Null values are undefined and unknown values and represented by the NULL keyword. When executing queries, it becomes important sometimes to extract NULL and NOT NULL rows separately. To support this purpose, SQL Server provides IS NULL and its negation IS NOT NULL to be included with the WHERE condition clause.

Try It: Using IS NULL Operator

Open a New Query window in SQL Server Management Studio. Enter the following query, and click Execute. You should see the results shown in Figure 5-19.

```
select Title, FirstName, MiddleName, LastName
from Person.Contact
where MiddleName is null
```

How It Works

You specify four columns of the Contact table.

```
select Title, FirstName, MiddleName, LastName
from Person.Contact
```

You specify the WHERE condition based on whether MiddleName is null. Hence, it filters 8,499 records for the person's contact details; all the listed records have their MiddleName as NULL.

```
where MiddleName is null
```

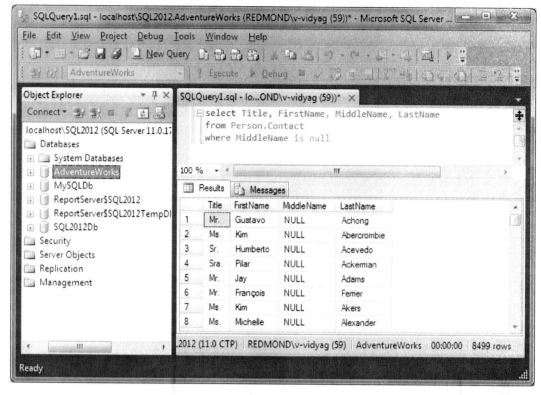

Figure 5-19. Using the IS NULL operator

Try It: Using the IS NOT NULL Operator

Open a New Query window in SQL Server Management Studio. Enter the following query, and click Execute. You should see the results shown in Figure 5-20.

```
select Title, FirstName, MiddleName, LastName
from Person.Contact
where MiddleName is not null
```

How It Works

You specify four columns of the Contact table.

```
select Title, FirstName, MiddleName, LastName
from Person.Contact
```

You specify the WHERE condition based on whether MiddleName is not null. Hence, it filters 11,473 records for the person's contact details; all the listed records have a defined MiddleName.

```
where MiddleName is not null
```

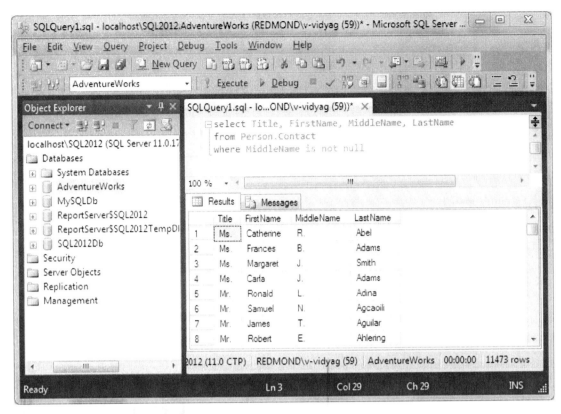

Figure 5-20. *Using the IS NOT NULL operator*

Joins

Most queries require information from more than one table. *A join* is a relational operation that produces a table by retrieving data from two (not necessarily distinct) tables and matching their rows according to a *join specification*.

Different types of joins exist, which you'll look at individually, but keep in mind that every join is a *binary* operation; that is, one table is joined to another, which may be the same table since tables can be joined to themselves. The join operation is a rich and somewhat complex topic. The next sections will cover the basics.

Inner Joins

An inner join is the most frequently used join. It returns only those rows that satisfy the join specification. Although in theory any relational operator (such as > or <) can be used in the join specification, the equality operator (=) is almost always used. Joins using the equality operator are called *natural joins*.

The basic syntax for an inner join is as follows:

```
select
      <select list>
from
      left-table INNER JOIN right-table
      ON
      <join specification>
```

Notice that INNER JOIN is a binary operation, so it has two operands, left-table and right-table, which may be base tables or anything that can be queried (for example, a table produced by a subquery or by another join). The ON keyword begins the join specification, which can contain anything that could be used in a WHERE clause.

Table Aliasing

Table aliasing is a technique used to assign a short nickname to a table or each individual table needed in any SQL query. Though you can use full table name, repeating the table name again and again in a query is a cumbersome process.

Hence, table aliasing makes it very easy when you have to specify column names that either may exist in multiple tables or you want to use different columns from a particular table; therefore, it becomes very important to specify <Table Name>.<Column Name>.

Refer to the following query, in which we are aliasing Production.Product as PP and Production.ProductReview to PPR. Next, when it comes to use columns from these tables, we use the defined aliases.

Also, remember these aliases are temporary, and their life span is until the query is executed. After a query execution, you can't reuse the same alias for any other query. Hence, the scope of an alias is within the defined query and life span is until the query is executed.

Try It: Writing an Inner Join

Let's retrieve a list of products, the product IDs, and their ReviewerName, Comments, and Rating entries.

Open a New Query window in SQL Server Management Studio (remember to make AdventureWorks your query context). Enter the following query, and click Execute. You should see the results shown in Figure 5-21.

```
select PP.ProductID, PP.Name, PPR.ReviewerName, PPR.Comments, PPR.Rating
from Production.Product PP inner join Production.ProductReview PPR
on PP.ProductID = PPR.ProductID
```

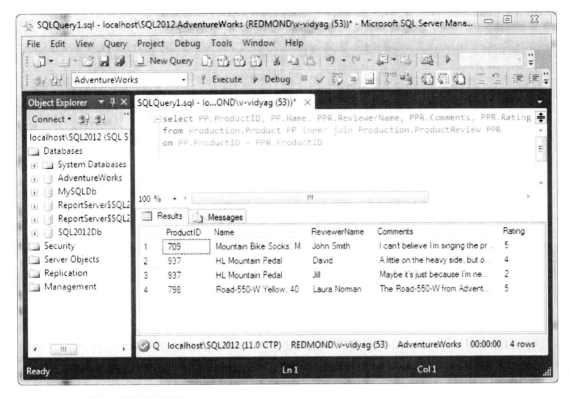

Figure 5-21. *Using INNER JOIN*

How It Works

Let's start with the SELECT list.

```
select PP.ProductID, PP.Name, PPR.ReviewerName, PPR.Comments, PPR.Rating
```

Since you're selecting columns from two tables, you need to identify which table a column comes from, which you do by prefixing the table name and a dot (.) to the column name. This is known as *disambiguation*, or removing ambiguity so the database manager knows which column to use. Though this has to be done only for columns that appear in both tables, the best practice is to qualify all columns with their table names.

The following FROM clause specifies both the tables and their aliases you're joining and the kind of join you're using:

```
from Production.Product PP inner join Production.ProductReview PPR
```

It specifies an inner join of the Production.Product and Production.ProductReview tables.

It also specifies the criteria for joining the primary key ProductID of the Product table with the foreign key ProductId of the ProductReview table.

```
on PP.ProductID = PPR.ProductID
```

The inner join on <u>ProductID</u> produces a table composed of five columns: ProductID, Name, ReviewerName, Comments, and Rating. The data is retrieved from rows in Production.Product and Production.ProductReview where their ProductID columns have the same value. Any rows in Orders that don't match rows in Employees are ignored, and vice versa. (This isn't the case here, but you'll see an example soon.) An inner join always produces only rows that satisfy the join specification.

■ **Tip** Columns used for joining don't have to appear in the SELECT list. If you want, you can omit that column.

Outer Joins

Outer joins return *all* rows from (at least) one of the joined tables even if rows in one table don't match rows in the other. Three types of outer joins exist: left outer join, right outer join, and full outer join. The terms *left* and *right* refer to the operands on the left and right of the JOIN operator. (Refer to the basic syntax for the inner join, and you'll see why we called the operands left-table and right-table.) In a left outer join, all rows from the left table will be retrieved whether they have matching rows in the right table. Conversely, in a right outer join, all rows from the right table will be retrieved whether they have matching rows in the left table. In a full outer join, all rows from both tables are returned.

■ **Tip** Left and right outer joins are logically equivalent. It's always possible to convert a left join into a right join by changing the operator and flipping the operands or a right join into a left with a similar change. So, only one of these operators is actually needed. Which one you choose is basically a matter of personal preference, but a useful rule of thumb is to use either left or right but not both in the same query. The query optimizer won't care, but humans find it much easier to follow a complex query if the joins always go in the same direction.

When is this useful? Quite frequently. In fact, whenever a parent-child relationship exists between tables, despite that referential integrity is maintained, some parent rows may not have related rows in the child table, since child rows may be allowed to have null foreign key values and therefore not match any row in the parent table.

Try It: Using LEFT OUTER JOIN

To list all ProductID and ProductName entries, even those that haven't been reviewed yet and have no associated ReviewerName, Comments, and Rating, open a New Query window in SQL Server Management Studio (remember to make AdventureWorks your query context). Enter the following query, and click Execute. You should see the results shown in Figure 5-22.

```
select PP.ProductID, PP.Name, PPR.ReviewerName, PPR.Comments, PPR.Rating
from Production.Product PP left outer join Production.ProductReview PPR
on PP.ProductID = PPR.ProductID
```

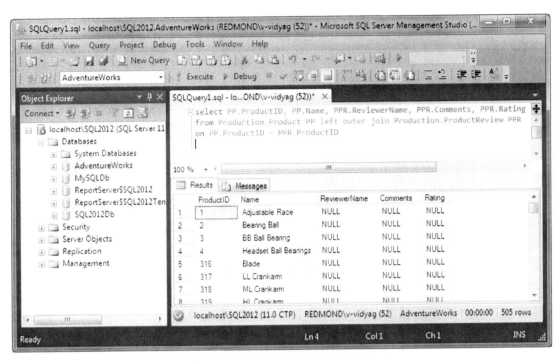

Figure 5-22. *Using LEFT OUTER JOIN*

How It Works

Let's start with the SELECT list.

```
select PP.ProductID, PP.Name, PPR.ReviewerName, PPR.Comments, PPR.Rating
```

Since you're selecting columns from two tables, you need to identify which table a column comes from, which you do by prefixing the table name and a dot (.) to the column name. This is known as *disambiguation,* or removing ambiguity so the database manager knows which column to use. Though this has to be done only for columns that appear in both tables, the best practice is to qualify all columns with their table names.

The following FROM clause specifies both the tables you're joining and the kind of join you're using:

```
from Production.Product PP left outer join Production.ProductReview PPR
```

It specifies a left outer join of the Production.Product and Production.ProductReview tables.

It also specifies the criteria for joining the primary key ProductID of the Product table with the foreign key ProductId of the ProductReview table.

```
on PP.ProductID = PPR.ProductID
```

The left outer join on ProductID produces a table composed of five columns: ProductID, Name, ReviewerName, Comments, and Rating. All the data is retrieved from rows in Production.Product, which is the left table, and matching and unmatching data from Production.ProductReview where their ProductID columns have the matching or even unmatching values.

Try It: Using RIGHT OUTER JOIN

To list all ProductID and ProductName columns and details based on those that have been reviewed, open a New Query window in SQL Server Management Studio (remember to make AdventureWorks your query context). Enter the following query, and click Execute. You should see the results shown in Figure 5-23.

```
select PP.ProductID, PP.Name, PPR.ReviewerName, PPR.Comments, PPR.Rating
from Production.Product PP right outer join Production.ProductReview PPR
on PP.ProductID = PPR.ProductID
```

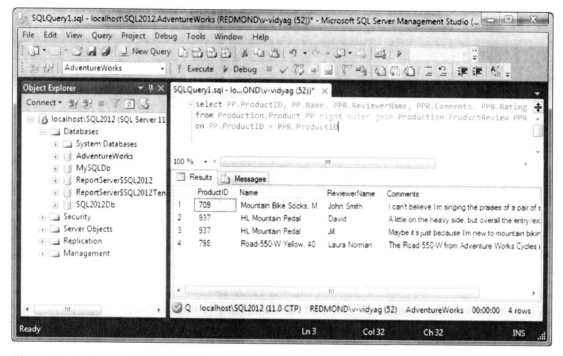

Figure 5-23. Using LEFT OUTER JOIN

How It Works

Let's start with the SELECT list.

```
select PP.ProductID, PP.Name, PPR.ReviewerName, PPR.Comments, PPR.Rating
```

Since you're selecting columns from two tables, you need to identify which table a column comes from, which you do by prefixing the table name and a dot (.) to the column name. This is known as *disambiguation,* or removing ambiguity so the database manager knows which column to use. Though this has to be done only for columns that appear in both tables, the best practice is to qualify all columns with their table names.

The following FROM clause specifies both the tables you're joining and the kind of join you're using:

```
from Production.Product PP right outer join Production.ProductReview PPR
```

It specifies a right outer join of the Production.Product and Production.ProductReview tables.

It also specifies the criteria for joining the primary key ProductID of the Product table with the foreign key ProductId of the ProductReview table.

```
on PP.ProductID = PPR.ProductID
```

The right outer join on ProductID produces a table composed of five columns: ProductID, Name, ReviewerName, Comments, and Rating. All the data is retrieved from rows in Production.ProductReview, which is the right table, and matching and unmatching data from Production.ProductReview where their ProductID columns have the matching or even unmatching values.

Other Joins

The SQL standard also provides for FULL OUTER JOIN, UNION JOIN, and CROSS JOIN (and even NATURAL JOIN, basically an inner join using equality predicates), but these are much less used and beyond the scope of this book. We won't provide examples, but this section contains a brief summary of them.

A FULL OUTER JOIN is like a combination of both the LEFT and RIGHT OUTER joins. All rows from both tables will be retrieved, even if they have no related rows in the other table.

A UNION JOIN is unlike outer joins in that it doesn't match rows. Instead, it creates a table that has all the rows from both tables. For two tables, it's equivalent to the following query:

```
select
      *
from
      table1
union all
select
      *
from
      table2
```

The tables must have the same number of columns, and the data types of corresponding columns must be compatible (able to hold the same types of data).

A CROSS JOIN combines all rows from both tables. It doesn't provide for a join specification, since this would be irrelevant. It produces a table with all columns from both tables and as many rows as the product of the number of rows in each table. The result is also known as a *Cartesian product*, since that's the mathematical term for associating each element (row) of one set (table) with all elements of another set. For example, if there are five rows and five columns in table A and ten rows and three columns in table B, the cross join of A and B would produce a table with fifty rows and eight columns. Not only is this join operation virtually inapplicable to any real-world query, but it's also a potentially very expensive process for even small real-world databases. (Imagine using it for production tables with thousands or even millions of rows.)

Summary

In this chapter, we covered how to construct database queries using SQL features such as range, list, IS NULL operators, aggregate functions, DATETIME functions, GROUP BY clauses, joins, and pattern matching.

In the next chapter, you will learn about creating stored procedures.

CHAPTER 6

Using Stored Procedures

A *stored procedure* is a collection of SQL statements that allows you to perform a task repeatedly. You can create the procedure once and reuse it any number of times in your program. This can improve the maintainability of your application and allow applications to access the database in a uniform and optimized manner. The goals of this chapter are to get you acquainted with stored procedures by creating and modifying them in SQL Server 2012 and to explain how C# programs can interact with them. This chapter covers the following:

- Creating stored procedures
- Modifying stored procedures
- Displaying the definitions of stored procedures
- Renaming stored procedures
- Working with stored procedures in C#
- Deleting stored procedures

Creating Stored Procedures

Stored procedures can have *parameters* that are used for input or output. Stored procedures can have a single integer *return value* (which defaults to zero) and can return zero or more result sets. They can be called from client programs or other stored procedures. They are powerful indeed and are becoming the preferred mode for much database programming, particularly for multitier applications and web services, since (among their many benefits) they can dramatically reduce network traffic between clients and database servers.

Note If you are using the AdventureWorks2008R2 database, then a few table name changes will apply. For example, in my code example, I used the Person.Contact table, which is actually named Person.Person in AdventureWorks2008R2. If you come across any such instance, replace Person.Contact with Person.Person.

Try It: Working with Stored Procedures in SQL Server

Let's create a stored procedure using SQL Server Management Studio that produces a list of the contact details of a person in the AdventureWorks database. It requires no input and doesn't need to set a return value.

1. Open SQL Server Management Studio, and in Connect to Server dialog select localhost\SQL2012 as the server name; then click Connect.

2. In the Object Explorer, expand the Databases node, select the AdventureWorks database, and click the New Query pane. Enter the following query, and click Execute. You should see the results in Figure 6-1. Create procedure sp_Select_All_PersonContact As select Contact.Title, Contact.FirstName, Contact.LastName from Person.Contact

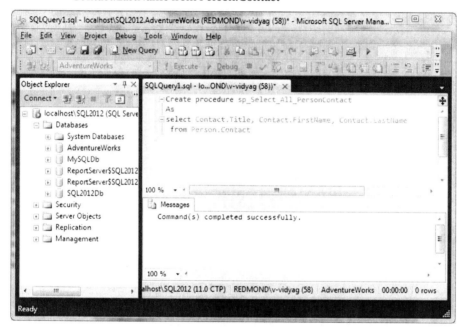

Figure 6-1. Creating a stored procedure using SQL Server Management Studio

3. To execute the stored procedure, enter the command as shown in Figure 6-2, and click Execute. You should see the results shown in Figure 6-2.

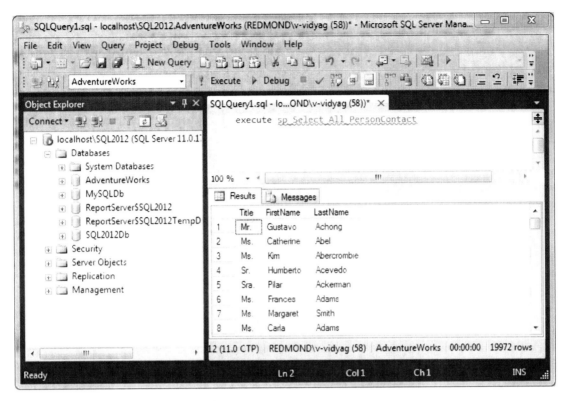

Figure 6-2. Executing the stored procedure

How It Works

You use the CREATE PROCEDURE to create stored procedures. The AS keyword separates the signature (the procedure's name and parameter list, but here you define no parameters) of the stored procedure from its body (the SQL that makes up the procedure).

```
Create procedure sp_Select_All_PersonContact
As
select Contact.Title, Contact.FirstName, Contact.LastName
 from Person.Contact
```

SQL Server Management Studio submitted the CREATE PROCEDURE statement, and once the stored procedure was created, you ran it from the query pane by writing the following statement:

```
execute sp_Select_All_PersonContact
```

That's it! There's nothing complicated about creating stored procedures.

■ **Note** The prefix sp_ is a T-SQL convention that usually indicates that the stored procedure is coded in SQL. The prefix xp_ (for "extended procedure") is used to indicate that the stored procedure isn't written in SQL. (However, not all sp_ stored procedures provided by SQL Server are written in SQL.) By the way, hundreds of sp_ (and other) stored procedures are provided by SQL Server 2012 to perform a wide variety of common tasks.

Try It: Creating a Stored Procedure with an Input Parameter

Let's create a stored procedure that produces a list of contacts for a given title of any person. We'll pass the title to the stored procedure for use in a query.

1. Enter the following query, and click Execute. You should see the message "command(s) completed successfully" in the results pane.

```
Create procedure sp_Contact_By_Title
 @Title nvarchar(8)
 As
select Contact.Title, Contact.FirstName, Contact.LastName
 from Person.Contact
 where Contact.Title = @Title
```

2. To execute the stored procedure, enter the command along with the value for the parameter, select the following statement, and then click Execute. You should see the results shown in Figure 6-3.

```
execute sp_Contact_By_Title 'Mr.'
```

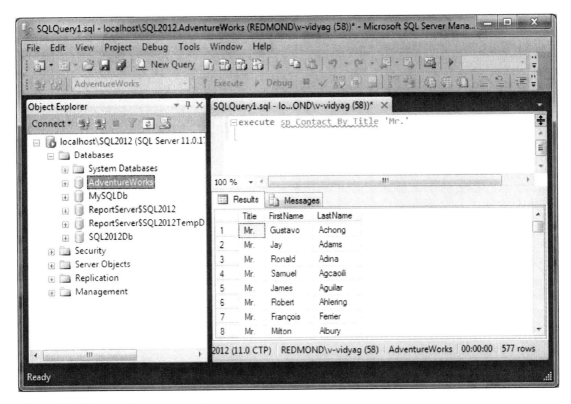

Figure 6-3. *Using an input parameter*

How It Works

The CREATE PROCEDURE statement created a stored procedure that has one input parameter. Parameters are specified between the procedure name and the AS keyword. Here you specified only the parameter name and datatype, so by default it is an input parameter. Parameter names start with @.

```
Create procedure sp_Contact_By_Title
 @Title nvarchar(8)
 As
```

This parameter is used in the WHERE clause of the query.

```
where Contact.Title = @Title
```

Try It: Creating a Stored Procedure with an Output Parameter

Output parameters are usually used to pass values between stored procedures. In other words, they are used to return a value like a function in a programming language, so let's write a stored procedure with an output parameter so we can use it in a C# program later. I'll also show how to return a value other than zero.

3.   Enter the following query, and click Execute. You should see the message "command(s) completed successfully" in the results pane.

```
Create procedure sp_CountContacts_By_Title
@Title nvarchar(8),
@TitleCount int= 0 output
As
select Contact.Title, Contact.FirstName, Contact.LastName
from Person.Contact
where Contact.Title = @Title

Select @TitleCount = count(*)
from Person.Contact
where Title=@Title

return @TitleCount
```

You have made the stored procedure, and now you need to test it; in order to do so, enter the following statements in the query pane, making sure you either replace the earlier statements or select only these statements while executing.

```
Declare @return_value int,
              @TitleCount int

      Execute @return_value=sp_CountContacts_By_Title
              @Title='Mr.',
              @TitleCount=@TitleCount output

      Select 'Total Title Count' =@return_value
```

If you look at the status bar in Figure 6-3 in the bottom-right corner, you will notice that the total returned rows were 577; this is reflected in Figure 6-4 as Total Title Count.

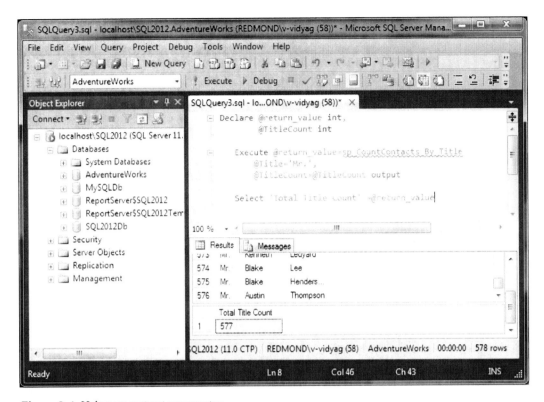

Figure 6-4. *Using an output parameter*

How It Works

You added an output parameter, @TitleCount, like this:

```
Create procedure sp_CountContacts_By_Title
 @Title nvarchar(8),
 @TitleCount int= 0 output
 As
```

You assigned it a default value of zero. The keyword output marks it as an output parameter. You also added an additional query:

```
select Contact.Title, Contact.FirstName, Contact.LastName
 from Person.Contact
 where Contact.Title = @Title
```

You assigned the scalar returned by the new query to the output parameter in the SELECT list:

```
    @TitleCount = count(*)then you returned the same value
```

```
return @TitleCount
```

The COUNT function returns an integer, so this was a convenient way to demonstrate how to use the RETURN statement.

■ **Tip** Input parameters can also be assigned default values.

Modifying Stored Procedures

You use the `Alter Procedure procedure_name` statement to modify an existing stored procedure.

Try It: Modifying Your Trivial Stored Procedure

1. Here you are modifying the sp_Select_All_PersonContact stored procedure shown in Figure 6-1 by adding an Order by clause. (See Figure 6-5.)

```
Alter procedure sp_Select_All_PersonContact
As
select Contact.Title, Contact.FirstName, Contact.LastName
 from Person.Contact
Order by Contact.LastName
```

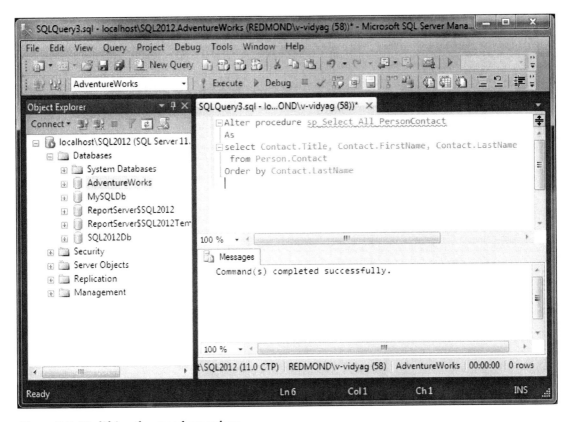

Figure 6-5. Modifying the stored procedure

2. Execute the stored procedure by writing the statement as shown in Figure 6-6, and notice that the employee names are now sorted (whereas if you look at the Figure 6-2, the records are not sorted).

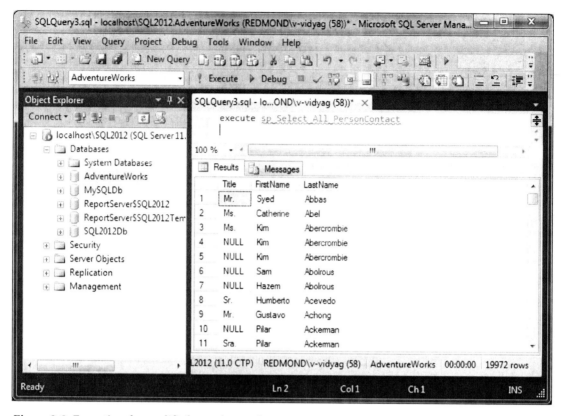

Figure 6-6. Executing the modified stored procedure

How It Works

After you've executed the ALTER PROCEDURE statement, the stored procedure is updated in the database.

```
Alter procedure sp_Select_All_PersonContact
```

You also added the Order by clause while modifying the procedure.

```
order by Contact.LastName
```

Displaying the Definition of Stored Procedures

SQL Server offers a way to view the definition of the objects created in the database. This is known as *metadata retrieval*. The information about objects is stored in some predefined system stored procedures that can be retrieved whenever required.

Try It: Viewing the Definition of Our Stored Procedure

1. Enter the following statement in the query pane:

```
Execute sp_helptext 'sp_Select_All_Employees'
sp_helptext 'sp_Select_All_PersonContact'
```

2. Go to the Query menu, point to Results To, click Results to Text, and then click Execute. You will see the same definition that you have specified for your stored procedure. You can see the output in Figure 6-7.

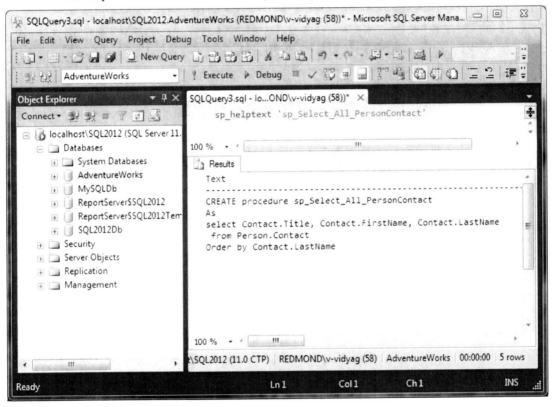

Figure 6-7. Displaying the definition of the stored procedure

How It Works

The statement sp_helptext is a predefined SQL Server stored procedure that accepts an object name as a parameter and shows the definition of the object passed to the sp_helptext as the parameter.

```
sp_helptext 'sp_Select_All_PersonContact'
```

■ **Note** sp_helptext doesn't work with table objects. In other words, you can't see the definition of the CREATE TABLE statement used while creating the table object.

Renaming Stored Procedures

SQL Server allows you to rename the objects. The following statement will allow you to change the stored procedure name. sp_rename is a predefined stored procedure that allows to rename the objects.

Try It: Renaming a Stored Procedure

1. Enter the following statement in the query pane:

```
sp_rename 'sp_Select_All_PersonContact,
      'sp_Select_All_ContactDetails'
```

2. Click Execute, and you will see the following message in the results pane:

■ **Caution** Changing any part of an object name could break scripts and stored procedures.

Even though the stored procedure sp_rename has been executed successfully, it still shows the caution message.

3. Now go to the Object Browser, expand the AdventureWorks database node, expand Programmability, right-click the Stored Procedures node, and select Refresh.

4. Expand the Stored Procedures node, and notice that sp_Select_All_PersonContact has been renamed to sp_Select_All_ContactDetails. You should see screen shown in Figure 6-8.

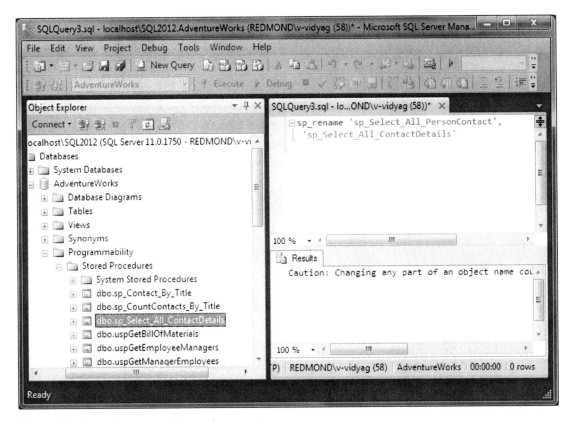

Figure 6-8. Renaming a stored procedure

How It Works

The statement sp_rename is a predefined SQL Server stored procedure that accepts an object's old name and the object's new name as parameters.

```
sp_rename 'sp_Select_All_PersonContact,
                     'sp_Select_All_ContactDetails'
```

■ **Note** sp_rename works very well with most of the objects when you want to rename them, such as tables, columns, and other objects.

Deleting Stored Procedures

Once a stored procedure is created, you can delete it if you don't need its functionality. `Drop Procedure procedure_name` is the basic syntax for this.

Note Because we will require these created stored procedures, if you choose to delete one in the following exercise, please then re-create it so any dependencies will not be lost.

Try It: Deleting a Stored Procedure

Let's delete our first store procedure (`sp_Select_All_PersonContact`), which we have just renamed to `sp_Select_All_ContactDetails`.

1. Enter the following statement (replace the query with this statement) in the query pane, and click Execute:

   ```
   Drop procedure sp_Select_All_ContactDetails
   ```

2. You will see the following message:

   ```
   Command(s) completed successfully.
   ```

3. After deleting the stored procedure, navigate to the Object Explorer, and expand the AdventureWorks database node; then expand Programmability, right-click the Stored Procedures node, and select Refresh. Notice that the procedure sp_Select_All_ContactDetails has been deleted (see Figure 6-9), and it is not listed in the Object Explorer anymore, as you can see in Figure 6-8.

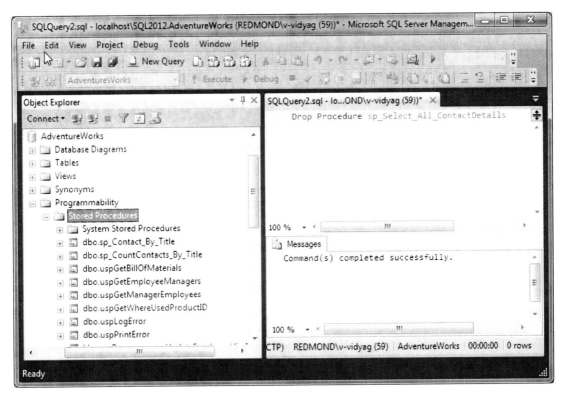

Figure 6-9. Deleting a stored procedure

Summary

In this chapter, you created stored procedures, and you developed an understanding of what's involved in creating, executing, and modifying a stored procedure from SSMS. You saw that calling stored procedures isn't inherently different from executing queries and statements. You simply create appropriate command parameters for the stored procedure parameters you need to use. In the next chapter, you will learn how to use SQL queries to produce XML output.

CHAPTER 7

Using XML

XML has been around for many years; with the release of the Microsoft .NET technology, XML has become even more popular. Microsoft's development tools and technologies contain built-in features to support XML. The advantage of using XML and its related technologies is that it is the major foundation of both the Internet and .NET.

My goal in this chapter is to introduce you to the most essential XML concepts and terminology and the basic techniques for using XML with SQL Server 2012. This will enable you to handle some common programming tasks while writing a software application.

This chapter will cover the following:

- Defining XML

- Understanding why to use XML

- Benefits of storing data as XML

- Understanding XML documents

- Understanding the XML declaration

- Converting relational data to XML

- Storing and retrieving XML documents using the xml data type

Defining XML

XML stands for eXtensible Markup Language. XML is derived from Standard Generalized Markup Language (SGML). XML is a *metalanguage*. A metalanguage isn't used for programming but rather for defining other languages, and the languages XML defines are known as *markup languages*. Markup is exactly what it implies: a means of "marking up" something. The XML document is in the form of a text document, and it can be read by both humans and computers.

> **Note** In essence, each XML document is an instance of a language defined by the XML elements used in the document. The specific language may or may not have been explicitly defined, but professional use of XML demands carefully planning one's XML *vocabulary* and specifying its definition in a *schema* that can be used to validate that documents adhere to both the syntax and the semantics of a vocabulary. XML Schema Definition (XSD) is the language for defining XML vocabularies.

The World Wide Web Consortium (W3C) developed XML in 1996. Intended to support a wide variety of applications, XML was used by the W3C to create eXtensible HTML (XHTML), an XML vocabulary. Since 1996, the W3C has developed a variety of other XML-oriented technologies, including eXtensible Stylesheet Language (XSL), which provides the same kind of facility for XHTML that Cascading Style Sheets (CSS) does for HTML, and XSL Transformations (XSLT), which is a language for transforming XML documents into other XML documents.

Why XML

XML is a multipurpose, extensible data representation technology. XML increases the possibilities for applications to consume and manipulate data. XML is different from the relational data; XML data can be structured, semistructured, or unstructured. XML support in SQL Server 2012 is fully integrated with the relational engine and query optimizer, allowing you to retrieve and modify XML data and even convert between XML and relational data representations.

Benefits of Storing Data As XML

XML is a platform-independent, data-representation format that offers certain benefits over a relational format for specific data representation requirements.

Storing data as XML offers many benefits:

- Since XML is self-describing, applications can consume XML data without knowing the schema or structure. XML data is always arranged hierarchically in a tree structure. The XML tree structure must always have a root, or parent node, which is known as the XML *document*.

- XML maintains document ordering. Because XML is arranged in a tree structure, maintaining node order becomes easy.

- XML Schema is used to define valid XML document structure.

- Because of XML's hierarchical structure, you can search inside the tree structures. XQuery and XPath are the query languages designed to search XML data.

- Data stored as XML is extensible. It is easy to manipulate XML data by inserting, modifying, and deleting nodes.

Note Well-formed XML is an XML document that meets a set of constraints specified by the W3C recommendation for XML 1.0. For example, well-formed XML must contain a root-level element, and any other nested elements must open and close properly without intermixing.

SQL Server 2005 validates some of the well-formedness constraints. Some rules such as the requirement for a root-level element are not enforced. For a complete list of well-formedness requirements, refer to the W3C recommendations for XML 1.0 at www.w3.org/TR/REC-xml.

Understanding XML Documents

An XML document could be a physical file on a computer, a data stream over a network (in theory, formatted so a human could read it, but in practice, often in compressed binary form), or just a string in memory. It has to be complete in itself, however, and even without a schema, it must obey certain rules.

The most fundamental rule is that XML documents must be *well-formed*. At its simplest, this means that overlapping elements aren't allowed, so you must close all *child* elements before the end tag of their *parent* element. For example, this XML document is well-formed:

```
<states>
    <state>
        <name>Delaware</name>
        <city>Dover</city>
        <city>Wilmington</city>
    </state>
</states>
```

It has a *root* (or *document*) element, states, delimited by a start tag, <states>, and an end tag, </states>. The root element is the parent of the state element, which is in turn the parent of a name element and two city elements. An XML document can have only one root element.

Elements may have *attributes*. For example, the previous document could be rewritten as follows, where name is used as an attribute with the state element:

```
<states>
    <state name="Delaware">
        <city>Dover</city>
        <city>Wilmington</city>
    </state>
</states>
```

It retains the same information, replacing the name element that occurs only once with a name attribute and changing the *content* of the original element (Delaware) into the *value* of the attribute ("Delaware"). An element may have any number of attributes, but it may not have duplicate attributes, so the city elements weren't candidates for replacement.

Elements may have content (text data or other elements), or they may be *empty*. For example, if you want (just for the sake of argument) to keep track of how many states are in the document, you could use an empty element to do it:

```
<states>
   <controlinfo count="1"/>
   <state name="Delaware">
      <city>Dover</city>
      <city>Wilmington</city>
   </state>
</states>
```

The empty element, controlinfo, has one attribute, count, but no content. Note that it isn't delimited by start and end tags but exists within an *empty element tag* (that starts with < and ends with />).

An alternative syntax for empty elements, using start and end tags, is also valid:

```
<controlinfo count="1"></controlinfo>
```

Many programs that generate XML use this form.

■ **Note** Though it's easy to design XML documents, designing them well is as much a challenge as designing a database. Many experienced XML designers disagree over the best use of attributes and even whether attributes should be used at all (without attributes, empty elements have virtually no use). While elements may in some ways map more ideally to relational data, this doesn't mean attributes have no place in XML design. After all, XML isn't intended to (and in principle, can't) conform to the relational model of data. In fact, you'll see that a "pure" element-only design can be more difficult to work with in T-SQL.

Understanding the XML Declaration

In addition to elements and attributes, XML documents can have other parts, but most of them are important only if you really need to delve deeply into XML. Though it is optional, the *XML declaration* is one part that should be included in an XML document to precisely conform to the W3C recommendation. If used, it must occur before the root element in an XML document.

The XML declaration is similar in format to an element, but it has question marks immediately next to the angle brackets. It always has an attribute named version; currently, this has two possible values: "1.0" and "1.1". (A couple other attributes are defined but aren't required.) So, the simplest form of an XML declaration is as follows:

```
<?xml version="1.0" ?>
```

XML has other aspects, but this is all you need to get started. In fact, this may be all you'll ever need to be quite effective. As you'll see, we don't use any XML declarations (or even more important things such as XML schemas and namespaces) for our XML documents, yet our small examples work well, are representative of fundamental XML processing, and could be scaled up to much larger XML documents.

Converting Relational Data to XML

A SELECT query returns results as a row set. You can optionally retrieve results of a SQL query as XML by specifying the FOR XML clause in the query. SQL Server 2005 enables you to extract relational data into XML form, by using the FOR XML clause in the SELECT statement. SQL Server 2005 extends the FOR XML capabilities, making it easier to represent complex hierarchical structures and add new keywords to the modify the resulting XML structure.

■ **Note** In Chapter 13, I show how to extract data from a data set, convert it to XML, and write it to a file with the data set's WriteXml method.

The FOR XML clause converts result sets from a query into an XML structure, and it provides four modes of formatting:

- FOR XML RAW
- FOR XML AUTO
- FOR XML PATH
- FOR XML EXPLICIT

We'll use the first two in examples to show how to generate XML with a query.

Using FOR XML RAW

The RAW mode transforms each row in the query result set into an XML element identified as row for each row displayed in the result set. Each column name in the SELECT statement is added as an attribute to the row element while displaying the result set.

By default, each column value in the row set that is not NULL is mapped to an attribute of the row element.

Try It: Using FOR XML RAW (Attribute-centric)

1. Let's produce the SQL query result in raw XML format. FOR XML RAW is the statement we will use to produce the output, as you will see in the following steps. In the Object Explorer, expand the Databases node, select the AdventureWorks database, and click the New Query window. Enter the following query, and click Execute:

```
select  Person.Contact.Title, Person.Contact.FirstName, Person.Contact.LastNamefrom
Person.Contact
where  Person.Contact.Title ='Mr.'
for xml raw
```

2. You will see a link in the results pane of the query pane. Click the link, and you should see the results shown in Figure 7-1.

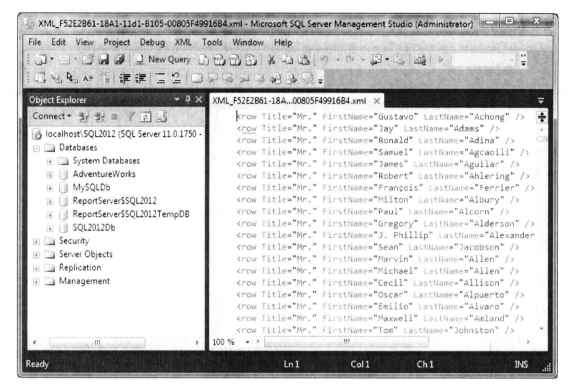

Figure 7-1. Using FOR XML RAW

How It Works

RAW mode produces very "raw" XML. It turns each row in the result set into an empty XML row element and uses an attribute for each of the column values, using the alias names we specified in the query as the attribute names. It produces a string composed of all the elements.

RAW mode doesn't produce an XML document, since it has as many root elements (raw) as there are rows in the result set, and an XML document can have only one root element.

Try It: Using FOR XML RAW (Element-centric)

Changing the formatting from attribute-centric (as shown in the previous example) to element-centric means that a new element will be created for each column. To achieve this, you need to add the ELEMENTS keyword after the FOR XML RAW clause, as shown in the following query.

1. Replace the existing query in query pane with the following query, and click Execute:

```
select  Person.Contact.Title, Person.Contact.FirstName, Person.Contact.LastNamefrom
Person.Contact
where  Person.Contact.Title ='Mr.'
for xml raw, elements
```

2.   You will see a link in the results pane of the query pane. Click the link, and you should see the results in Figure 7-2.

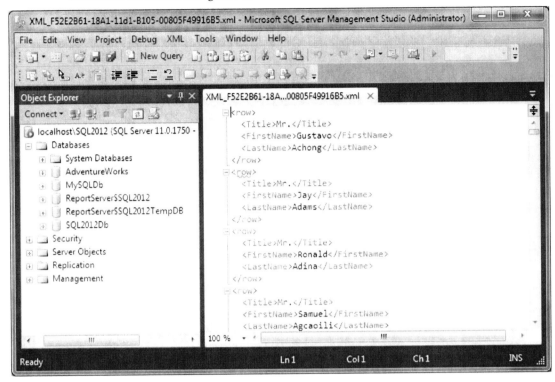

Figure 7-2. *Using FOR XML RAW ELEMENTS*

How It Works

RAW ELEMENTS mode produces very "element-centric" XML. It turns each row in the result set where each column is converted into an attribute.

RAW ELEMENTS mode also doesn't produce an XML document, since it has as many root elements (raw) as there are rows in the result set, and an XML document can have only one root element.

Try It: Renaming the row Element

For each row in the result set, the RAW mode generates an element called row. You can optionally specify another name for this element by specifying an optional argument to the RAW mode, as shown in this query. To achieve this, you need to add an alias after the FOR XML RAW clause, as shown in the following query.

1.   Replace the existing query in query window with the following query, and click Execute:

```
select  Person.Contact.Title, Person.Contact.FirstName, Person.Contact.LastNamefrom
Person.Contact
where  Person.Contact.Title ='Mr.'
for xml raw ('PersonDetails'), elements
```

2. You will see a link in the results pane of the query pane. Click the link, and you should see the results in Figure 7-3.

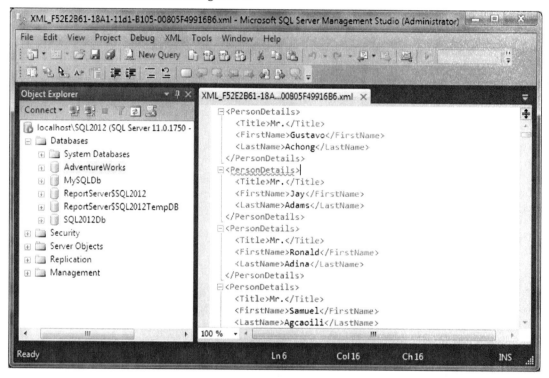

Figure 7-3. Renaming the row element

How It Works

RAW ('alias') mode produces output where the row element is renamed into the alias specified in the query.

Because the ELEMENTS directive is added in the query, the result is element-centric, which is why the row element is renamed with the alias specified. If you don't add the ELEMENTS keyword in the query, then the output will be attribute-centric, and the row element will be renamed to the alias specified in the query.

Observations About XML RAW Formatting

The following are tips about XML RAW:

- XML RAW does not provide a root node, which is why the XML structure is not a well-formed XML document.

- Since XML RAW supports attribute- and element-centric formatting, all the columns must be formatted in the same way. Hence, it is not possible to have an XML structure returned with both the XML attributes and XML elements.

- XML RAW generates a hierarchy where all the elements in the XML structure are at the same level.

Using FOR XML AUTO

AUTO mode returns query results as nested XML elements. This does not provide much control over the shape of the XML generated from a query result. As such, AUTO mode queries are useful if you want to generate simple hierarchies.

Each table in the FROM clause, from which at least one column is listed in the SELECT clause, is represented as an XML element. The columns listed in the SELECT clause are mapped to attributes or subelements.

Try It: Using FOR XML AUTO

Let's produce the SQL query result as nested XML elements. FOR XML AUTO is the statement we will use to produce the output, as you will see in following steps:

1. Replace the existing query in query pane with the following query, and click Execute:

```
select  Person.Contact.Title, Person.Contact.FirstName, Person.Contact.LastName
from Person.Contact
where  Person.Contact.Title ='Mr.'
for xml auto
```

2. You will see a link in the results pane of the query pane. Click the link, and you should see the results in Figure 7-4.

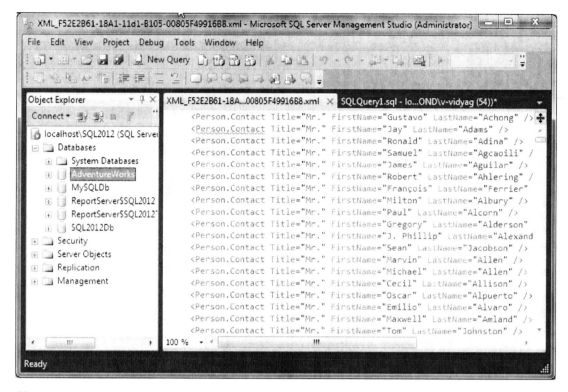

Figure 7-4. *Using FOR XML AUTO*

How It Works

Three columns, Contact.Title, Contact.FirstName, and Contact.LastName , reference the Person.Contact table. Therefore, an Person.Contact element is added, and the three columns are added as attributes of Person.Contact.

Observations About XML AUTO Formatting

Here are tips about XML AUTO:

- XML AUTO does not provide a root node, which is why the XML structure is not a well-formed XML document.

- Since XML AUTO supports attribute- and element-centric formatting, all the columns must be formatted in the same way. Hence, it is not possible to have an XML structure returned with both the XML attributes and XML elements.

- XML AUTO does not provide a renaming mechanism the way XML RAW does, whereas XML AUTO uses the table and column names and aliases if present.

Using the XML Datatype

SQL Server 2012 has a datatype, xml, that is designed not just for holding XML documents (which are essentially characters strings and can be stored in any character column big enough to hold them) but also for processing XML documents. When I discussed parsing an XML document into a DOM tree, I didn't mention that once it's parsed, the XML document can be updated. You can change element contents and attribute values, and you can add and remove element occurrences to and from the hierarchy.

You won't update XML documents here, but the xml datatype provides methods to do it. It is a very different kind of SQL Server datatype, and describing how to exploit it would take a book of its own—maybe more than one. The focus here will be on what every database programmer needs to know: how to use the xml type to store and retrieve XML documents.

Note There are so many ways to process XML documents (even in ADO.NET and with SQLXML, a support package for SQL Server 2000) that only time will tell if incorporating such features into a SQL Server datatype is worth the effort. Because XML is such an important technology, being able to process XML documents purely in T-SQL does offer many possibilities, but right now it's unclear how much more about the xml data type you'll ever need to know. At any rate, this chapter will give you what you need to know to start experimenting with it.

Try It: Creating a Table to Store XML

To create a table to hold XML documents, follow these steps:

1. In the Object Explorer, select the previously created database SQL2012Db, and click New Query.

Note For the purpose of keeping AdventureWorks clean, I am using the SQL2012Db database; you may want to execute the following statement in the same or another database.

---

2. In query pane, type the following query, and click Execute:

```
create table xmltest
(
   xid  int not null primary key,
   xdoc xml not null
)
```

How It Works

This works in the same way that the CREATE TABLE statement is expected to work without the xml datatype. Though I've said the xml datatype is different from other SQL Server datatypes, columns of xml type are defined just like any other columns. (But they can't be used in primary keys.)

Now, you'll insert your XML documents into xmltest and query it to see that they were stored.

Try It: Storing and Retrieving XML Documents

To insert your XML documents, follow these steps:

1. Replace the code in the SQL edit window with the code in Listing 7-1.

Listing 7-1. Inserting XML Documents into xmltest

```
insert into xmltest
values(
1,
'
<states>
    <state>
        <abbr>CA</abbr>
        <name>California</name>
        <city>Berkeley</city>
        <city>Los Angeles</city>
        <city>Wilmington</city>
    </state>
    <state>
        <abbr>DE</abbr>
        <name>Delaware</name>
        <city>Newark</city>
        <city>Wilmington</city>
    </state>
</states>
'
)

insert into xmltest
values(
2,
'
<states>
    <state abbr="CA" name="California">
        <city name="Berkeley"/>
        <city name="Los Angeles"/>
        <city name="Wilmington"/>
    </state>
    <state abbr="DE" name="Delaware">
        <city name="Newark"/>
        <city name="Wilmington"/>
    </state>
```

```
</states>
'
)
```

2. Run the two INSERT statements, and then display the table with select * from
   xmltest. You see the two rows displayed. Click the xdoc column in the first row,
   and you should see the XML shown in Figure 7-5.

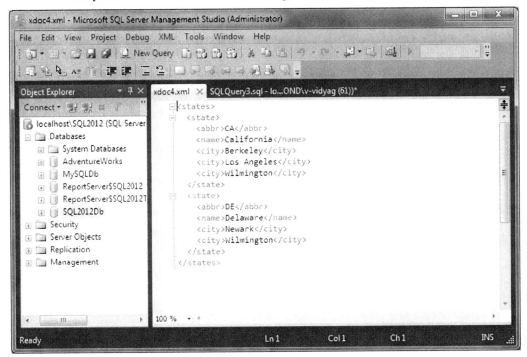

Figure 7-5. *Viewing an XML document*

How It Works

This works like all INSERTs work. You simply provide the primary keys as integers and the XML
documents as strings. The query works just as expected too.

Summary

This chapter covered the fundamentals of XML that every C# programmer needs to know. It also showed
you how to use the most frequently used T-SQL features for extracting XML from tables and querying
XML documents like tables. Finally, I discussed the xml data type and gave you some practice using it.

How much more you need to know about XML or T-SQL and ADO.NET facilities for using XML
documents depends on what you need to do. For many, this chapter may be all you ever really need to
know about XML. For those who do more sophisticated XML processing, you now have a strong
foundation for experimenting on your own. In the next chapter, you will learn about transactions.

Understanding Transactions

For any business, transactions play a key role. They may comprise many individual operations and even other transactions. Transactions are essential for maintaining data integrity both for multiple related operations and when multiple users update the database concurrently.

This chapter will talk about the concepts related to transactions and how transactions can be used in SQL Server 2012.

In this chapter, I'll cover the following:

- What is a transaction?

- When to use transactions

- Understanding ACID properties

- Transaction design

- Transaction state

- Specifying transaction boundaries

- T-SQL statements allowed in a transaction

- Local transactions in SQL Server 2012

- Distributed transactions in SQL Server 2012

- Guidelines to code efficient transactions

- How to code transactions

What Is a Transaction?

A *transaction* is a set of operations performed so all operations are guaranteed to succeed or fail as one unit.

A common example of a transaction is the process of transferring money from a checking account to a savings account. This involves two operations: deducting money from the checking account and adding it to the savings account. Both must succeed together and be *committed* to the accounts, or both must fail together and be *rolled back* so that the accounts are maintained in a consistent state. Under no circumstances should money be deducted from the checking account but not added to the savings account (or vice versa). By using a transaction, both the operations, namely, debit and credit, can be guaranteed to succeed or fail together. So, both accounts remain in a consistent state all the time.

When to Use Transactions

You should use transactions when several operations must succeed or fail as a unit. The following are some frequent scenarios where using transactions is recommended:

- In batch processing, where multiple rows must be inserted, updated, or deleted as a single unit

- Whenever a change to one table requires that other tables be kept consistent

- When modifying data in two or more databases concurrently

- In distributed transactions, where data is manipulated in databases on different servers

When you use transactions, you place locks on data pending permanent change to the database. No other operations can take place on locked data until the lock is released. You could lock anything from a single row up to the whole database. This is called *concurrency,* which means how the database handles multiple updates at one time.

In the bank example, locks ensure that two separate transactions don't access the same accounts at the same time. If they did, either deposits or withdrawals could be lost.

■ **Note** It's important to keep transactions pending for the shortest period of time. A lock stops others from accessing the locked database resource. Too many locks, or locks on frequently accessed resources, can seriously degrade performance.

Understanding ACID Properties

A transaction is characterized by four properties, often referred to as the *ACID properties:* atomicity, consistency, isolation, and durability.

■ **Note** The term ACID was coined by Andreas Reuter in 1983.

Atomicity: A transaction is atomic if it's regarded as a single action rather than a collection of separate operations. So, only when all the separate operations succeed does a transaction succeed and is committed to the database. On the other hand, if a single operation fails during the transaction, everything is considered to have failed and must be undone (rolled back) if it has already taken place. In the case of the order-entry system of the Northwind database, when you enter an order into the Orders and Order Details tables, data will be saved together in both tables, or it won't be saved at all.

Consistency: The transaction should leave the database in a consistent state—whether or not it completed successfully. The data modified by the transaction must comply with all the constraints placed on the columns in order to maintain data integrity. In the case of Northwind, you can't have rows in the Order Details table without a corresponding row in the Orders table, because this would leave the data in an inconsistent state.

Isolation: Every transaction has a well-defined boundary—that is, it is isolated from another transaction. One transaction shouldn't affect other transactions running at the same time. Data modifications made by one transaction must be isolated from the data modifications made by all other transactions. A transaction sees data in the state it was in before another concurrent transaction modified it, or it sees the data after the second transaction has completed, but it doesn't see an intermediate state.

Durability: Data modifications that occur within a successful transaction are kept permanently within the system regardless of what else occurs. Transaction logs are maintained so that should a failure occur, the database can be restored to its original state before the failure. As each transaction is completed, a row is entered in the database transaction log. If you have a major system failure that requires the database to be restored from a backup, you could then use this transaction log to insert (roll forward) any successful transactions that have taken place.

Every database server that offers support for transactions enforces these four ACID properties automatically.

Transaction Design

Transactions represent real-world events such as bank transactions, airline reservations, remittance of funds, and so forth.

The purpose of transaction design is to define and document the high-level characteristics of transactions required on the database system, including the following:

- Data to be used by the transaction

- Functional characteristics of the transaction

- Output of the transaction

- Importance to users

- Expected rate of usage

There are three main types of transactions:

- *Retrieval transactions*: Retrieves data from display on the screen

- *Update transactions*: Inserts new records, deletes old records, or modifies existing records in the database

- *Mixed transactions*: Involves both retrieving and updating data

Transaction State

In the absence of failures, all transactions complete successfully. However, a transaction may not always complete its execution successfully. Such a transaction is termed *aborted*.

A transaction that completes its execution successfully is said to be *committed*. Figure 8-1 shows that if a transaction has been partially committed, it will be committed but only if it has not failed; and if the transaction has failed, it will be aborted.

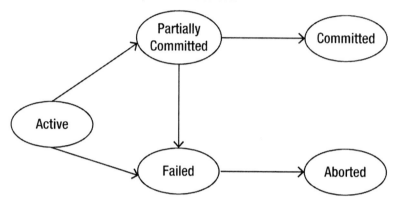

Figure 8-1. States of a transaction

Specifying Transaction Boundaries

SQL Server transaction boundaries help you identify when SQL Server transactions start and end by using API functions and methods:

- *Transact-SQL statements:* Use the BEGIN TRANSACTION, COMMIT TRANSACTION, COMMIT WORK, ROLLBACK TRANSACTION, ROLLBACK WORK, and SET IMPLICIT_TRANSACTIONS statements to delineate transactions. These are primarily used in DB-Library applications and in T-SQL scripts, such as the scripts that are run using the osql command-prompt utility.

- *API functions and methods:* Database APIs such as ODBC, OLE DB, ADO, and the .NET Framework SQLClient namespace contain functions or methods used to delineate transactions. These are the primary mechanisms used to control transactions in a database engine application.

Each transaction must be managed by only one of these methods. Using both methods on the same transaction can lead to undefined results. For example, you should not start a transaction using the ODBC API functions and then use the T-SQL COMMIT statement to complete the transaction. This would not notify the SQL Server ODBC driver that the transaction was committed. In this case, use the ODBC SQLEndTran function to end the transaction.

T-SQL Statements Allowed in a Transaction

You can use all T-SQL statements in a transaction, except for the following statements: ALTER DATABASE, RECONFIGURE, BACKUP, RESTORE, CREATE DATABASE, UPDATE STATISTICS, and DROP DATABASE.

Also, you cannot use `spdboption` to set database options or use any system procedures that modify the master database inside explicit or implicit transactions.

Local Transactions in SQL Server 2012

All database engines are supposed to provide built-in support for transactions. Transactions that are restricted to only a single resource or database are known as *local transactions*. Local transactions can be in one of the following four transaction modes:

- *Autocommit transactions*: Autocommit mode is the default transaction management mode of SQL Server. Every T-SQL statement is committed or rolled back when it is completed. If a statement completes successfully, it is committed; if it encounters any errors, it is bound to roll back. A SQL Server connection operates in autocommit mode whenever this default mode has not been overridden by any type transactions.

- *Explicit transactions*: Explicit transactions are those in which you explicitly control when the transaction begins and when it ends. Prior to SQL Server 2000, explicit transactions were also called *user-defined* or *user-specified* transactions.

  T-SQL scripts for this mode use the `BEGIN TRANSACTION`, `COMMIT TRANSACTION`, and `ROLLBACK TRANSACTION` statements. Explicit transaction mode lasts only for the duration of the transaction. When the transaction ends, the connection returns to the transaction mode it was in before the explicit transaction was started.

- *Implicit transactions*: When you connect to a database using SQL Server Management Studio and execute a DML query, the changes are automatically saved. This occurs because, by default, the connection is in autocommit transaction mode. If you want no changes to be committed unless you explicitly indicate so, you need to set the connection to implicit transaction mode.

  You can set the database connection to implicit transaction mode by using `SET IMPLICIT TRANSACTIONS ON|OFF`.

  After implicit transaction mode has been set to `ON` for a connection, SQL Server automatically starts a transaction when it first executes any of the following statements: `ALTER TABLE`, `CREATE`, `DELETE`, `DROP`, `FETCH`, `GRANT`, `INSERT`, `OPEN`, `REVOKE`, `SELECT`, `TRUNCATE TABLE`, and `UPDATE`.

  The transaction remains in effect until a `COMMIT` or `ROLLBACK` statement has been explicitly issued. This means that when, say, an `UPDATE` statement is issued on a particular record in a database, SQL Server will maintain a lock on the data scoped for data modification until either a `COMMIT` or `ROLLBACK` is issued. In case neither of these commands is issued, the transaction will be automatically rolled back when the user disconnects. This is why it is not a best practice to use implicit transaction mode on a highly concurrent database.

- *Batch-scoped transactions*: A connection can be in batch-scoped transaction mode, if the transaction running in it is Multiple Active Result Sets (MARS) enabled. Basically, MARS has an associated batch execution environment, because it allows ADO.NET to take advantage of SQL Server 2012's capability of having multiple active commands on a single connection object.

When MARS is enabled, you can have multiple interleaved batches executing at the same time, so all the changes made to the execution environment are scoped to the specific batch until the execution of the batch is complete. Once the execution of the batch completes, the execution settings are copied to the default environment. Thus, a connection is said to be using batch-scoped transaction mode if it is running a transaction, has MARS enabled on it, and has multiple batches running at the same time.

MARS allows executing multiple interleaved batches of commands. However, MARS does not let you have multiple transactions on the same connection; it allows only having Multiple Active Result Sets.

Distributed Transactions in SQL Server 2012

In contrast to local transactions, which are restricted to a single resource or database, *distributed transactions* span two or more servers, which are known as *resource managers*. Transaction management needs to be coordinated among the resource managers via a server component known as a *transaction manager* or *transaction coordinator*. SQL Server can operate as a resource manager for distributed transactions coordinated by transaction managers such as the Microsoft Distributed Transaction Coordinator (MS DTC).

A transaction with a single SQL Server that spans two or more databases is actually a distributed transaction. SQL Server, however, manages the distributed transaction internally.

At the application level, a distributed transaction is managed in much the same way as a local transaction. At the end of the transaction, the application requests the transaction to be either committed or rolled back. A distributed commit must be managed differently by the transaction manager to minimize the risk that a network failure might lead you to a situation when one of the resource managers is committing instead of rolling back the transactions because of failure caused by various reasons. This critical situation can be handled by managing the commit process in two phases, also known as *two-phase commit:*

- *Prepare phase*: When the transaction manager receives a commit request, it sends a prepare command to all of the resource managers involved in the transaction. Each resource manager then does everything required to make the transaction durable, and all buffers holding any of the log images for other transactions are flushed to disk. As each resource manager completes the prepare phase, it returns success or failure of the prepare phase to the transaction manager.

- *Commit phase*: If the transaction manager receives successful prepares from all of the resource managers, it sends a COMMIT command to each resource manager. If all of the resource managers report a successful commit, the transaction manager sends notification of success to the application. If any resource manager reports a failure to prepare, the transaction manager sends a ROLLBACK statement to each resource manager and indicates the failure of the commit to the application.

Guidelines to Code Efficient Transactions

I recommend you use the following guidelines while coding transactions to make them as efficient as possible:

- *Do not require input from users during a transaction.*

  Get all required input from users before a transaction is started. If additional user input is required during a transaction, roll back the current transaction and restart the transaction after the user input is supplied. Even if users respond immediately, human reaction times are vastly slower than computer speeds. All resources held by the transaction are held for an extremely long time, which has the potential to cause blocking problems. If users do not respond, the transaction remains active, locking critical resources until they respond, which may not happen for several minutes or even hours.

- *Do not open a transaction while browsing through data, if at all possible.*

  Transactions should not be started until all preliminary data analysis has been completed.

- *Keep the transaction as short as possible.*

  After you know the modifications that have to be made, start a transaction, execute the modification statements, and then immediately commit or roll back. Do not open the transaction before it is required.

- *Make intelligent use of lower cursor concurrency options, such as optimistic concurrency options.*

  In a system with a low probability of concurrent updates, the overhead of dealing with an occasional "somebody else changed your data after you read it" error can be much lower than the overhead of always locking rows as they are read.

- *Access the least amount of data possible while in a transaction.*

  The smaller the amount of data that you access in the transaction, the fewer the number of rows that will be locked, reducing contention between transactions.

How to Code Transactions

The following three T-SQL statements control transactions in SQL Server:

- `BEGIN TRANSACTION`: This marks the beginning of a transaction.

- `COMMIT TRANSACTION`: This marks the successful end of a transaction. It signals the database to save the work.

- `ROLLBACK TRANSACTION`: This denotes that a transaction hasn't been successful and signals the database to roll back to the state it was in prior to the transaction.

Note that there is no `END TRANSACTION` statement. Transactions end on (explicit or implicit) commits and rollbacks.

Coding Transactions in T-SQL

You'll use a stored procedure to practice coding transactions in SQL. It's an intentionally artificial example but representative of transaction-processing fundamentals. It keeps things simple so you can focus on the important issue of what can happen in a transaction. That's what you really need to understand, especially when you code the transaction-related activity in a C# application later in this book.

Warning Using ROLLBACK and COMMIT inside stored procedures typically requires careful consideration of what transactions may already be in progress and have led to the stored procedure call. The example runs by itself, so you don't need to be concerned with this here, but you should always consider whether it's a potential issue.

Try It: Creating a Parent-Child Relationship

Before you code a transaction, let's create two tables.

1. Open SQL Server Management Studio, and in Object Explorer, select the previously created database SQL2012Db, right-click, and click New Query.

2. Enter the SQL statement in Listing 8-1 to create tables with a primary key and foreign key (in other words, the parent-child relationship). The Person table will have a primary key column that will be referenced by the PersonDetails table via a foreign key column.

Listing 8-1. Create Parent-Child Relationship create table Person

```
(
   PersonID nvarchar(5) primary key not null,
   FirstName nvarchar(10) not null,
   Company nvarchar(15)
)

    create table PersonDetails
    (
        PersonID nvarchar(5) foreign key references dbo.Person(PersonID),
        Address nvarchar(30)
    )
```

3. Now click Execute. You will see the status as "Command(s) completed successfully," as shown in Figure 8-2.

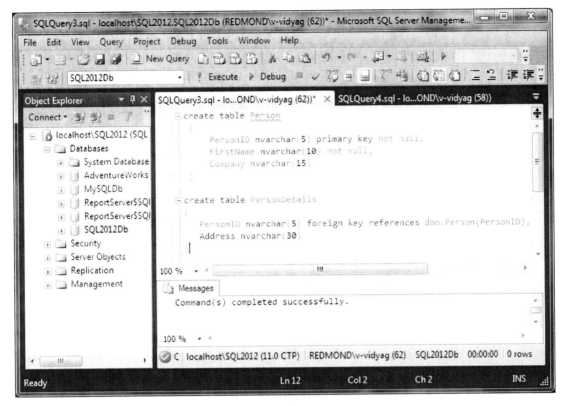

Figure 8-2. Executing the create table statement (parent-child relationship)

4. Next let's insert some data into the Person and PersonDetails tables; execute the statement in Listing 8-2, and click Execute.

Listing 8-2. Create Parent-Child Relationship

```
Insert into Person
values('Vidvr','Vidya Vrat','Lionbridge Inc'),
      ('Rupag','Rupali', 'Pearl Solutions')
```

This statement should show the status "(2 row(s) affected)."

A child can have only those records that map to the parent; hence, we can insert only child records in PersonDetails for those PersonIDs that are already available in the Person table.

```
Insert into PersonDetails
values('Vidvr','Bellevue WA 98007'),
      ('Rupag', 'Bellevue WA 98007')
```

As you can see, the child table's PersonID matches with the parent table.

So, now we have a perfect parent-child relationship, where we have two parent records and two matching child records in the Person and PersonDetails tables, as shown in Figure 8-3.

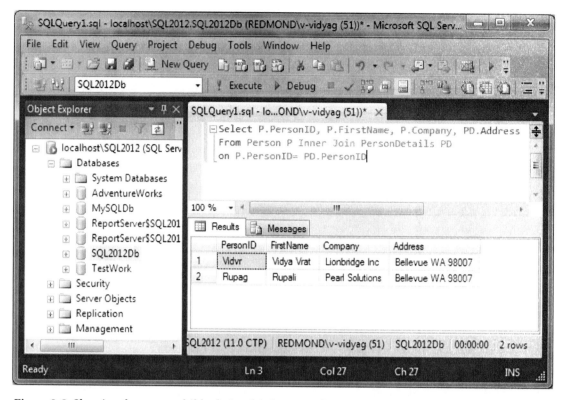

Figure 8-3. Showing the parent-child relationship between the Person and PersonDetails tables

Try It: Coding a Transaction in T-SQL

Follow these steps to code a transaction:

1. Here, you'll code a transaction based on the Person and PersonDetails tables, where we will make use of SQL Server's primary key and foreign key rules to understand how transactions work. The Person table has three columns. Two columns, PersonID and FirstName, don't allow null values, and PersonID is also a primary key column; that is, only unique values are allowed. Also, the last column, Company, allows null values.

   Similarly, the PersonDetails table is a foreign key or child table; it has a PersonID column, which is a foreign key column and reference to Person.PersonID. It also has an Address column. The child or foreign key table can have only those records that have a matching primary key column value available in the parent or primary key table, as shown in Figure 8-3. If a child record that is inserted doesn't have a matching parent or primary key value, then it will result in an error and not be inserted into the child table.

2. In Object Explorer, select the SQL2012Db database, and click the New Query button.

3. Create a stored procedure named sp_Trans_Test using the code in Listing 8-3.

Listing 8-3. *spTransTest*

```
create procedure sp_Trans_Test
      @newpersonid nvarchar(5),
      @newfirstname nvarchar(10),
      @newcompanyname nvarchar(15),
      @oldpersonid nvarchar(5)
as
      declare @inserr int
      declare @delerr int
      declare @maxerr int

      set @maxerr = 0

      begin transaction

      -- Add a person
      insert into person (personid, firstname, company)
      values(@newpersonid, @newfirstname, @newcompanyname)

      -- Save error number returned from Insert statement
      set @inserr = @@error
      if @inserr > @maxerr
        set  @maxerr  = @inserr

      -- Delete a person
      delete from person
      where personid = @oldpersonid

      -- Save error number returned from Delete statement
      set @delerr = @@error
      if @delerr > @maxerr
        set  @maxerr  = @delerr
-- If an error occurred, roll back
if @maxerr <> 0
      begin
        rollback
        print  'Transaction  rolled  back'
      end
else
      begin
        commit
        print  'Transaction  committed'
      end
print 'INSERT error number:' + cast(@inserr as nvarchar(8))
print 'DELETE error number:' + cast(@delerr as nvarchar(8))
```

```
return @maxerr
```

4. Enter the following query in the same query pane as the Listing 8-3 code. Select the statement, as shown in Figure 8-2, and then click Execute to run the query.

```
exec sp_Trans_Test 'Pearl', 'Vamika ', null,'Agraw'
```

5. The results pane should show a return value of zero, and you should see the same messages as in Figure 8-4.

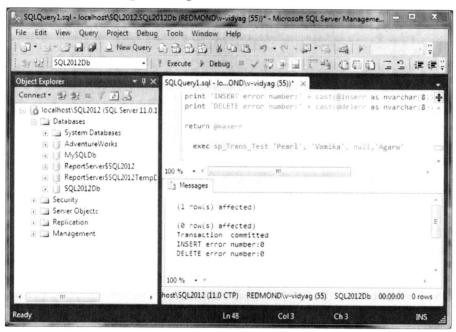

Figure 8-4. *Executing the stored procedure*

In the same query pane, enter the following SELECT statement:

```
Select * from Person
```

Select the statement as shown in Figure 8-3, and then click the Execute button. You will see that the person named Vamika has been added to the table, as shown on the Results tab in Figure 8-3.

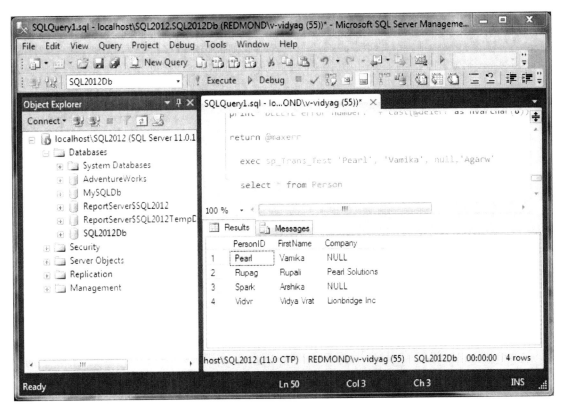

Figure 8-5. Row inserted in a transaction

6. Add another person with parameter values. Enter the following statement, and execute it as you've done previously with other similar statements.

```
exec sp_Trans_Test 'Spark', 'Arshika ', null,'Agarw'
```

7. You should get the same results shown earlier in Figure 8-4 in the Messages tab.

8. Try the SELECT statement shown in Figure 8-4 one more time. You should see that Arshika has been added to the Person table. Both Vamika and Arshika have no child records in the PersonDetails table.

How It Works

In the stored procedure, you define four input parameters:

```
create procedure sp_Trans_Test

    @newpersonid nvarchar(5),
    @newfirstname nvarchar(10),
    @newcompanyname nvarchar(15),
    @oldpersonid nvarchar(5)
as
```

You also declare three local variables:

```
declare @inserr int
declare @delerr int
declare @maxerr int
```

These local variables will be used with the stored procedure, so you can capture and display the error numbers returned, if any, from the INSERT and DELETE statements.

You mark the beginning of the transaction with a BEGIN TRANSACTION statement and follow it with the INSERT and DELETE statements that are part of the transaction. After each statement, you save the return number for it.

```
begin      transaction

--  Add  a  person
insert into person (personid, firstname, company)
values(@newpersonid, @newfirstname, @newcompanyname)

--      Save error number returned from Insert statement
set     @inserr = @@error
if @inserr > @maxerr
        set  @maxerr  =   @inserr

-- Delete a person
delete from person
where personid = @oldpersonid

--      Save error number returned from Delete statement
set     @delerr = @@error
if @delerr > @maxerr
        set  @maxerr  =   @delerr
```

Error handling is important at all times in SQL Server, and it's never more so than inside transactional code. When you execute any T-SQL statement, there's always the possibility that it may not succeed. The T-SQL @@ERROR function returns the error number for the last T-SQL statement executed. If no error occurred, @@ERROR returns zero.

@@ERROR is reset after every T-SQL statement (even SET and IF) is executed, so if you want to save an error number for a particular statement, you must store it before the next statement executes. That's why you declare the local variables @inserr, @delerr, and @maxerr.

If @@ERROR returns any value other than 0, an error has occurred, and you want to roll back the transaction. You also include PRINT statements to report whether a rollback or commit has occurred.

```
-- If an error occurred, roll back
if  @maxerr <> 0
      begin
        rollback
        print  'Transaction  rolled  back'
      end
else
      begin
        commit
        print  'Transaction  committed'
      end
```

▧ **Tip** T-SQL (and standard SQL) supports various alternative forms for keywords and phrases. You've used just ROLLBACK and COMMIT here.

Then you add some more instrumentation so you can see what error numbers are encountered during the transaction.

```
print 'INSERT error number:' + cast(@inserr as nvarchar(8))
print 'DELETE error number:' + cast(@delerr as nvarchar(8))
return @maxerr
```

Now let's look at what happens when you execute the stored procedure. You run it twice, first by adding Pearl and next by adding Spark, but you also enter the same nonexistent person Agarw to delete each time. If all statements in a transaction are supposed to succeed or fail as one unit, why does the INSERT succeed when the DELETE doesn't delete anything?

Figure 8-4 should make everything clear. Both the INSERT and DELETE return error number 0. The reason DELETE returns error number 0 even though it has not deleted any rows is that when a DELETE doesn't find any rows to delete, T-SQL doesn't treat that as an error. In fact, that's why you use a nonexistent person. Excluding these recently added people Pearl and Spark, other records have child records in the PersonDetails table, as shown in Figure 8-3; therefore, you can't delete the existing people unless you delete their details from the PersonDetails table first.

Try It: What Happens When the First Operation Fails

In this example, you'll try to insert a duplicate person and delete an existing person. Add Pearl and delete Spark by entering the following statement, and then click the Execute button:

```
exec sp_Trans_Test 'Pearl', 'Vamika', null,'Spark'
```

The result should appear as in Figure 8-6.

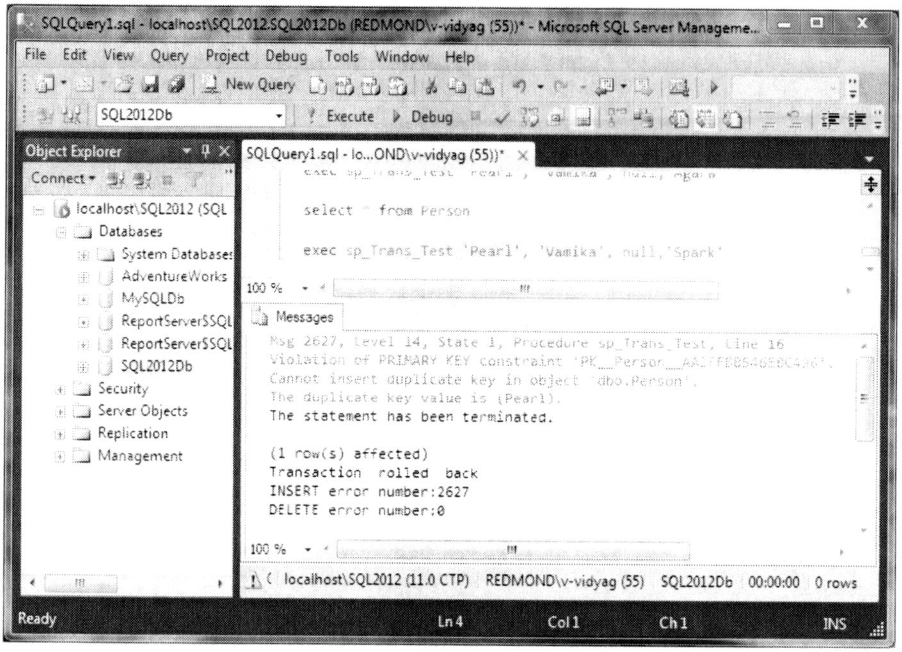

Figure 8-6. *First operation failed, second operation rolled back*

In the Messages pane shown in Figure 8-6, note that the entire transaction was rolled back because the INSERT failed and was terminated with error number 2627 (whose error message appears at the top of the window). The DELETE error number was 0, meaning it executed successfully but was rolled back. (If you check the table, you'll find that Spark still exists in the Person table.)

How It Works

Since Pearl already exists and the Person table's PersonID column is the primary key and can contain only unique values, SQL Server prevents the insertion of a duplicate, so the first operation fails. The second DELETE statement in the transaction is executed, and Spark is deleted since it doesn't have any child records in the PersonDetails table; but because gmaxerr isn't 0 (it's 2627, as you see in the Results pane), you roll back the transaction by undoing the deletion of Spark. As a result, you see all the records in the table as it is.

Try It: What Happens When the Second Operation Fails

In this example, you'll insert a valid new person and try to delete a person who has child records in the PersonDetails table.

Add ag and delete Vidvr by entering the following statement, and then click the Execute button:

```
exec sp_Trans_Test 'ag', 'Agarwal ',null, 'Vidvr'
```

The result should appear as in Figure 8-7.

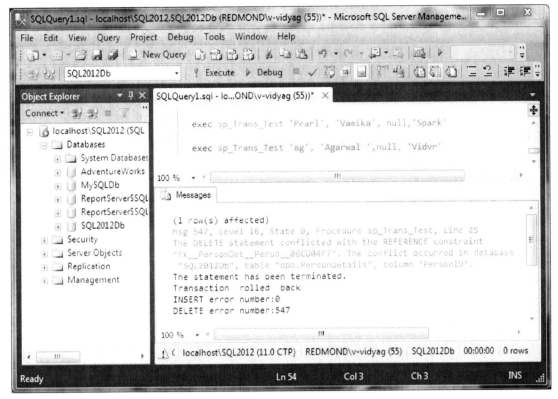

Figure 8-7. Second operation failed, first operation rolled back

In the Messages pane shown in Figure 8-7, note that the transaction was rolled back because the DELETE failed and was terminated with error number 547 (the message for which appears at the top of the window). The INSERT error number was 0, so it apparently executed successfully but was rolled back. (If you check the table, you'll find ag is not a person.)

How It Works

Since ag doesn't exist, SQL Server inserts the row, so the first operation succeeds. When the second statement in the transaction is executed, SQL Server prevents the deletion of customer Vidvr because it has child records in the PersonDetails table, but since gmaxerr isn't 0 (it's 547, as you see in the Results pane), the entire transaction is rolled back.

Try It: What Happens When Both Operations Fail

In this example, you'll try to insert an invalid new person, in other words, one with a duplicate name, and try to delete an undeletable one, in other words, one that has child records in the PersonDetails table.

Add Pearl, and delete customer Rupag by entering the following statement, and then click the Execute button:

```
exec sp_Trans_Test 'Pearl', 'Vamika', null,'Rupag'
```

The result should appear as in Figure 8-8.

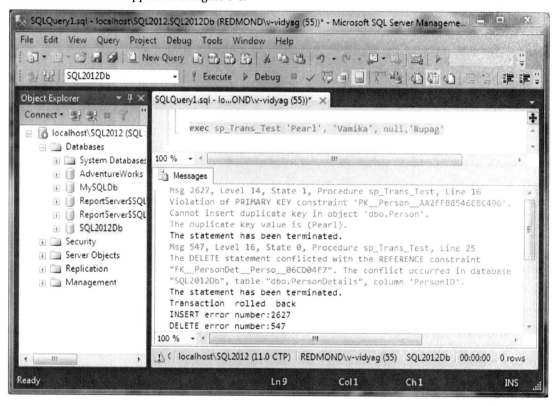

Figure 8-8. *Both operations rolled back*

In the Messages pane shown in Figure 8-8, note that the transaction was rolled back (even though neither statement succeeded, so there was nothing to roll back) because gmaxerr returns 2627 for the INSERT and 547 for the DELETE. Error messages for both failing statements are displayed at the top of the window.

How It Works

By now, you should understand why both statements failed. This happened because the first statement couldn't insert a duplicate record and the second statement couldn't delete a record that has associated child records. This is why the Message pane in Figure 8-8 shows both the errors explicitly mentioning duplicate keys and conflicting references with child records.

Summary

This chapter covered the fundamentals of transactions, including concepts such as understanding what transactions are, ACID properties, local and distributed transactions, guidelines for writing efficient transactions, and coding transactions in T-SQL. Although this chapter provided just the fundamentals of transactions, you now know enough about coding transactions to handle basic transactional processing and to implement it with later chapters using C# and ADO.NET.

In the next chapter, you'll learn about the fundamentals of Windows Forms.

Working with Data Using ADO.NET

Building Windows Forms Applications

This chapter covers Windows Forms and how to develop Windows Forms applications using C# 2012. In this chapter, we'll cover the following:

- Understanding Windows Forms

- User interface design principles

- Best practices for user interface design

- Working with Windows Forms

- Understanding the Design and Code views

- Sorting properties in the Properties window

- Setting the properties of solutions, projects, and Windows forms

- Working with controls

- Setting dock and anchor properties

- Adding a new form to the project

- Implementing an MDI form

Understanding Windows Forms

Windows Forms, also known as WinForms, is the name of the graphical user interface (GUI) application programming interface (API) included as part of Microsoft's .NET Framework, providing access to the native Microsoft Windows interface elements by wrapping the existing Windows API in managed code.

WinForms are the basic building blocks of the user interface. They work as containers to host controls that allow you to present an application. WinForms is the most commonly used interface for an application's development, although other types of applications are also available such as console applications and services. But WinForms offers the best possible way to interact with the user and accepts user input in the form of key presses or mouse clicks.

User Interface Design Principles

The best mechanism for interacting with any application is often a user interface. Therefore, it becomes important to have an efficient design that is easy to use. When designing the user interface, your primary consideration should be the people who will use the application. They are your target audience, and knowing your target audience makes it easier for you to design a user interface that helps users learn and use your application. A poorly designed user interface, on the other hand, can lead to frustration and inefficiency if it causes the target audience to avoid or even discard your application.

Forms are the primary element of a Microsoft Windows application. As such, they provide the foundation for each level of user interaction. Various controls, menus, and so on, can be added to forms to supply specific functionality. In addition to being functional, your user interface should be attractive and inviting to the user.

Best Practices for User Interface Design

The user interface provides a mechanism for users to interact with your application. Therefore, an efficient design that is easy to use is of paramount importance. The following are some guidelines for designing user-friendly, elegant, and simple user interfaces.

Simplicity

Simplicity is an important aspect of a user interface. A visually "busy" or overly complex user interface makes it harder and more time-consuming to learn the application. A user interface should allow a user to quickly complete all interactions required by the program, but it should expose only the functionality needed at each stage of the application. When designing your user interface, you should keep program flow and execution in mind so that users of your application will find it easy to use. Controls that display related data should be grouped together on the form. ListBox, ComboBox, and CheckBox controls can be used to display data and allow users to choose between preset options.

The use of a tab order (the order by which users can cycle through controls on a form by pressing the Tab key) allows users to rapidly navigate fields.

Trying to reproduce a real-world object is a common mistake when designing user interfaces. For instance, if you want to create a form that takes the place of a paper form, it is natural to attempt to reproduce the paper form in the application. This approach might be appropriate for some applications, but for others, it might limit the application and provide no real user benefit, because reproducing a paper form can limit the functionality of your application. When designing an application, think about your unique situation and try to use the computer's capabilities to enhance the user experience for your target audience.

Default values are another way to simplify your user interface. For example, if you expect 90 percent of the users of an application to select Washington in a State field, make Washington the default choice for that field.

Information from your target audience is paramount when designing a user interface. The best information to use when designing a user interface is input from the target audience. Tailor your interface to make frequent tasks easy to perform.

Position of Controls

The location of controls on your user interface should reflect their relative importance and frequency of use. For example, if you have a form that is used to input both required information and optional information, the controls for the required information are more important and should receive greater prominence. In Western cultures, user interfaces are typically designed to be read from left to right and from top to bottom. The most important or frequently used controls are most easily accessed at the top of a form. Controls that will be used after a user completes an action on a form, such as a Submit button, should follow the logical flow of information and be placed at the bottom of the form.

It is also necessary to consider the relatedness of information. Related information should be displayed in controls that are grouped together. For example, if you have a form that displays information about a customer, a purchase order, or an employee, you can group each set of controls on a Tab control that allows a user to easily move back and forth between displays.

Aesthetics is also an important consideration in the placement of controls. You should try to avoid forms that display more information than can be understood at a glance. Whenever possible, controls should be adequately spaced to create visual appeal and ease of accessibility.

Consistency

Your user interface should exhibit a consistent design across each form in your application. An inconsistent design can make your application seem disorganized or chaotic, hindering adoption by your target audience. Don't ask users to adapt to new visual elements as they navigate from form to form.

Consistency is created through the use of colors, fonts, size, and types of control employed throughout the application. Before any actual application development takes place, you should decide on a visual scheme that will remain consistent throughout the application.

Aesthetics

Whenever possible, a user interface should be inviting and pleasant. Although clarity and simplicity should not be sacrificed for the sake of attractiveness, you should endeavor to create an application that will not dissuade users from using it.

Color

Judicious use of color helps make your user interface attractive to the target audience and inviting to use. It is easy to overuse color, however. Loud, vibrant colors might appeal to some users, but others might have a negative reaction. When designing a background color scheme for your application, the safest course is to use muted colors with broad appeal.

Always research any special meanings associated with color that might affect user response to your application. If you are designing an application for a company, you might consider using the company's corporate color scheme in your application. When designing for international audiences, be aware that certain colors might have cultural significance. Maintain consistency, and do not overdo the color.

Always think about how color might affect usability. For example, gray text on a white background can be difficult to read and thus impairs usability. Also, be aware of usability issues related to color blindness. Some people, for example, are unable to distinguish between red and green. Therefore, red text on a green background is invisible to such users. Do not rely on color alone to convey information. Contrast can also attract attention to important elements of your application.

Fonts

Usability should determine the fonts you choose for your application. For usability, avoid fonts that are difficult to read or highly embellished. Stick to simple, easy-to-read fonts such as Palatino or Times New Roman. Also, as with other design elements, fonts should be applied consistently throughout the application. Use cursive or decorative fonts only for visual effects, such as on a title page if appropriate, and never to convey important information.

Images and Icons

Pictures and icons add visual interest to your application, but careful design is essential to their use. Images that appear "busy" or distract the user will hinder use of your application. Icons can convey information, but again, careful consideration of end-user response is required before deciding on their use. For example, you might consider using a red octagon similar to a U.S. stop sign to indicate that users might not want to proceed beyond that point in the application. Whenever possible, icons should be kept to simple shapes that are easily rendered in a 16-by-16-pixel square.

Working with Windows Forms

To work with Windows Forms, you need to create a Windows Forms Application project using Visual Studio 2012. To do so, click Start   All Programs   Visual Studio 2012, and from the list shown choose Microsoft Visual Studio 2012. This will open the Visual Studio start page. Click File ➤ New ➤ Project. Now you will see the New Project dialog box from which you can choose the Windows Forms Application template, as shown in Figure 9-1.

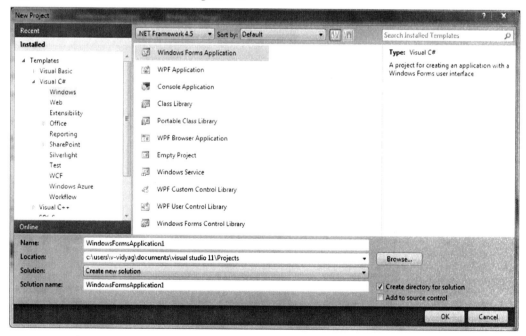

Figure 9-1. Choosing the Windows Forms Application project template

By default, the project is named as WindowsFormsApplication1 (the next would be WindowsFormsApplication2, and so on). You can enter another name for your project in the Name text box when you choose the project template, or you can rename your project later.

Once you have chosen the Windows Forms Application template and desired name and location, click OK. This will open the Visual Studio integrated development environment (IDE), called such because it has all the development-related tools, windows, dialog boxes, options, and so forth, embedded (or integrated) inside one common window, which makes the development process easier.

In the IDE, you will see that a Windows form named Form1.cs has been added as you open the project, and on the right side you can also see the Solution Explorer window. You also need to know about one more window called the Properties window. If the Properties window is not available below the Solution Explorer window, you can open it by clicking View   Properties Window or pressing F4. Now the development environment will look like Figure 9-2.

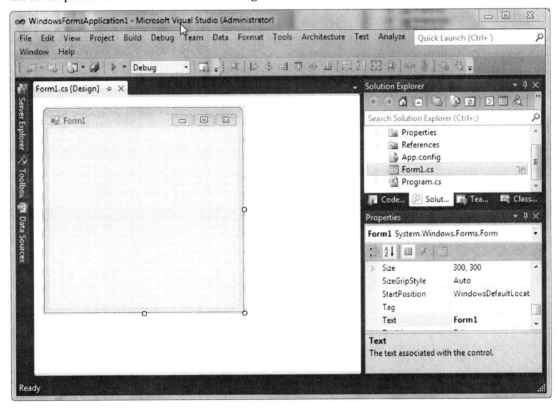

Figure 9-2. IDE with Solution Explorer and the Properties window

Because this is a Windows Forms Application project, you will be working with controls or tools that allow you to achieve functionality in the form of a GUI. You can pick the controls from the Toolbox, shown on the left side of the Windows form in the development environment. If you hover your mouse pointer on the Toolbox tab, the Toolbox window will open; expand the All Windows Forms tool set, as shown in Figure 9-3. You can pick controls from there and drop them on the surface of the Windows form.

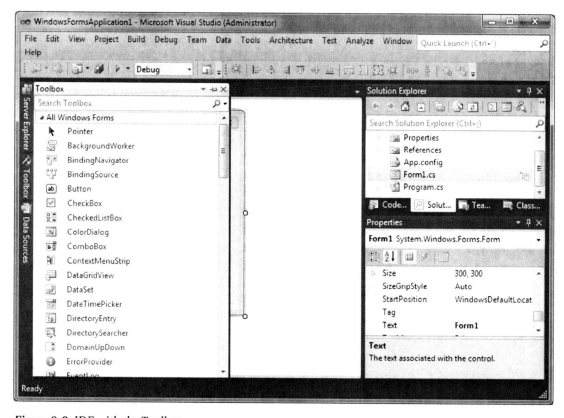

Figure 9-3. IDE with the Toolbox

Understanding the Design and Code Views

You mainly deal with two views in the Visual Studio IDE: the Design view and the Code view. When you open the Visual Studio IDE, by default it displays the Design view, as shown in Figure 9-3. The Design view allows you to drag controls and drop them onto the form. You can use the Properties window to set the properties of objects and forms or other files shown in Solution Explorer. Solution Explorer also allows you to rename the project, forms, or even other files included in the project. You can rename these objects by selecting them, right-clicking, and selecting Rename from the context menu.

Basically, the Design view gives you a visual way to work with the controls, objects, project files, and so forth. You'll want to use the other view available in the Visual Studio IDE, Code view, when you are working with code to implement the functionality behind the visual controls sitting on the surface of your Windows forms.

To switch from the Design view to the Code view, click View   Code or right-click the Windows form in Design view and select View Code. Either method will open the Code view for you, as shown in Figure 9-4.

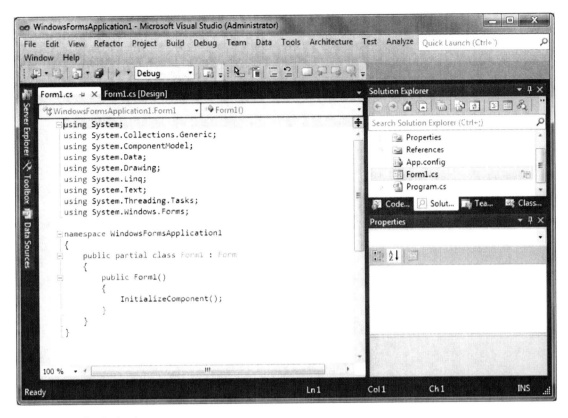

Figure 9-4. The Code view

The Code view displays all the code functionality. In Figure 9-4, note the Form1.cs tab (in which you see the Code view) is beside the Form1.cs [Design] tab, which is actually the Design view of the Windows form Form1; these tabs allow you to switch between all the GUI elements of the Design view and the related code in Code view that helps you to achieve functionality. Interestingly, if you tried accessing the Toolbox while in the Code view, you would see that there are no controls in the Toolbox. But when you switch back to the Design view, you'll find the Toolbox is fully loaded with the controls.

To switch back to the Design view, right-click the form in the Code view and select View Designer; you will see that now you are back to the Design view and can continue working with the visual elements, or *controls*.

You can also use Solution Explorer to switch between the Design and Code views by selecting your desired Windows form (in case you have multiple Windows forms open), right-clicking, and choosing either View Code or View Designer. This will open either the Code or Design view of the selected Windows form.

Sorting Properties in the Properties Window

Each object such as a form control has a lot of properties you may need to set while working with any application. To help you navigate the many properties listed in the Properties window, you can sort them by either category or alphabetically. Let's look at each of these sorting options.

Categorized View

The Categorized view organizes properties in the form of sets of properties, and each set has a name to describe that collection of properties; for example, there are categories named Appearance, Behavior, Data, Design, Focus, and so on. You can switch to the Categorized view by clicking the icon on the very left of the toolbar shown at the top of the Properties window.

In Figure-9-5, which shows the Categorized view, under the Appearance category, you will see all properties listed that define the look and feel of the object (in this case, a form). Note the other categories also shown in Figure 9-5.

■ **Note** We have intentionally kept the other categories in the collapsed mode in Figure 9-5, just to show you all the categories. When you switch to the Categorized view, you will see that all the categories are expanded by default.

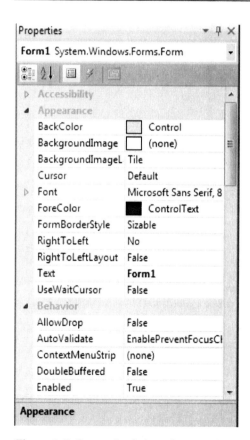

Figure 9-5. Categorized view of properties

Alphabetical View

The Alphabetical view organizes properties in ascending order by name from *a* to *z*. You can switch to the Alphabetical view by clicking the icon second from the left on the toolbar shown in the top of the Properties window.

In Figure 9-6, which shows this view, all the properties listed are organized alphabetically. Working with the Alphabetical view, rather than the Categorized view, makes life much easier. For example, say you are seeking the Font property. In the Categorized view, you have to know under which category this property is located to find it. However, if you have properties organized in the Alphabetical view, you can easily locate this property because it begins with the letter *F*, so you know whether you need to go back or forward to find this property for your control.

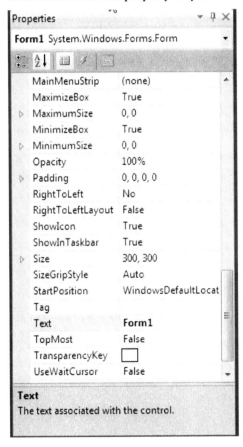

Figure 9-6. *Alphabetical view of properties*

Setting the Properties of Solutions, Projects, and Windows Forms

Before you begin putting controls on the Windows form, you need to learn how to modify some property values of the solution, project, and form you created earlier (shown previously in Figure 9-2).

Select the WindowsFormsApplication1 solution, go to the Properties window, and set its Name property value to Chapter9.

■ **Note** In some cases you may not be able to see the solution (`.sln`) file in Visual Studio. To have a solution file listed, such as Solution Chapter9 (1 project), as shown in Figure 9-7, you have to click Tools Options, go to the Project and Solutions tab, choose General, check the "Always show solution" option, and click OK.

Select the WindowsFormsApplication1 project in Solution Explorer, go to the Properties window, and modify the Project File property value, which defines the file name of the project, to appear as `WinApp.csproj`.

Now change the name of Windows form: select `Form1.cs` in Solution Explorer, in the Properties window modify the File Name property from `Form1.cs` to `WinApp.cs`, and click Yes in the dialog box that appears.

Now click Form1, located in the Solution Explorer window. Once Form1 is selected, you will see that the list of properties has changed in the Properties window. Select the Text property and modify its value from Form1 to Windows Application. The Text property defines the name shown on the title bar of the form.

After setting the properties for your solution, project, and Windows form, the IDE will look like Figure 9-7.

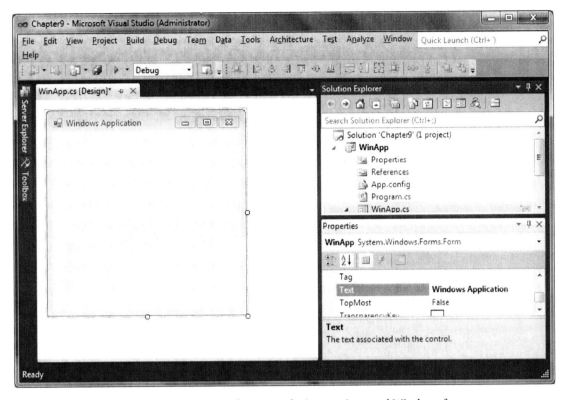

Figure 9-7. IDE after setting the properties for your solution, project, and Windows form

Working with Controls

Now that you have your Windows Forms application in place, you can start working with the controls.

The basic element of any Windows application is the control, which plays a key role by providing the visual meaning of the code functionality embedded in an application.

The most commonly used controls are Label, Button, TextBox, RadioButton, CheckBox, ListBox, ComboBox, MenuStrip, and ContextMenuStrip. Applications cannot exist without these controls, so you'll see how you can incorporate some of them into your application.

Try It: Working with the Label, TextBox, and Button Controls

In this exercise, you'll create a Windows Forms application with three labels, two text boxes, and a button. The application will accept your name as input and then flash a "Welcome" message in the form of a dialog box.

1. Go to the project named WinApp located under the solution named Chapter9, which you created earlier (refer to Figure 9-7). Ensure that you are in the Design view.

2. Drag a Label control onto the form, and position it at the top middle of the form. Select this label, navigate to the Properties window, and set the following properties:

    a. Set the Name property to lblWelcome.

    b. Set the Text property to Welcome.

    c. Select the Font property, click the ellipsis button, and specify the size of the Label control as 16 points in the Size drop-down list.

    d. Set the TextAlign property to TopCenter.

■ **Tip** You can also double-click any control in the Toolbox to add it to the form. The difference between dragging a control and double-clicking is that while dragging, you can position the control as you desire on the form. But if you just double-click a control, it will be added to the top-left corner; therefore, if you prefer it in a different location, you still have to drag it there.

---

3. Drag two more Label controls onto the form, and put them below the "Welcome" text, a little toward the left of the form. Select the first label, navigate to the Properties window, and set the Name property to lblFirstName and the Text property to First Name.

4. Now select the second label, navigate to the Properties window, and set its Name property to lblLastName and its Text property to Last Name.

5. Drag two TextBox controls onto the form, and put the TextBox named textBox1 in front of the First Name label and the TextBox named textBox2 in front of the Last Name label.

6. Select textBox1, go to the Properties window, and set its Name property to txtFname. Select textBox2, and in the Properties window set its Name property to txtLname.

7. Drag a Button control onto the form, and place it below the Label and TextBox controls. Select the Button control, go to the Properties window, change the Name property to btnSubmit, and then set its Text property to Submit.

Now you have your GUI design of the application ready; it should resemble the form shown in Figure 9-8.

Figure 9-8. *GUI design of the Windows Application form*

It's time to add functionality and switch to the Code view. You are going to read in the First Name and Last Name values supplied by the user and flash a message on a click of the Submit button, which means you need to put all the functionality behind the Submit button's click event, which will eventually read the values from the TextBox controls. To achieve this, continue with these steps:

8. Double-click the Submit button. This will take you to the Code view, and you will see that the btnSubmitClick event template has been added to the Code view window. Now you will add the code to show a dialog box, with a greeting and welcome message for the entered first name and last name. To do so, you will use MessageBox class; this class provides a Show() function to display a dialog box with the provided information. Now let's add the following code inside this btnSubmitClick event to achieve the desired functionality of a dialog, with a message, a caption in dialog box's title bar, an OK button, a Cancel button, and an information icon displayed:

```
MessageBox.Show("Hello" + ' ' + txtFname.Text + ' ' + txtLname.Text + ' ' +
"Welcome to the Windows Application","Welcome", MessageBoxButtons.OKCancel,
         MessageBoxIcon.Information);
```

Now your Code view will show the button's click event code, as shown in Figure 9-9.

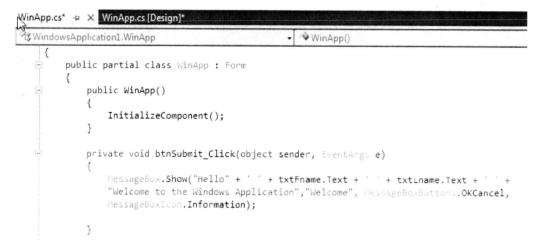

Figure 9-9. Code view of your Button click event with MessageBox.Show

9. Now click Build ▶ Build Solution, and ensure that you see the following message in the Output window:

```
========== Build: 1 succeeded or up-to-date, 0 failed, 0 skipped ==========
```

10. Now it's time to run and test the application. To do so, press Ctrl+F5. Visual Studio 2012 will load the application.

11. Enter values in the First Name and Last Name text boxes, and then click the Submit button; you will see a message similar to the one shown in Figure 9-10.

Figure 9-10. *Running the Windows Application form*

How It Works

Visual Studio comes with a lot of features to help developers while writing code. One of these features is that you can just double-click the GUI element for which you want to add the code, and you will be taken to the code associated with the GUI element in the Code view. For example, when you double-click the Submit button in the Design view, you are taken to the Code view, and the btnSubmitClick event template automatically gets generated.

To achieve the functionality for this control, you add the following code:

```
MessageBox.Show("Hello" + ' ' + txtFname.Text + ' ' + txtLname.Text + ' ' +
    "Welcome to the Windows Application","Welcome", MessageBoxButtons.OKCancel,
    MessageBoxIcon.Information);
```

MessageBox.Show() is a .NET Windows Forms method that pops up a message box based on provided arguments. To display a "Welcome" message with the first name and last name specified by the user in the message box, you apply a string concatenation approach while writing the code.

In the code segment, you hard-code the message "Hello Welcome to the Windows Application," but with the first name and last name of the user appearing after the word *Hello* and concatenated with the rest of the message, "Welcome to the Windows Application."

For readability, you also add single space characters (' ') concatenated by instances of the + operator in between the words and values you are reading from the Text property of txtFnam and txtLname. If you do not include the single space character (' ') during string concatenation, the words will be run into each other, and the message displayed in the message box will be difficult to read.

The second parameter you are provided with is Caption, which is the title of the dialog. We hard-coded this as "Welcome," and then we chose our button set through MessageBoxButtons.OKCancel. The final argument we passed is MessageBoxIcon and used an information type icon.

■ **Note** MessageBox.Show() is very powerful and handy function; you may want to play a little more with various choices that IntelliSense shows for the MessageBoxButtons and MessageBoxIcon type arguments.

Setting Dock and Anchor Properties

Prior to Visual Studio 2005, resizing Windows forms would require you to reposition and/or resize controls on those forms. For instance, if you had some controls on the left side of a form and you tried to resize the form by stretching it toward the right side or bringing it back toward the left, the controls wouldn't readjust themselves according to the width of the resized form. Developers were bound to write code to shift controls accordingly to account for the user resizing the form. This technique was very code heavy and not so easy to implement.

With Visual Studio 2005 and onwards came two new properties, Anchor and Dock, which are easy to set at design time. The same Dock and Anchor properties are available with Visual Studio 2012, and they solve the problem with the behavior of controls that users face while resizing forms.

Dock Property

The Dock property allows you to attach a control to one of the edges of its parent. The term *parent* applies to Windows forms, because Windows forms contain the controls that you drag and drop on them. By default, the Dock property of any control is set to None.

For example, a control docked to the top edge of a form will always be connected to the top edge of the form, and it will automatically resize in the left and right directions when its parent is resized.

The Dock property for a control can be set by using the provided graphical interface in the Properties window, as shown in Figure 9-11.

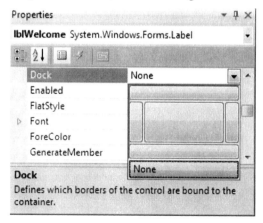

Figure 9-11. Setting the Dock property

Anchor Property

When a user resizes a form, the controls maintain a constant distance from the edges of their parent form with the help of the Anchor property. The default value for the Anchor property for any control is set to Top, Left, which means that this control will maintain a constant distance from the top and left edges of the form. The Anchor property can be set by using the provided graphical interface in the Properties window, as shown in Figure 9-12.

Because of the default setting of Anchor property to Top, Left, if you try to resize a form by stretching it toward the right side, you will see that its controls are still positioned on the left rather than shifting to the center of the form to adjust to the size of the form after resizing is done.

If opposite edges, for example, Left and Right, are both set in the Anchor property, the control will stretch when the form is resized. However, if neither of the opposite edges is set in the Anchor property, the control will float when the parent is resized.

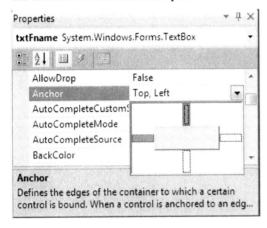

Figure 9-12. Setting the Anchor property

Try It: Working with the Dock and Anchor Properties

In this exercise, you will use the existing Windows Forms application named WinApp, which you created previously in the chapter. You will see how to modify this application in such a way that when you resize the form, its controls behave accordingly and keep the application presentable for the user.

Go to Solution Explorer and open the WinApp project. Open the WinApp form in the Design view.

1. Select the form by clicking its title bar; you will see handles around form's border, which allow you to resize the form's height and width.

2. Place the cursor on the handle of the right border, and when the mouse pointer becomes double-headed, click and stretch the form toward the right side. You will see that the form's width increases, but the controls are still attached to the left corner of the form.

3. Similarly, grab the handle located on the bottom of the form and try to increase the height of the form. You will notice that the controls are still attached to the top side of the form.

Take a look at Figure 9-13, which shows a resized (height and width) form and the position of the controls. The controls appear in the top-left corner because their Dock property values are None and their Anchor property values are Top, Left.

Figure 9-13. *Resized form and position of controls*

Now you will try to set the Dock and Anchor properties for the controls and then retest the application.

4. Select the Label control named lbl Welcome, and set the Text value to Welcome. Go to the Properties window. Select the AutoSize property, and set its value to False (default value is True).

5. Resize the width of the Label control to the width of the form, and adjust the Label control to the top border of the form. Set this control's TextAlign property to Top, Center.

6. Set the Dock property for the Label control from None to Top, which means you want the label to always be affixed with the top border of the form.

7. Now select all the remaining controls (two Labels, two TextBoxes, and one Button) either by scrolling over all of them while holding down the left mouse button or by selecting each with a click while pressing down either the Shift or Ctrl key.

8. Once you have selected all the controls, go to the Properties window. You will see listed all the properties common to the controls you have selected on the form.

9. Select the Anchor property; modify its value from the default Top, Left to Top, Left, and Right. This will allow you to adjust the controls accordingly as soon as you resize the form. The controls will also grow in size accordingly to adjust to the width of the form, as you can see in Figure 9-14.

Figure 9-14. The effect of the Anchor property setting Top, Left, Right on a resized form

Note The Anchor property has very interesting behaviors; you can try setting this property in various combinations and see the effects when you resize your form.

10. Return the form to its previous size so you can see the effects of setting another Anchor property.

11. Select all the controls again as you did in step 8. Set the Anchor property to Top only and try resizing the form now. You will notice that the controls are floating in the middle of the form when you resize it, as you can see in Figure 9-15.

Figure 9-15. The effect of the Anchor property setting Top on a resized form

12. Save the changes in your project by clicking File ➤ Save All.

How It Works

When you resize the form, it will behave according to the settings of the Dock and Anchor properties.

In the first instance, you set the Dock property of the Label control to Top, which allows this Label control to be affixed to the top border of the form and span the entire width of the form. Setting the Anchor property of the remaining controls to Top, Left, and Right shifts the controls in such a manner that they will maintain a constant distance from the left and right borders of the form.

Adding a New Form to the Project

Any real-world or enterprise application will obviously need multiple Windows forms to perform business functionality. By default, every project opens with only one Windows form, but you are free to add more.

Try It: Adding a New Form to the Windows Project

In this exercise, you will add another Windows form to your project. You will also work with ListBox, ComboBox, RadioButton, and CheckBox controls. In this new form, you will add data from two different text boxes to a ListBox and a ComboBox, respectively.

1. Navigate to Solution Explorer and select the WinApp project, right-click, and click Add Windows form. This will add a new Windows form in your project.

2. In the Add New Item dialog box displayed, change the form's name from Form1.cs to UserInfo.cs. Click Add. The new form with the name UserInfo will be added to your project.

3. Ensure that the newly added form UserInfo is open in the Design view. Select the UserInfo form by clicking the form's titlebar, navigate to the Properties window, and set the Size property's Width to 455 and Height to 251.

4. Drag a Label control onto the form; select this control, navigate to the Properties window, and set the following properties:

   a. Set the Name property to lblCountry.

   b. Set the AutoSize property to false.

   c. Set the Location property's X to 12 and Y to 26.

   d. Set the Size property's Width to 71 and Height to 13.

   e. Set the Text property to Enter Country.

5. Drag a TextBox control in front of the lblCountry label. Select this control, navigate to the Properties window, and set the following properties:

   a. Set the Name property to txtCountry.

   b. Set the Location property's X to 97 and Y to 19.

    c.   Set the Size property's Width to 129 and Height to 20.

    d.   Drag another Label below lblCountry, select this control, navigate to the Properties window, and set the following properties:

    e.   Set the Name property to lblState.

    f.   Set the AutoSize property to false.

    g.   Set the Location property's X to 12 and Y to 65.

    h.   Set the Size property's Width to 60 and Height to 13.

    i.   Set the Text property to Enter State.

6.   Drag a TextBox control in front of the lblState label. Select this control, navigate to the Properties window, and set the following properties:

    a.   Set the Name property to txtState.

    b.   Set the Location property's X to 97 and Y to 58.

    c.   Set the Size property's Width to 129 and Height to 20.

7.   Drag a ListBox control onto the UserInfoInfo form on the right side of the TextBox control you have added. Select this control, navigate to the Properties window, and set the following properties:

    a.   Set the Name property to lstCountry.

    b.   Set the Location property's X to 280 and Y to 12.

    c.   Set the Size property's Width to 129 and Height to 82.

8.   Drag a ComboBox below the just-added ListBox. Select this control, navigate to the Properties window, and set the following properties:

    a.   Set the Name property to cboState.

    b.   Set the Location property's X to 280 and Y to 117.

    c.   Set the Size property's Width to 129 and Height to 21.

9.   Drag two CheckBoxes below the Label controls, and name them chkPostalMail and chkEMail; set their Text property to Postal Mail and E-Mail, respectively.

10. Drag two RadioButtons below the TextBox controls, and name rdbMale and rdbFemale; set their Text property to Male and Female, respectively.

11. Drag a Button control to the UserInfo form to the left side below the CheckBox controls; select this control, navigate to the Properties window, and set the following properties:

    a.   Set the Name property to btnAdd.

    b.   Set the Location property's X to 12 and Y to 165.

    c.   Set the Size property's Width to 75 and Height to 23.

    d.   Set the Text property to Add.

12. Drag a Button control next to the Add button; select this control, navigate to the Properties window, and set the following properties:

    a.   Set the Name property to btnRemoveCountry.

    b.   Set the Location property's X to 105 and Y to 165.

    c.   Set the Size property's Width to 95 and Height to 23.

    d.   Set the Text property to Remove Country.

13. Drag a Button control next to the Remove Country button; select this control, navigate to the Properties window, and set the following properties:

    a.   Set the Name property to btnRemoveState.

    b.   Set the Location property's X to 220 and Y to 165.

    c.   Set the Size property's Width to 86 and Height to 23.

    d.   Set the Text property to Remove State.

14. Drag a Button control next to the Remove State button; select this control, navigate to the Properties window, and set the following properties:

    a.   Set the Name property to btnShowDetails.

    b.   Set the Location property's X to 327 and Y to 165.

    c.   Set the Size property's Width to 100 and Height to 23.

    d.   Set the Text property to Show Details.

Now you are done with the design part of the UserInfo form; while dragging and dropping the controls, you should place the controls to create a visually appealing layout, as shown in Figure 9-16.

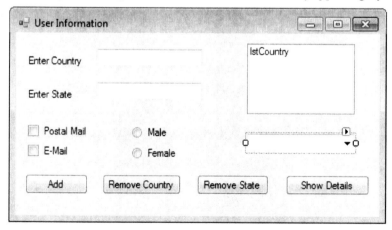

Figure 9-16. GUI design of the UserInfo form

You want the user to add a name in the TextBoxes and click the Add button, after which the country will be added to the ListBox and the state will be added to ComboBox. Accordingly, the Remove button will remove the country or state, and Show Details will show the selection made with a CheckBox and RadioButton. To do so, you need to write the code functionality behind the click event of all these buttons one by one.

15. Double-click the Add button and write the following code inside the btnAdd_Click event, which will read the country and state name entered into the textboxes and add them to the ListBox and ComboBox.

```
lstCountry.Items.Add(txtCountry.Text);
txtCountry.Clear();
    cboState.Items.Add(txtState.Text);
txtState.Clear();
```

16. Double-click the Remove Country button, and write the following code inside the btnRemoveCountry_Click event, which will remove the selected country from the ListBox named lstCountry:

```
lstCountry.Items.Remove(lstCountry.SelectedItem);
```

17. Double-click the Remove State button, and write the following code inside the btnRemoveState_Click event, which will remove the selected state from the ComboBox named cboState.

```
cboState.Items.Remove(cboState.SelectedItem);
```

18. Double-click the Show Details button, and write the following code inside the btnShowDetails_Click event, which will show the options selected via a CheckBox and RadioButton.

```
if (chkEmail.Checked == true || chkPostalMail.Checked == true &&
rdbMale.Checked == true)
{
```

19. MessageBox.Show("Hello Mr, you will be contacted by either USPS or email", "Information", MessageBoxButtons.OKCancel, MessageBoxIcon.Information);

```
}
else
    if (chkEmail.Checked == true || chkPostalMail.Checked == true
        && rdbFemale.Checked == true)
    {
        MessageBox.Show("Hello Mam, you will be contacted by either USPS or email",
"Information", MessageBoxButtons.OKCancel,
        MessageBoxIcon.Information);
}
```

20. Go to the Build menu and select Build Solution. You should see a message indicating a successful build.

21. Keep your current project open, because you'll need it immediately for the next exercise. (Don't worry, we'll explain how this and the next exercise work afterward.)

Try It: Setting the Start-up Form

Setting the start-up form in a Visual C# project is a little tricky, so I wanted to break it into its own exercise. To set a start-up form, you need to follow these steps:

1. In the project you modified in the previous exercise, navigate to Solution Explorer, open the `Program.cs` file, and look for the following code line:

```
Application.Run(new WinApp());
```

This code line ensures the WinApp form will be the first form to run all the time because this is the first form called Form1, which was already added and you renamed it when you began this project; in order to set the UserInfo form as the start-up form, you need to modify this statement a little, as follows:

```
Application.Run(new UserInfo());
```

2. Build the solution, and run and test the application by pressing Ctrl+F5. The UserInfo application form will be loaded.

3. Enter a country and state name in the appropriate text boxes and click the Add button; you will see that the names you entered have been added to the ListBox and ComboBox, as shown in Figure 9-17.

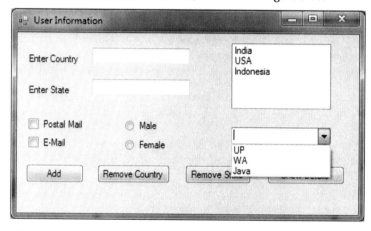

Figure 9-17. *Using ListBox and ComboBox withUserInfo Windows Forms application*

4. Select both the CheckBoxes and one of the RadioButton, and click the ShowDetails button; you will see that a message box is displayed, as shown in Figure 9-18.

Figure 9-18. Using CheckBox and RadioButton with UserInfo Windows Forms application

How It Works

Let's take a look at the "Adding a New Form to the Windows Project" task first and understand the code, button by button and line by line.

First you have an Add button, which adds the country and state to the ListBox and ComboBox. The ListBox and ComboBox controls have a collection named Items, and this collection can contain a list of items, which is why you use it here. Next you call up the Add method of the Items collection, and finally you pass the value entered in the TextBox to the ListBox's or ComboBox's Items collection's Add method, as shown here:

```
lstCountry.Items.Add(txtCountry.Text);
```

Also, once an item is added, for a better user experience, it is advisable to clear the text box so a user can type a new value with ease.

```
txtCountry.Clear();
```

You repeat the same for the ComboBox:

```
cboState.Items.Add(txtState.Text);
txtState.Clear();
```

For the Remove Country and Remove State buttons, you follow a similar approach as the Items collection, but this time instead of Add() you call the Remove() method, and as you know, the prerequisites for an item removal is that and item has to be selected first either in the ListBox or the ComboBox. Hence, the code seeks a SelectedItem to be passed to the Remove() method.

```
lstCountry.Items.Remove(lstCountry.SelectedItem);
```

```
cboState.Items.Remove(cboState.SelectedItem);
```

Now for the Show Details button, you have used some conditional logic to produce different message based on your selection, specifically with the Male and Female radio buttons.

The CheckBox and RadioButton controls offer a property named Checked, which can be either true or false, that is, checked or not checked. You build a condition around these and then show a message box.

```
if (chkEmail.Checked == true || chkPostalMail.Checked == true &&
    rdbMale.Checked == true)
{
    MessageBox.Show("Hello Mr, you will be contacted by either USPS or
                email", "Information",MessageBoxButtons.OKCancel,
                MessageBoxIcon.Information);
}
else
    if (chkEmail.Checked == true || chkPostalMail.Checked == true &&
        rdbFemale.Checked == true)
    {
        MessageBox.Show("Hello Mam, you will be contacted by either USPS or
                    email", "Information", MessageBoxButtons.OKCancel,
                    MessageBoxIcon.Information);
    }
```

In the "Setting the Startup Form" task, you create an instance of the AddName form in the Program.cs file, as shown in the following code:

```
Application.Run(new UserInfo());
```

Implementing an MDI Form

The term *multiple document interface* (MDI) means to have a GUI interface that allows multiple documents or forms under one parent form or window.

Visualize the working style of Microsoft Word: you are allowed to open multiple documents in one parent window, and all the documents will get listed in the Window menu, from which you can choose whichever you want to read, instead of having the individual documents open in their own windows, which makes it difficult to handle all of the documents and covers your screen with a lot of open windows.

Having an individual window for each instance of the same application is termed *single document interface* (SDI); applications such as Notepad, MS Paint, Calculator, and so on, are SDI applications. SDI applications get opened only in their own windows and can become difficult to manage, unlike when you have multiple documents or forms open inside one MDI interface.

Hence, MDI applications follow a parent form and child form relationship model. MDI applications allow you to open, organize, and work with multiple documents at the same time by opening them under the context of the MDI parent form; therefore, once opened, they can't be dragged out of it like an individual form.

The parent (MDI) form organizes and arranges all the child forms or documents that are currently open. You might have seen such options in many Windows applications under a Windows menu, such as Cascade, Tile Vertical, and so on.

Try It: Creating an MDI Parent Form with a Menu Bar

In this exercise, you will create an MDI form in the WinApp project. You will also see how to create a menu bar for the parent form, which will allow you to navigate to all the child forms. To do so, follow these steps:

1. Navigate to Solution Explorer, select the WinApp project, right-click, and select Add Windows form. Change the Name value from `Form1.es` to `ParentForm.es`, and click Add.

2. Select the newly added ParentForm in the Design view. Select the ParentForm form by clicking the form's title bar, navigate to the Properties window, and set the following properties:

   a. Set the IsMdiContainer property to True (the default value is False). Notice that the background color of the form has changed to dark gray.

   b. Set the Size property's Width to 546 and Height to 411.

3. Drag a MenuStrip control to the ParentForm. In the top-left corner, you should now see a drop-down showing text Type Here. Enter the text **Open Forms** in the drop-down. This will be your main, top-level menu.

4. Now under the Open Forms menu, add a submenu by entering the text **Win App**.

5. Under the Win App submenu, enter **User Info**.

6. Now click the top menu, Open Forms, and on the right side of it, type **Help**. Under the Help menu, enter **Exit**.

7. Now, click the top menu, on the right side of Help, type **Windows**.

8. Under the Windows menu, add the following options as separate submenus: **Cascade**, **Tile Horizontal**, **Tile Vertical**, and **Arrange Icons**. These will help in arranging the child forms.

9. Now it's time to attach code to the submenus you have added under the main menu Open Forms. First, you'll add code for the submenu Win App, which basically will open the WinApp form. In the Design view, double-click the Win App submenu, which will take you to the Code view. Under the `click` event, add the following code:

```
WinApp objWA = new WinApp();
            objWA.Show();
```

10. Now to associate functionality with the User Info submenu: double-click this submenu, and under the `click` event add the following code:

```
UserInfo objUI = new UserInfo();
    objUI.Show();
```

To associate functionality with the Exit submenu located under the Help main menu, double-click Exit, and under the `click` event add the following code:

```
    Application.Exit();
```

11. Now you have the form-opening code functionality in place, and you are almost set to run the application. But first, you need to set ParentForm as the start-up object. To do so, open `Program.cs`, and modify the `Application.Run(new UserInfo());` statement to the following:

    ```
    Application.Run(new ParentForm());
    ```

12. Now build the solution, and run the application by pressing F5; the MDI application will open and should look like Figure 9-19.

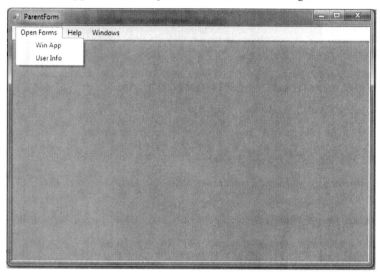

Figure 9-19. Running an MDI form application

13. Now if you will click Win App and then User Info, both the forms will open one by one. These forms can be opened and dragged outside of the MDI form. This is not an expected behavior from a MDI application, as shown in Figure 9-20. This issue will be addressed later in this chapter.

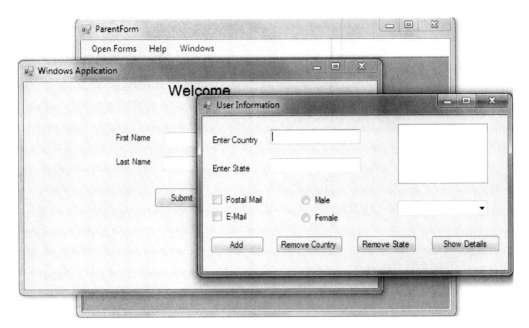

Figure 9-20. Running an MDI form application

How It Works

Each windows form is a class and exposes a Show() function by an instance created for it. You use the following code, which is creating an object and then invoking the Show() method. This opens the other form from the MDI parent form.

This creates an instance of the WinApp form and opens it for you:

```
WinApp objWA = new WinApp();
objWA.Show();
```

The following code creates an instance of the UserInfo form and opens it for you:

```
UserInfo objUI = new UserInfo();
objUI.Show();
```

You close the application with the following code:

```
Application.Exit();
```

Try It: Opening an MDI Child Form Within an MDI Application

As mentioned and shown in Figure 9-20, the problem is that even though the MDI form shows a parent menu, the forms are still able to open outside, and context is moved from a form to another. You can try clicking the title bar of each the open form, and you will see how you can move back and forth with these opened forms.

In this exercise, you will overcome this problem and associate all the forms you created earlier as MDI child forms to the main MDI parent form you created in the previous task.

1. In the project you modified in the previous exercise, you'll first make the WinApp form an MDI child form. To do so, you need to set the `MdiParent` property of the child form's object to the MDI parent form itself, but in the Code view. You have already added functionality in the previous task (opening the WinApp form); just before the line where you are calling the Show() method, add the following code (this code can be found under Win App menu click event):

```
                    objWA.MdiParent=this;
After adding this line, the code will appear as follows:
                    WinApp objWA = new WinApp();
                    objWA.MdiParent = this;
                    objWA.Show();
```

Note `this` is a C# language keyword that represents the current instance of the class. In this case, it refers to ParentForm. Because you are writing this code inside ParentForm, you can use the `this` keyword for the same.

---

2. Now you will make the UserInfo form an MDI child form. To do so, you need to set the `MdiParent` property to the name of the MDI parent form but in the Code view. Add the following code as you did in the previous step (this code can be found under the User Info menu click event):

```
            objUI.MdiParent=this;
```

After adding this line, the code will appear as follows:

```
                    UserInfo objUI = new UserInfo();
                    objUI.MdiParent=this;
                     objUI.Show();
```

3. Now build the solution, and run the application by pressing F5; the MDI application will open and should appear as shown in Figure 9-21.

4. Click Open Form Win App; the WinApp form should open. Again, open the main menu and click User Info. Both the forms should now be open inside your main MDI parent form application, and unlike before, you will not be able to drag these out of your MDI parent form (as shown in Figure 9-20). Figure 9-21 shows the expected behavior of an MDI application with opened form(s).

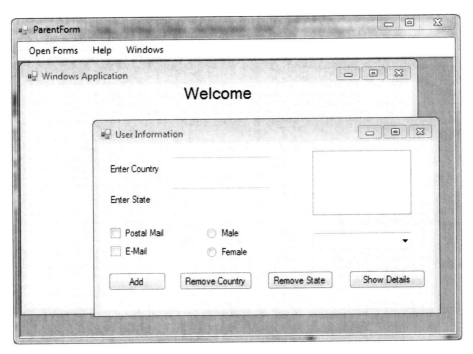

Figure 9-21. Opening child forms inside an MDI form application

5. Because both the forms are open inside one MDI parent, it becomes easier to work with them, and they are not draggable outside of MDI parent. Switch back and forth between these forms by clicking their title bars.

6. Once you are done with the forms, close the application by selecting Help Exit.

How It Works

As you noticed in earlier exercise, the only issue discussed was that child forms opened and were able to be dragged outside. In other words, they didn't really belong to a parent form. An MDI application is about claiming a form with a menu bar as an MDI parent so all the child forms can open inside it.

To do so, first an object of the child form needs to be created:

```
WinApp objWA = new WinApp();
```

But before we really invoke the Show() method on the objWA, you need to tell the object who is its parent so it operates from within the MDI parent form. To accomplish this, you will use the this keyword, which represents the current form class.

```
objWA.MdiParent = this;
```

You have object created and its context set to MDI parent form, so now it's a perfect time to call Show() method, which will launch the form so you can work with it.

```
        objWA.Show();
```

The wa.MdiParent=this; line tells the child form which form is its parent. Because you want all the child forms to appear inside ParentForm and you write the code inside the MDI parent form, you can use the this keyword to represent the current object.

Set the previous suggested changes for UserInfo as well.

```
        UserInfo objUI = new UserInfo();
            objUI.MdiParent=this;
            objUI.Show();
```

Try It: Arranging MDI Child Forms Within an MDI Application

Multiple forms will open within one MDI window, so once you have a few open, your MDI application will be cluttered. It's hard to move forms around to shift you focus from one to another. Hence, it is prime concern to have a mechanism that allows you to arrange the forms in an organized manner.

For example, in most applications you can arrange the forms and then cascade them so you can see the stack of open forms. Or you can tile them vertically or horizontally so you can see multiple forms side by side. You can even minimize all the open forms and arrange them as an icon.

To accomplish this, in this exercise you will add the Windows menu as shown in Figure 9-22.

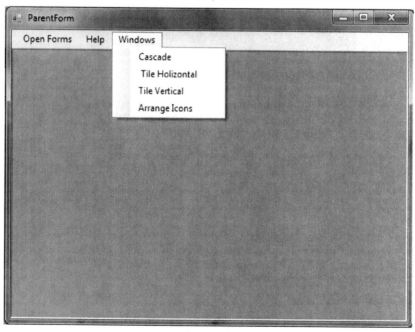

Figure 9-22. Windows menu of MDI form application to arrange child forms

.NET's Windows Forms offers the LayoutMdi method, which takes the MdiLayout enumeration to rearrange the child forms in an MDI parent form. There are four modes you can arrange your forms into: Cascade, Tile Horizontal, Tile Vertical, and ArrangeIcons.

1. Open the ParentForm in the Design view, and click the Windows menu, as shown in Figure 9-22.

2. Double-click the first option, Cascade, under Windows, and it will take you to its click event. Add the following code:

    ```
    LayoutMdi(MdiLayout.Cascade);
    ```

3. Double-click Tile Horizontal, and in the Code view under the click event, add the following code:

    ```
    LayoutMdi(MdiLayout.TileHorizontal);
    ```

4. Double-click the Tile Vertical, and in the Code view under the click event, add the following code:

    ```
    LayoutMdi(MdiLayout.TileVertical);
    ```

5. Double-click Tile Vertical, and in the Code view under the click event, add the following code:

    ```
    LayoutMdi(MdiLayout.ArrangeIcons);
    ```

6. Now build the solution, and run the application by pressing F5; the MDI application will open. After it opens, go to the Open Forms menu and click Win App and User Info one by one. It is important to have at least two forms open in the MDI parent form.

Now go to Windows menu and try the available options by clicking Cascade, then Arrange Vertical, then Arrange Horizontal, and finally Arrange Icons. When you will try these options, Tile Vertical will show the child forms arranged like Figure 9-23.

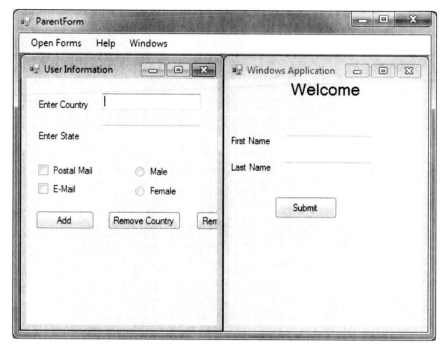

Figure 9-23. *Arranging (Tile Vertical) child forms in the MDI form application*

Summary

In this chapter, you learned about Windows Forms and the design principles associated with graphical user interface design. You also learned the importance of commonly ignored features, such as font styles and colors, as well as their impact on applications and their effect on large numbers of users. You also worked with the most commonly used Windows controls and properties that solve the resizing problem of Windows forms. You looked at the importance of MDI applications, and then you created an MDI application with menu controls, arranging the child forms in an MDI application.

In the next chapter, you will learn about ADO.NET application design.

CHAPTER 10

Introduction to ADO.NET

In industry, most applications can't be built without having interaction with a database. Databases serve the purpose of data storage so the data can be retrieved later via either a SQL query or a database application. Almost every software application running interacts with either one or multiple databases. Therefore, the front end needs a mechanism to connect with databases, and ADO.NET serves that purpose. Most of the .NET applications that require database functionality are dependent on ADO.NET. In this chapter, we'll cover the following:

- Understanding ADO.NET
- The motivation behind ADO.NET
- Moving from ADO to ADO.NET
- Understanding ADO.NET architecture
- Understanding the SQL Server data provider
- Understanding the OLE DB data provider
- Understanding the ODBC data provider
- Data providers as APIs

Understanding ADO.NET

Before .NET, developers used data access technologies such as ODBC, OLE DB, and ActiveX Data Object (ADO). With the introduction of .NET, Microsoft created a new way to work with data, called ADO.NET.

ADO.NET is a set of classes exposing data access services to .NET programmers, providing a rich set of components for creating distributed, data-sharing applications. ADO.NET is an integral part of the .NET Framework and provides access to relational, XML, and application data. ADO.NET classes are found in System.Data.dll.

This technology supports a variety of development needs, including the creation of front-end database clients and middle-tier business objects used by applications, tools, languages, and Internet browsers. Hence, ADO.NET helps connect the UI, or presentation layer, of your application with the data source or database.

The Motivation Behind ADO.NET

With the evolution of application development, applications have become *loosely coupled,* an architecture where components are easier to maintain and reuse without relying on implementation details of other components. More and more of today's applications use XML to encode data to be passed over network connections, and that is how different applications running on different platforms can interoperate.

ADO.NET was designed to support disconnected data architecture, tight integration with XML, common data representation with the ability to combine data from multiple and varied data sources, and optimized facilities for interacting with a database, all native to the .NET Framework.

During the development of ADO.NET, Microsoft wanted to include the following features:

- *Leverage for the current ADO knowledge:* ADO.NET's design addresses many of the requirements of today's application development model. At the same time, the programming model stays as similar as possible to ADO, so current ADO developers do not have to start from scratch. ADO.NET is an intrinsic part of the .NET Framework yet is familiar to ADO programmers.

  ADO.NET also coexists with ADO. Although most new .NET-based applications will be written using ADO.NET, ADO remains available to the .NET programmer through .NET COM interoperability services.

- *Support for the n-tier programming model:* The concept of working with a disconnected record set has become a focal point in the programming model. ADO.NET provides premium-class support for the disconnected, n-tier programming environment. ADO.NET's solution for building n-tier database applications is the DataSet.

- *Integration of XML support:* XML and data access are closely tied. XML is about encoding data, and data access is increasingly becoming about XML. The .NET Framework not only supports web standards but also is built entirely on top of them.

XML support is built into ADO.NET at a fundamental level. The XML classes in the .NET Framework and ADO.NET are part of the same architecture; they integrate at many different levels. You therefore no longer have to choose between the data access set of services and their XML counterparts; the ability to cross over from one to the other is inherent in the design of both.

Moving from ADO to ADO.NET

ADO is a collection of ActiveX objects that are designed to work in a constantly *connected* environment. It was built on top of OLE DB (which we'll look at in the "Understanding the OLE DB Data Provider" section). OLE DB provides access to non-SQL data as well as SQL databases, and ADO provides an interface designed to make it easier to work with OLE DB providers.

However, accessing data with ADO (and OLE DB under the hood) means you have to go through several layers of connectivity before you reach the data source. Just as OLE DB is there to connect to a large number of data sources, an older data access technology, Open Database Connectivity (ODBC), is still there to connect to even older data sources such as dBase and Paradox. To access ODBC data sources using ADO, you use an OLE DB provider for ODBC (since ADO works directly only with OLE DB), thus adding more layers to an already multilayered model.

With the multilayered data access model and the connected nature of ADO, you could easily end up sapping server resources and creating a performance bottleneck. ADO served well in its time, but ADO.NET has some great features that make it a far superior data access technology.

ADO.NET Isn't a New Version of ADO

ADO.NET is a completely new data access technology, with a new design that was built entirely from scratch. Let's first get this cleared up: ADO.NET *doesn't* stand for ActiveX Data Objects .NET. Why? For many reasons, but the following are the two most important ones:

- ADO.NET is an integral part of .NET, not an external entity.

- ADO.NET isn't a collection of ActiveX components.

The name ADO.NET is analogous to ADO because Microsoft wanted developers to feel at home using ADO.NET and didn't want them to think they'd need to "learn it all over again," as mentioned earlier, so Microsoft purposely named and designed ADO.NET to offer similar features implemented in a different way.

During the design of .NET, Microsoft realized that ADO wasn't going to fit in. ADO was available as an external package based on Component Object Model (COM) objects, requiring .NET applications to explicitly include a reference to it. In contrast, .NET applications are designed to share a single model, where all libraries are integrated into a single framework, organized into logical namespaces, and declared public to any application that wants to use them. It was wisely decided that the .NET data access technology should comply with the .NET architectural model. So, ADO.NET was born.

ADO.NET is designed to accommodate both connected and disconnected access. Also, ADO.NET embraces the fundamentally important XML standard, much more than ADO did, since the explosion in XML use came about after ADO was developed. With ADO.NET, not only can you use XML to transfer data between applications, but you can also export data from your application into an XML file, store it locally on your system, and retrieve it later when you need it.

Performance usually comes at a price, but in the case of ADO.NET, the price is definitely reasonable. Unlike ADO, ADO.NET doesn't transparently wrap OLE DB providers; instead, it uses *managed data providers* that are designed specifically for each type of data source, thus leveraging their true power and adding to overall application speed and performance.

ADO.NET also works in both connected and disconnected environments. You can connect to a database, remain connected while simply reading data, and then close your connection, which is a process similar to ADO. Where ADO.NET really begins to shine is in the disconnected world. If you need to edit database data, maintaining a continuous connection would be costly on the server. ADO.NET gets around this by providing a sophisticated disconnected model. Data is sent from the server and cached locally on the client. When you're ready to update the database, you can send the changed data back to the server, where updates and conflicts are managed for you.

In ADO.NET, when you retrieve data, you use an object known as a *data reader*. When you work with disconnected data, the data is cached locally in a relational data structure, either a *data table* or a *data set*.

ADO.NET and the .NET Base Class Library

A data set (a `DataSet` object) can hold large amounts of data in the form of tables (`DataTable` objects), their relationships (`DataRelation` objects), and constraints (`Constraint` objects) in an in-memory cache, which can then be exported to an external file or to another data set. Since XML support is integrated into ADO.NET, you can produce XML schemas and transmit and share data using XML documents. Table 10-1 describes the namespaces in which ADO.NET components are grouped.

Table 10-1. ADO.NET Namespaces

Namespace	Description
System.Data	Classes, interfaces, delegates, and enumerations that define and partially implement the ADO.NET architecture
System.Data.Common	Classes shared by .NET Framework data providers
System.Data.Design	Classes that can be used to generate a custom-typed data set
System.Data.Odbc	The .NET Framework data provider for ODBC
System.Data.OleDb	The .NET Framework data provider for OLE DB
System.Data.Sql	Classes that support SQL Server–specific functionality
System.Data.OracleClient	The .NET Framework data provider for Oracle
System.Data.SqlClient	The .NET Framework data provider for SQL Server
System.Data.SqlServerCe	The .NET Compact Framework data provider for SQL Server Mobile
System.Data.SqlTypes	Classes for native SQL Server data types
Microsoft.SqlServer.Server	Components for integrating SQL Server and the CLR

Since XML support has been closely integrated into ADO.NET, some ADO.NET components in the System.Data namespace rely on components in the System.Xml namespace. So, you sometimes need to include both namespaces as references in Solution Explorer.

These namespaces are physically implemented as assemblies, and if you create a new application project in VCSE, references to the assemblies should automatically be created, along with the reference to the System assembly. However, if they're not present, simply perform the following steps to add the namespaces to your project:

1. Right-click the References item in Solution Explorer; then click Add Reference.

2. A dialog box with a list of available references displays. Select System.Data, System.Xml, and System (if not already present) one by one (hold down the Ctrl key for multiple selections); then click the Select button.

3. Click OK, and the references will be added to the project.

Tip Though we don't use it in this book, if you use the command-line C# compiler, you can use the following compiler options to include the reference of the required assemblies: /r:System.dll /r:System.Data.dll /r:System.Xml.dll.

As you can see from the namespaces, ADO.NET can work with older technologies such as OLE DB and ODBC. However, the SQL Server data provider communicates directly with SQL Server without adding an OLE DB or Open Database Connectivity (ODBC) layer, so it's the most efficient form of connection. Likewise, the Oracle data provider accesses Oracle directly.

Note All major DBMS vendors support their own ADO.NET data providers. We'll stick to SQL Server in this book, but the same kind of C# code is written regardless of the provider.

Understanding ADO.NET Architecture

ADO.NET offers two types of architectural components to build data-centric applications: connected and disconnected. Within Microsoft .NET Framework, ADO.NET is housed in the namespace System.Data (the assembly name is System.Data.dll), so all the classes and functions for connected and disconnected components live in the same namespace. Hence, it is important to add a reference of System.Data to your application irrespective of the connected or disconnected architecture style you have chosen or will choose later.

Figure 10-1 presents the most important architectural features of ADO.NET. We'll discuss them in far greater detail in later chapters.

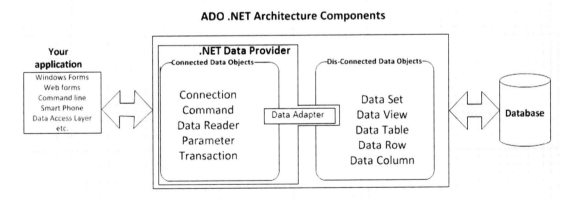

Figure 10-1. ADO.NET architecture

Connected Data Objects

ADO.NET's connected architecture relies on a consistent database connection to access data and perform any operations on the retrieved data. ADO.NET offers the following objects to help you build your application with a connected architecture:

- Connection: This is the main, or core, object for any database-oriented application. As you might imagine, without knowing a data source's statistics such as where it is located, what database you would like to connect with, what user name and password it requires, and so on, it would be impossible to establish a connection and perform any data-related activity. Each .NET provider provides its own Connection object that offers features targeted to specific data sources.

- Command: This object represents the handling of statements that your application will be using to perform data-oriented tasks, such as reading data or inserting or modifying data. Hence, any SQL statement is actually executed via a Command object.

- DataReader: DataReader involves creating an instance of the Command object and then creating a DataReader by calling Command.ExecuteReader for data retrieval from your data source, the returned data can be fetched in a read-only way through a DataReader object. Data retrieval behavior of DataReader is also known as a *read-forward-only fire-hose cursor with fast speed*.

- Parameter: Parameter has always been an important part of any programming model. Similarly, it is important in ADO.NET programming when it comes to passing values to Command. A Parameter can be a value passed or returned to/from a stored procedure or an argument passed to a SQL query.

- DataAdapter: DataAdapter is the object ADO.NET exposes to bridge the gap between connected and disconnected architectures to let applications establish a connection and sync data into and from the data source.

Disconnected Data Objects

ADO.NET's connected architecture relies on a consistent database connection to access data and perform any operations on the retrieved data. However, in today's complex distributed application environments, it is not possible to rely on a dedicated database connection to retrieve and modify data.

To help you meet your business requirements and work with ease in your distributed environment, you can utilize ADO.NET's disconnected architecture; it offers flexible application design and helps organizations save database connections. Hence, data can be retrieved and then stored locally on the device in the form of a DataSet object. The retrieved DataSet can be modified by users on their local devices such as laptops, handhelds, tablets, and so on, and once that's done, they can sync the changes into the central data source. Disconnected architecture utilizes expansive resources like Connection in a very optimum way (that is, to open late and close early).

ADO.NET offers the following objects to help you build your application with a disconnected architecture:

- DataSet: DataSet is the core architectural component of ADO.NET to make disconnected applications. A data set can be considered a subset of data. A data set supports disconnected, independent caching of data in a relational fashion, updating the data source as required. A data set contains one or more data tables.

- DataTable: DataTable is a row-and-column representation that provides much the same logical view as a physical table in a database. For example, you can store the data from a database's table in an ADO.NET DataTable and manipulate the data as needed.

- DataRow: As you know, a table always consists of rows. In a similar manner, ADO.NET's DataTable consists of rows of the DataRowCollection type. This DataRowCollection is an enumerable collection of DataRow objects. When new data is added to the DataTable, a new DataRow is added.

- DataColumn: Just like any other column in a database table, ADO.NET's DataTable consists of a DataColumn of the DataColumnCollection type.

- DataView: DataView in ADO.NET serves a purpose similar to a view in a database. Usually a view in a databse provides a predefined, organized, or filtered set of records. Similarly, a DataView provides filtered or sorted records from a DataTable. Just like a database table can have multiple views, so too can the DataTable have multiple data views on it.

Understanding .NET Data Providers

ADO.NET consists of various data providers that allow an easy and predefined object model to communicate with various industry databases such as SQL Server, Oracle, Microsoft Access, and many others.

There are various database providers, so each data provider has its own namespace. In fact, each data provider is essentially an implementation of interfaces in the System.Data namespace, specialized for a specific type of data source.

For example, if you use SQL Server, you should use the SQL Server data provider (System.Data.SqlClient) because it's the most efficient way to access SQL Server.

The OLE DB data provider supports access to older versions of SQL Server as well as to other databases, such as Access, DB2, MySQL, and Oracle. However, native data providers (such as System.Data.OracleClient) are preferable for performance, since the OLE DB data provider works through two other layers, the OLE DB service component and the OLE DB provider, before reaching the data source.

Figure 10-2 illustrates the difference between using the SQL Server and OLE DB data providers to access a SQL Server database.

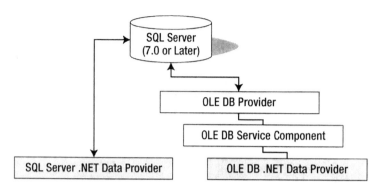

Figure 10-2. SQL Server and OLE DB data provider differences

If your application connects to an older version of SQL Server (6.5 or older) or to more than one kind of database server at the same time (for example, an Access and an Oracle database connected simultaneously), only then should you choose to use the OLE DB data provider.

No hard-and-fast rules exist; you can use both the OLE DB data provider for SQL Server and the Oracle data provider (System.Data.OracleClient) if you want, but it's important you choose the best provider for your purpose. Given the performance benefits of the server-specific data providers, if you use SQL Server, 99 percent of the time you should be using the System.Data.SqlClient classes.

Before we look at what each kind of data provider does and how it's used, you need to be clear on their core functionality. Each .NET data provider is designed to do the following two things very well:

- Provide access to data with an active connection to the data source

- Provide data transmission to and from disconnected data sets and data tables

Database connections are established by using the data provider's Connection class (for example, System.Data.SqlClient.SqlConnection). Other components such as data readers, commands, and data adapters support retrieving data, executing SQL statements, and reading or writing to data sets or data tables, respectively.

As you've seen, each data provider is prefixed with the type of data source it connects to (for instance, the SQL Server data provider is prefixed with Sql), so its connection class is named SqlConnection. The OLE DB data provider's connection class is named OleDbConnection.

Let's understand the three data providers that can be used with SQL Server.

Understanding the SQL Server Data Provider

The .NET data provider for SQL Server is in the System.Data.SqlClient namespace. Although you can use System.Data.OleDb to connect with SQL Server, Microsoft has specifically designed the System.Data.SqlClient namespace to be used with SQL Server, and it works in a more efficient and optimized way than System.Data.OleDb. The reason for this efficiency and optimized approach is that this data provider communicates directly with the server using its native network protocol instead of through multiple layers.

Table 10-2 describes some important classes in the SqlClient namespace.

Table 10-2. Commonly Used SqlClient *Classes*

Classes	Description
SqlCommand	Executes SQL queries, statements, or stored procedures
SqlConnection	Represents a connection to a SQL Server database
SqlDataAdapter	Represents a bridge between a data set and a data source
SqlDataReader	Provides a forward-only, read-only data stream of the results
SqlError	Holds information on SQL Server errors and warnings
SqlException	Defines the exception thrown on a SQL Server error or warning
SqlParameter	Represents a command parameter
SqlTransaction	Represents a SQL Server transaction

Another namespace, System.Data.SqlTypes, maps SQL Server data types to .NET types, both enhancing performance and making developers' lives a lot easier.

Understanding the OLE DB Data Provider

Outside .NET, OLE DB is still Microsoft's high-performance data access technology. The OLE DB data provider has been around for many years. If you've programmed for Microsoft Access in the past, you may recall using Microsoft Jet OleDb 3.5 or 4.0 to connect with the Microsoft Access database. You can use this data provider to access data stored in any format, so even in ADO.NET it plays an important role in accessing data sources that don't have their own ADO.NET data providers.

The .NET Framework data provider for OLE DB is in the namespace System.Data.OleDb. Table 10-3 describes some important classes in the OleDb namespace.

Table 10-3. Commonly Used OleDb *Classes*

Classes	Description
OleDbCommand	Executes SQL queries, statements, or stored procedures
OleDbConnection	Represents a connection to an OLE DB data source
OleDbDataAdapter	Represents a bridge between a data set and a data source
OleDbDataReader	Provides a forward-only, read-only data stream of rows from a data source
OleDbError	Holds information on errors and warnings returned by the data source

Classes	Description
OleDbParameter	Represents a command parameter
OleDbTransaction	Represents a SQL transaction

Notice the similarity between the two data providers SqlClient and OleDb. The differences in their implementations are transparent, and the user interface is fundamentally the same.

The ADO.NET OLE DB data provider requires that an OLE DB provider be specified in the connection string. Table 10-4 describes some OLE DB providers.

Table 10-4. Some OLE DB Providers

Provider	Description
DB2OLEDB	Microsoft OLE DB provider for DB2
SQLOLEDB	Microsoft OLE DB provider for SQL Server
MicrosoftJet.OLEDB.4.0	Microsoft OLE DB provider for Access (which uses the Jet engine)
MSDAORA	Microsoft OLE DB provider for Oracle
MSDASQL	Microsoft OLE DB provider for ODBC

Understanding the ODBC Data Provider

ODBC was Microsoft's original general-purpose data access technology. It's still widely used for data sources that don't have OLE DB providers or .NET Framework data providers. ADO.NET includes an ODBC data provider in the namespace System.Data.Odbc.

The ODBC architecture is essentially a three-tier process. An application uses ODBC functions to submit database requests. ODBC converts the function calls to the protocol (*call-level interface*) of a *driver* specific to a given data source. The driver communicates with the data source, passing any results or errors back up to ODBC. Obviously, this is less efficient than a database-specific data provider's direct communication with a database, so for performance it's preferable to avoid the ODBC data provider, since it merely offers a simpler interface to ODBC but still involves all the ODBC overhead. Table 10-5 describes some important classes in the Odbc namespace.

Table 10-5. Commonly Used Odbc Classes

Classes	Description
OdbcCommand	Executes SQL queries, statements, or stored procedures
OdbcConnection	Represents a connection to an ODBC data source
OdbcDataAdapter	Represents a bridge between a data set and a data source
OdbcDataReader	Provides a forward-only, read-only data stream of rows from a data source
OdbcError	Holds information on errors and warnings returned by the data source
OdbcParameter	Represents a command parameter
OdbcTransaction	Represents a SQL transaction

Data Providers Are APIs

The .NET Framework data providers, sophisticated as they are (and you'll learn plenty about exploiting their sophistication later), are simply APIs for accessing data sources, most often relational databases. (ADO.NET is essentially one big API of which data providers are a major part.)

Newcomers to ADO.NET are often understandably confused by the Microsoft documentation. They read about Connection, Command, DataReader, and other ADO.NET objects, but they see no classes named Connection, Command, or DataReader in any of the ADO.NET namespaces. The reason is that data provider classes implement *interfaces* in the System.Data namespace. These interfaces define the data provider methods of the ADO.NET API.

The concept is simple. A data provider, such as System.Data.SqlClient, consists of classes whose methods provide a uniform way of accessing a specific kind of data source. This is true of all ADO.NET facilities, whatever kind of data source you need to access.

The SQL Server data provider is optimized to access SQL Server and can't be used for any other DBMS. The OLE DB data provider can access any OLE DB data source. The ODBC data provider lets you use an even older data access technology, again without knowing anything about it. Working at such an abstract level enabled you to do a lot more, and a lot more quickly, than you could have otherwise.

ADO.NET is not only an efficient data access technology but also an elegant one. Data providers are only one aspect of it. The art of ADO.NET programming is founded more on conceptualizing than on coding. First get a clear idea of what ADO.NET offers; then look for the right method in the right class to make the idea a reality.

Since conceptual clarity is so important, you can view (and refer to) connections, commands, data readers, and other ADO.NET components primarily as abstractions rather than merely objects used in database programs. If you concentrate on concepts, learning when and how to use relevant objects and methods will be easy.

Summary

In this chapter, you saw why ADO.NET was developed and how it supersedes other data access technologies in .NET. We gave an overview of its architecture and then focused on one of its core components, the data provider. You built three simple examples to practice basic data provider use and experience the uniform way data access code is written, regardless of the data provider. Finally, we offered the opinion that conceptual clarity is the key to understanding and using both data providers and the rest of the ADO.NET API. Next, we'll study the details of ADO.NET, starting with connections.

CHAPTER 11

Handling Exceptions

For the programs you write, you definitely care about fixing any errors or problems that are brought to your attention by the language compiler. However, there is a particular type of error that doesn't happen during compile time; instead, it occurs at runtime. As you progress into more complex application development, you have more chances of getting such runtime errors, known as *exceptions*. They can occur because the application is trying to open a connection to a nonexistent database, open a file that doesn't exist, or write to a file that is already open in read-only mode. This chapter will help you learn more about exceptions and how to handle them when they occur.

The System.Exception Class

In .NET, all exceptions are derived from the Exception class. The Exception class is defined inside the System namespace. Other derived exception classes are spread across many other namespaces such as SQLException, FileNotFoundException, IndexOutOfRangeException, and so on.

Hence, when you invoke some .NET functionality and something goes wrong at runtime, a function might throw an exception of a specific type. For example, if you connect to a nonexistent database, you will receive a runtime error, in other words, an exception of type SqlException. Similarly, if you try to open a file to read that doesn't exist, you will get a FileNotFound exception.

It is important to understand that all exceptions are derived from the System.Exception class. If you catch System.Exception, for example, that would cover all exceptions derived from System.Exception also. I will demonstrate this later in this chapter. Table 11-1 shows the properties exposed by the System.Exception class.

Table 11-1. System.Exception Properties

Property Name	Description
Data	Gets a collection of key-value pairs that contain user-defined information
HelpLink	Specifies the help file associated with this exception
InnerException	Gets the exception instance that caused the current exception
Message	Defines the text describing the exception
Source	Specifies the name of the provider that generated the exception

Property Name	Description
StackTrace	Defines a string representation of the call stack when the exception was thrown
TargetSite	Represents the method that throws the current exception

What Causes an Exception to Occur

Before we get into more details of how to handle an exception, let's see what an exception looks like when it occurs and how an application behaves in such a situation.

Many organizations today depend on log files to trace the activities happening on a system; you might have even seen or read some setup.log files. Hence, file handling is an important concept that can apply in many situations. For example, whatever you enter into a text box can be recorded into a log file, and later this information can be read from the stored file on the disk.

Assume you are given an application that reads the file path and file name from the user and opens the file. Normally, the application works fine, but in this case, an incorrect file name or path is provided, so an exception occurs.

Try It: Creating a File-Handling Application

In this exercise, you'll create a Windows Forms application with four labels, four text boxes, and two buttons. The application will accept some text and then save/write it to a file on disk; it will also take a file path as input and read the file content for you.

1. Create a new Windows Forms application project named Chapter11. When Solution Explorer opens, save the solution.

2. Rename the Chapter11 project to FileHandling and then rename Form1 to FileExceptionHandling.

3. Change the Text property of the FileExceptionHandling form to File-Read/Write.

4. Drag a Label control onto the form, and position it toward the top-left corner. Select this Label control, navigate to the Properties window, and set the following properties:

    a. Set the Name property to lblPathWrite.

    b. Set the Text property to Enter File Write Path.

5. Drag a TextBox control next to the Label control named lblPathWrite that you just dragged onto the form. Select this TextBox control, navigate to the Properties window, and set the following properties:

    a. Set the Name property to txtFileWritePath.

    b. Set the Size property to 301, 20.

6. Drag a Button control next to the TextBox control you just dragged onto the form. Select this Button control, navigate to the Properties window, and set the following properties:

      a.   Set the Name property to btnWriteToFile.

      b.   Set the Text property to Write To File.

7.   Drag a Label control onto the form, and position it below the Label control named Enter File Write Path. Select this Label control, navigate to the Properties window, and set the following properties:

      a.   Set the Name property to lblText.

      b.   Set the Text property to Enter your Text.

8.   Drag a TextBox control next to the Label control named lblText that you just dragged onto the form. Select this TextBox control, navigate to the Properties window, and set the following properties:

      a.   Set the Name property to txtFileText.

      b.   Set the Multiline property to True.

      c.   Set the Size property to 301, 60.

9.   Drag a Label control onto the form, and position it below the Label control named lblText. Select this Label control, navigate to the Properties window, and set the following properties:

      a.   Set the Name property to lblPathRead.

      b.   Set the Text property to Enter File Read Path.

Drag a TextBox control next to the Label control named lblPathWrite that you just dragged onto the form. Select this TextBox control, navigate to the Properties window, and set the following properties:

      a.   Set the Name property to txtFileReadPath.

      b.   Set the Size property to 301, 20.

10. Drag a Button control next to the TextBox control that you just dragged onto the form. Select this Button control, navigate to the Properties window, and set the following properties:

      a.   Set the Name property to btnReadFile.

      b.   Set the Text property to Read File.

11. Drag a Label control onto the form, and position it below the Label control named Enter File Read Path. Select this Label control, navigate to the Properties window, and set the following properties:

      a.   Set the Name property to lblFileContent.

      b.   Set the Text property to File Content.

12. Drag a TextBox control next to the Label control named lblText that you just dragged onto the form. Select this TextBox control, navigate to the Properties window, and set the following properties:

      a.   Set the Name property to txtFileContent.

b. Set the Multiline property to True.

c. Set the Size property to 301, 90.

13. Your FileExceptionHandling form will look like Figure 11-1.

Figure 11-1. *File-handling form in design view*

14. Now it's time to write the code.

15. Double-click the Write To File button, and start adding the code.

16. First add a using statement for file-related operations, navigate to the using statements in your code editor on the top, and the add following at the end:

```
using System.IO;
```

17. Now add the following code for writing text to the file from Listing11-1:

Listing11-1. *btnWriteToFile_Click*

```
StreamWriter sw = new StreamWriter(txtFileWritePath.Text, true);
sw.WriteLine(txtFileText.Text);
sw.Close();
```

18. Double-click the Read File button, and add the following code for reading content from a file from Listing 11-2:

```
Listing11-2: btnReadFile_ClickStreamReader sr = new StreamReader(txtFileReadPath.Text);
txtFileContent.Text = sr.ReadToEnd();
sr.Close();
```

19. Save the changes and build the application. You should see the message "Build Succeeded." Now it's time to run the application and do a file read-write operation. Press Ctrl+F5 to run the program.

Note It is important to understand that System.IO can read or write only those files with either a .txt or .log file extension. Also, such file-handling programs are based on a file path and file name. For demonstration purposes, I am using my laptop-specific path and a file name. These file paths and file names will not match what's on your system, so please modify the names of the directory and file name accordingly.

20. When the application launches, enter the file path in the first text box and then type the text you want to save in this file, as shown in Figure 11-2.

Note It is important to use the path of the file read and write as per your computer; also, make sure you have write permission to the specified drive/folder.

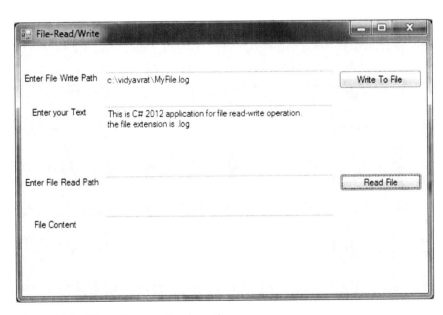

Figure 11-2. File write operation in action

21. Once you're done, click the Write To File button. You should be able to see your file created, as shown in Figure 11-3.

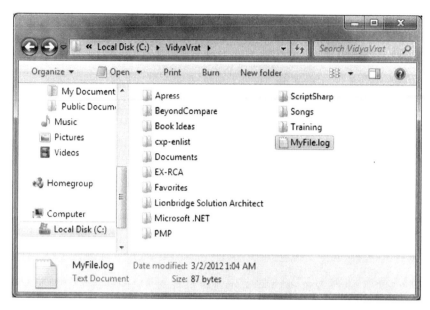

Figure 11-3. Log file created by the application

22. Now switch back to the running application, type the path where your file just got created in the Enter File Read Path text box, and click the Read File button. You should see the output shown in Figure 11-4.

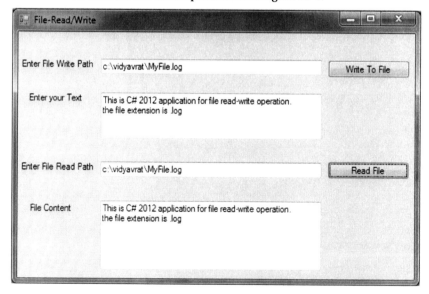

Figure 11-4. File write and read in action

Try It: Causing an Exception to Occur and Observing the Behavior

In this exercise, you'll continue to use the created application and then create a situation that will cause the exception to occur so you can observe the behavior.

1. Open the FileHandling project in Visual Studio 2012.

2. To cause an exception, you will perform only a file-read operation on the precreated file.

3. This time, you will run the application from the file Chapter11.exe, which is located in the project's bin\debug folder, as shown in Figure 11-5.

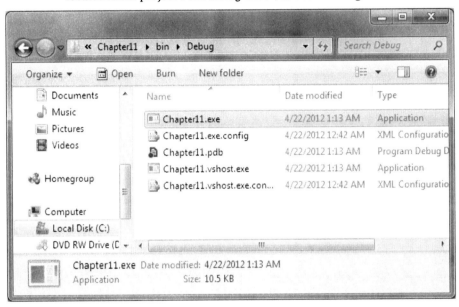

Figure 11-5. Running the program from its designated .exe from bin\debug

4. When the application loads, enter the following path in the Enter File Read Path text box: **c:\vidyavrat\MyLogFile.log**. As you probably recall, you saved the file as MyFile.log (refer to the earlier Figure11-2), but here you are intentionally passing the wrong file name, as shown in Figure 11-6.

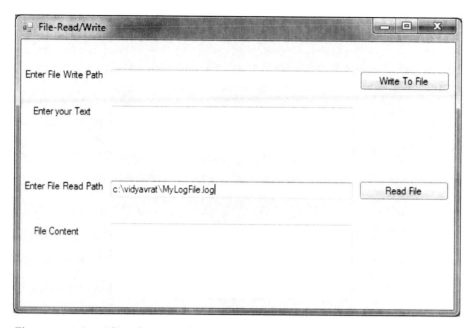

Figure 11-6. Providing the wrong file name to cause an exception

5. Now click the Read File button. Because this file name is incorrect, you will receive a strange-looking dialog with an unhandled exception, as shown in Figure 11-7.

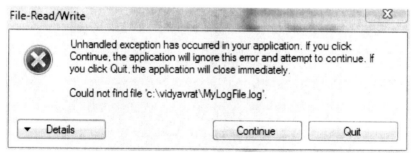

Figure 11-7. Exception dialog occurs when executing code through .exe

As you can see, this halts your application and leaves you with an unpleasant dialog, which is certainly not user-friendly.

6. Click Quit to exit the exception dialog. (If you clicked Continue, you would switch back to the application UI.)

7. To dig deeper, let's run the project from Visual Studio by pressing Ctrl+F5.

8. When the application loads, repeat the previous steps to enter an incorrect file name, and click Read File. You will get an exception. The difference now by running the program through Visual Studio is that it points to the code and exact details of the exception so you can add exception-handling code, as shown in Figure 11-8.

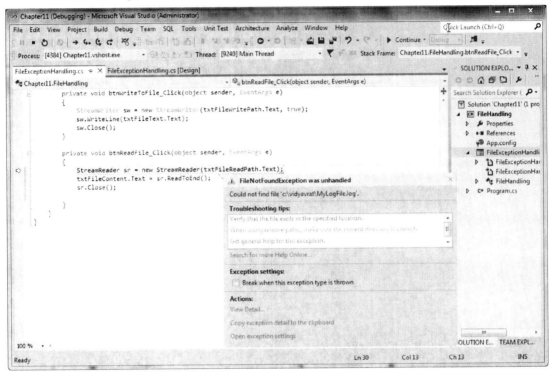

Figure 11-8. *Exception dialog occurs when executing code through Visual Studio*

As you can see, this is very informative for a developer. It explicitly says that the file name you provided does not exist or wasn't found, and it throws a `FileNotFoundException` exception.

Now, once this has occurred, there is no fix. You have to break the application by pressing Shift+F5, which will return you to your code view, and the application will stop running. But you now know what type of exception has occurred, so you can add code to handle it.

■ **Note** Exception handling is the main purpose of this chapter; an exercise later in the chapter will provide detailed steps on how to do this. For now, it is important to understand a few more conceptual aspects of exceptions.

Exploring the Type, Message, and StackTrace Properties of an Exception

Any .NET exception that occurs in Visual Studio or by running the EXE file is full of information to let the developer either handle it or investigate further. The Type, Message, and StackTrace properties serve this great purpose.

Type defines the category, or what kind of exception occurred. Whenever a .NET exception occurs, it shows the type of exception in the title bar of the dialog. As you can see, FileNotFoundException is mentioned on the title bar of the dialog in Figure-11-8.

You can find more information about any exception by clicking View Detail toward the bottom (under Actions) of the dialog, as shown in Figure 11-7. This applies to any exception you encounter within .NET.

Once you click View Detail, you will see another window open; it provides the exception snapshot. Expand this, and you will find a lot of information. Look for the Message property, which holds the exact message that your exception occurred with, as shown in Figure 11-9.

In most cases, developers want to add some extra text with this system-generated message. We cover how to do so later in this chapter.

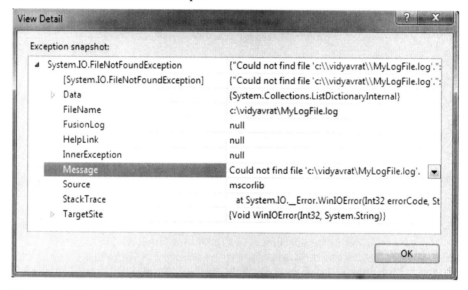

Figure 11-9. Exception's Message property

Other important information is exposed by the StackTrace property, which is mainly useful for people who want to debug the code and find out which line is actually causing the problem. Also, many organizations log such information into the Event Viewer or log files for their monitoring purposes.

Just below the Message property, you will find the StackTrace option; select it and then click the arrow pointing down on the right side of its description text, as shown in Figure 11-10.

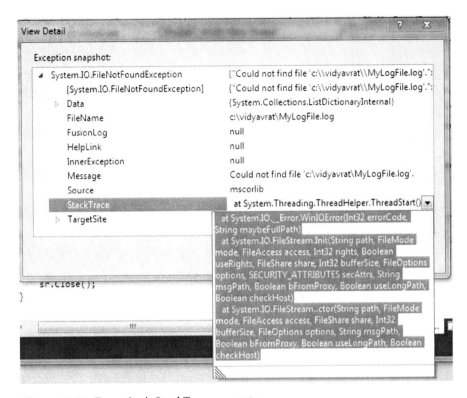

Figure 11-10. *Exception's StackTrace property*

As you will notice, this StackTrace property comes preselected, so you can copy and paste it with ease. Most of the bug-triage meetings have a lot of discussions about StackTrace, and whenever a manual tester talks about some runtime errors, most developers say, "Please provide me with the StackTrace!" because it can specify exactly where the issue is.

Now let's copy and paste this StackTrace into a Notepad file and investigate it, as shown in Figure 11-11. This image shows only the first half of the StackTrace. When you copy and paste, you will see the full details.

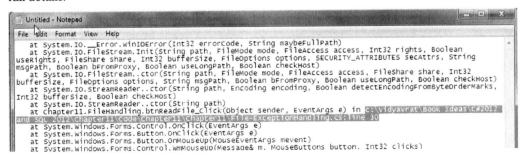

Figure 11-11. *Investigating the exception's StackTrace details*

If you look for the line shown selected in the figure, you will find out which file is causing this exception to occur, as well as which path and line number the problem is on.

Handling Exceptions

As you might have realized by now, exception handling is a technique you use to avoid any runtime errors and to handle them gracefully instead of issuing some awkward messages or having the application hang in front of the user.

Exception handling is mainly based on three keywords: try, catch, and finally. Any program can have one try, followed by one or many catch blocks, and then end with one finally block.

The try block holds any code that is throwing or can throw an exception. The catch block serves as a defensive mechanism and handles the exception that is being thrown. The finally block has unique behavior; it will execute in both situations: when an exception doesn't occur and when it does occur. So, the best code statements for finally are closing file streams, closing database connections, or even saying good-bye to a customer, and so on, but real-world applications consist of closing streams and connections instead. I will demonstrate this in the following exercise.

Try It: Adding Exception-Handling Statements

In this exercise, you'll continue to use the created application and then add exception-handling code blocks to handle such exceptions from being displayed in nonfriendly way to the user.

1. Open the FileHandling project in Visual Studio 2012.

2. Now double-click the Read File button and replace the code with the one in Listing 11-3.

Listing 11-3. btnReadFile_Click

```
StreamReader sr=null;
    try
    {
                    sr = new StreamReader(txtFileReadPath.Text);
            txtFileContent.Text = sr.ReadToEnd();
    }

    catch (FileNotFoundException ex)
    {
            MessageBox.Show(ex.Message + " " + "Please provide valid path and filename");
    }

    catch (DirectoryNotFoundException ex)
    {
            MessageBox.Show(ex.Message + " " + "Please provide valid Directory
            name", "File Read Error");
    }

    finally
    {
            if (sr != null)
            {
                sr.Close();
```

```
        }
    }
```

Build the application, and press Ctrl+F5 to run it. If you pass the wrong file name this time, it will actually throw an exception, but we are handling that, so a user-friendly message will be shown, as in Figure 11-12.

Figure 11-12. Exception handling with a catch block

As you can see, this dialog shows that you entered a wrong path or file name. Click OK, and it will take you back to the application for you to modify the path or file name correctly.

In such a file-handling applications, another scenario is when the user passes the wrong directory name. To handle that, you need a separate catch block to handle DirectoryNotFoundException. You have already added that, as shown in Listing 11-3. To test it now, change the path to a nonexisting folder name, and you will see a separate dialog saying "Provide valid Directory name."

How It Works

This file-read code is based on the Stream object, so you need to create a StreamReader object.

```
StreamReader sr=null;
```

Now you use this object in the try block to pass the file path and file name for reading the content.

```
try
{
    sr = new StreamReader(txtFileReadPath.Text);
    txtFileContent.Text = sr.ReadToEnd();
}
```

If a wrong file path or file name is provided, then it will throw a FileNotFoundException, so you need to provide a catch block to handle the exception.

```
catch (FileNotFoundException ex)
{
        MessageBox.Show(ex.Message + " " + "Please provide valid path and filename");
}
```

If a wrong directory name is provided, then it will throw a DirectoryNotFoundException, so you need to provide a catch block to handle the exception.

```
catch (DirectoryNotFoundException ex)
{
    MessageBox.Show(ex.Message + " " + "Please provide valid Directory
      name", "File Read Error");
}
```

In any case, whether the file is read or not, a Stream object needs to be closed. Performing such mandatory operations can be the best candidate for a finally block. Also, as you will notice in the case of an exception, the Stream object will not be initialized because the file name or path will not be found and so can't be closed.

Hence, you have to check whether the Stream object you created is null before you close it.

```
finally
{
        if (sr != null)
        {
            sr.Close();
        }
    }
}
```

Summary

In this chapter, you learned about exception handling and also how to handle exceptions thrown by a C# file I/O program. In the next chapters dedicated to ADO.NET, you will apply the exception-handling principles throughout the ADO .NET code.

Specifically, in the next chapter, you'll look at creating an ADO.NET connection to a SQL Server 2012 database.

CHAPTER 12

Making Connections

Before you can do anything useful with a database, you need to establish a *session* with the database server. You do this with an object called a *connection*, which is an instance of a class that implements the System.Data.IDbConnection interface for a specific data provider. In this chapter, you'll use various data providers to establish connections and look at problems that may arise and how to solve them. In this chapter, we'll cover the following:

- Introducing data provider connection classes

- Connecting to SQL Server with SqlConnection

- Improving your use of connection objects

- Connecting to SQL Server with OleDbConnection

Introducing the Data Provider Connection Classes

As you saw in Chapter 10, each data provider has its own namespace. Each has a connection class that implements the System.Data.IDbConnection interface. Table 12-1 summarizes the data providers supplied by Microsoft.

Table 12-1. Data Provider Namespaces and Connection Classes

Data Provider	Namespace	Connection Class
ODBC	System.Data.Odbc	OdbcConnection
OLE DB	System.Data.OleDb	OleDbConnection
Oracle	System.Data.OracleClient	OracleConnection
SQL Server	System.Data.SqlClient	SqlConnection
SQL Server CE	System.Data.SqlServerCe	SqlCeConnection

As you can see, the names follow a convention, using Connection prefixed by an identifier for the data provider. Since all connection classes implement System.Data.IDbConnection, the use of each one is similar. Each has additional members that provide methods specific to a particular database.

Connecting to SQL Server 2012 with SqlConnection

In this example, you'll connect to the SQL Server connect to the SQL Server 2012 AdventureWorks database.

Try It: Using SqlConnection

You'll write a very simple program just to open and check a connection.

1. In Visual Studio 2011, create a new Windows Console Application project named Chapter12. When Solution Explorer opens, save the solution.

2. Rename the Chapter12 project to ConnectionSQL. Rename the Program.cs file to ConnectionSql.cs, and replace the generated code with the code in Listing 12-1.

Listing 12-1. ConnectionSql.cs

```
using System;
using System.Data;
using System.Data.SqlClient;

namespace Chapter12
{
    class ConnectionSql
    {
      static  void  Main(string[]  args)
        {
                // Connection string (connection string key=value
                //might be different for you based on your environment
                string connString = @"server = .\sql2012; integrated security = true;";

                // Create connection
                SqlConnection  conn  =  new  SqlConnection(connString);

                try
                {
                        // Open connection
                        conn.Open();
                        Console.WriteLine("Connection opened.");
                }

                catch  (SqlException  ex)
                {
                        //  Display  error
                        Console.WriteLine("Error:  "  +  ex.Message  +  ex.StackTrace);
                }

                finally
                {
                        // Close connection
```

```
                conn.Close();
                Console.WriteLine("Connection closed.");
            }

            Console.ReadLine();
        }
    }
}
```

3. Run the application by pressing Ctrl+F5. If the connection is successful, you'll see the output in Figure 12-1.

Figure 12-1. Opening and closing a database connection

If the connection failed, you'll see an error message as in Figure 12-2. (You can get this by shutting down the SQL Server service first, with net stop mssql$<SQL Server instance name> entered at a command prompt. If you try this, remember to restart it with net start mssql$<SQL Server instance name>.) Or, the easy way would be to try passing wrong SQL instance name to the connection string.

```
file:///C:/VidyaVrat/C#2012 and SQL 2012/Chapter12/Code/Chapter12/ConnectionSql/bin/Debug/...
Error: A network-related or instance-specific error occurred while establishing
a connection to SQL Server. The server was not found or was not accessible. Veri
fy that the instance name is correct and that SQL Server is configured to allow
remote connections. (provider: SQL Network Interfaces, error: 26 - Error Locatin
g Server/Instance Specified)    at System.Data.SqlClient.SqlInternalConnection.On
Error(SqlException exception, Boolean breakConnection)
    at System.Data.SqlClient.TdsParser.ThrowExceptionAndWarning(TdsParserStateObj
ect stateObj)
    at System.Data.SqlClient.TdsParser.Connect(ServerInfo serverInfo, SqlInternal
ConnectionTds connHandler, Boolean ignoreSniOpenTimeout, Int64 timerExpire, Bool
ean encrypt, Boolean trustServerCert, Boolean integratedSecurity, SqlConnection
owningObject)
    at System.Data.SqlClient.SqlInternalConnectionTds.AttemptOneLogin(ServerInfo
serverInfo, String newPassword, Boolean ignoreSniOpenTimeout, Int64 timerExpire,
SqlConnection owningObject)
    at System.Data.SqlClient.SqlInternalConnectionTds.LoginNoFailover(String host
, String newPassword, Boolean redirectedUserInstance, SqlConnection owningObject
, SqlConnectionString connectionOptions, Int64 timerStart)
    at System.Data.SqlClient.SqlInternalConnectionTds.OpenLoginEnlist(SqlConnecti
on owningObject, SqlConnectionString connectionOptions, String newPassword, Bool
ean redirectedUserInstance)
    at System.Data.SqlClient.SqlInternalConnectionTds..ctor(DbConnectionPoolIdent
ity identity, SqlConnectionString connectionOptions, Object providerInfo, String
newPassword, SqlConnection owningObject, Boolean redirectedUserInstance)
    at System.Data.SqlClient.SqlConnectionFactory.CreateConnection(DbConnectionOp
```

Figure 12-2. Error if connection failed while connecting to SQL Server

Don't worry about the specifics of this message right now. Connections often fail for reasons that have nothing to do with your code. It may be because a server isn't started, as in this case, or because a password is wrong or because of some other configuration problem exists. You'll soon look at common problems in establishing database connections.

How It Works

Let's examine the code in Listing 12-1 to understand the steps in the connection process. First, you specify the ADO.NET and the SQL Server data provider namespaces so you can use the simple names of their members.

```
using System;
using System.Data;
using System.Data.SqlClient;
```

Then, you create a connection string. A *connection string* consists of parameters—in other words, key=value pairs separated by semicolons—that specify connection information. Although some parameters are valid for all data providers, each data provider has specific parameters it will accept, so it's important to know what parameters are valid in a connection string for the data provider you're using; this is explained in detail later in the chapter.

```
// Connection string
string connString = @"server = .\sql2012; integrated security = true;";
```

Let's briefly examine each of the connection string parameters in this example. The server parameter specifies the SQL Server instance to which you want to connect.

```
server =  .\sql2012;
```

In this statement, . (dot) represents the local server, and the name followed by the \ (slash) represents the SQL Server instance name running on the database server. So, here you have an instance of SQL Server 2012 named sql2012 running on the local server.

■ **Tip** (local) is an alternative to the . (dot) to specify the local machine, so .\sqlexpress can be replaced with (local)\sql2012, or you can write even localhost\sql2012.

The next clause indicates that you should use Windows Authentication (i.e., any valid logged-on Windows user can log on to SQL Server).

```
integrated security = true;
```

You could alternatively have used sspi instead of true, because they both have the same effect. Other parameters are available. You'll use one later to specify the database to which you want to connect.

Next you create a connection (a SqlConnection object), passing it the connection string. This doesn't create a database session. It simply creates the object you'll use later to open a session.

```
// Create connection
SqlConnection conn = new SqlConnection(connString);
```

Now you have a connection, but you still need to establish a session with the database by calling the Open method on the connection. If the attempt to open a session fails, an exception will be thrown, so you use a try statement to enable exception handling. You display a message after calling Open, but this line will be executed only if the connection was successfully opened.

```
try
{
        // Open connection
        conn.Open();
        Console.WriteLine("Connection opened.");
}
```

At this stage in the code, you'd normally issue a query or perform some other database operation over the open connection. However, we'll save that for later chapters and concentrate here on just connecting.

Next comes an exception handler in case the Open() fails, as shown in Figure 12-2 earlier in the chapter.

```
catch (SqlException ex)
{
        // Display error
        Console.WriteLine("Error: " + ex.Message + ex.StackTrace);
}
```

Each data provider has a specific exception class for its error handling; SqlException is the class for the SQL Server data provider. Specific information about database errors is available from the exception, but here you're just displaying its raw contents.

When you're finished with the database, you call Close() to terminate the session and then print a message to show that Close() was called.

```
finally
{
    // Close connection
    conn.Close();
    Console.WriteLine("Connection closed.");
}
```

You call Close() within the finally block to ensure it *always* gets called.

Console applications have a tendency to load the command window with output for a short time and close by itself. To hold the window on the screen so you can read and understand the output, invoke the ReadLine() method of the Console class. This will let the window stay until you press the Enter key.

```
Console.ReadLine();
```

▪ **Note** Establishing connections (database sessions) is relatively expensive. They use resources on both the client and the server. Although connections may eventually get closed through garbage collection or by timing out, leaving one open when it's no longer needed is a bad practice. Too many open connections can slow a server down or prevent new connections from being made.

Note that you can call Close( ) on a closed connection, and no exception will be thrown. So, your message would have been displayed if the connection had been closed earlier or even if it had never been opened. See Figure 12-2, where the connection failed but the close message is still displayed.

In one typical case, multiple calls to both Open( ) and Close( ) make sense. ADO.NET supports disconnected processing of data, even when the connection to the data provider has been closed. The pattern looks like this:

```
try
{
    // open connection
     conn.Open();
    // online processing (e.g., queries) here
    //
    conn.Close(); // close connection

    //
    // offline processing here
    //
       conn.Open(); // reopen connection
    //
  // online processing(e.g., INSERT/UPDATE/DELETE) here
 //
conn.Close(); // reclose connection
}

catch(SqlException ex)
{
    // error handling code here
}

finally
{
    // close connection
    conn.Close();
}
```

The finally block still calls Close( ), calling it unnecessarily if no exceptions are encountered, but this isn't a problem or expensive, and it ensures the connection will be closed. Although many programmers hold connections open until program termination, this is usually wasteful in terms of server resources. With *connection pooling*, opening and closing a connection as needed is actually more efficient than opening it once and for all.

That's it! You're finished with the first connection example. However, since you saw a possible error, let's look at typical causes of connection errors.

Debugging Connections to SQL Server

Writing the C# code to use a connection is usually the easy part of getting a connection to work. Problems often lie not in the code but rather in a mismatch in the connection parameters between the client (your C# program) and the database server. All appropriate connection parameters must be used and must have correct values. Even experienced database professionals often have problems getting a connection to work the first time.

More parameters are available than the ones shown here, but you get the idea. A corollary of Murphy's law applies to connections: If several things can go wrong, surely one of them will. Your goal is to check both sides of the connection to make sure all of your assumptions are correct and that everything the client program specifies is matched correctly on the server.

Often the solution is on the server side. If the SQL Server instance isn't running, the client will be trying to connect to a server that doesn't exist. If Windows Authentication isn't used and the user name and password on the client don't match the name and password of a user authorized to access the SQL Server instance, the connection will be rejected. If the database requested in the connection doesn't exist, an error will occur. If the client's network information doesn't match the server's, the server may not receive the client's connection request, or the server response may not reach the client.

For connection problems, using the debugger to locate the line of code where the error occurs usually doesn't help—the problem almost always occurs on the call to the Open method. The question is, why? You need to look at the error message.

A typical error is as follows:

```
Unhandled Exception: System.ArgumentException: Keyword not supported...
```

The cause for this is either using an invalid parameter or value or misspelling a parameter or value in your connection string. Make sure you've entered what you really mean to enter.

Figure 12-2 earlier showed probably the most common message when trying to connect to SQL Server. In this case, most likely SQL Server simply isn't running. Restart the SQL Server Express service with net start mssql$<your sql instance name>.

Other possible causes of this message are as follows:

- The SQL Server instance name is incorrect. For example, you used .\sqlexpress, but SQL Server was installed with a different name. It's also possible that SQL Server was installed as the default instance (with no instance name) or is on another machine (see the next section); correct the instance name if this is the case.

- SQL Server hasn't been installed—go back to Chapter 1 and follow the instructions there for installing SQL Server 2012 Express.

- A security problem exists—your Windows login and password aren't valid on the server. This is unlikely to be the problem when connecting to a local SQL Server Express instance, but it might happen in trying to connect to a SQL Server instance on another server.

- A hardware problem exists—again unlikely if you're trying to connect to a server on the same machine.

Security and Passwords in SqlConnection

There are two kinds of user authentication in SQL Server 2012. The preferred way is to use Windows Authentication (integrated security), as you do when following the examples in this book. SQL Server uses your Windows login to access the instance. Your Windows login must exist on the machine where SQL Server is running, and your login must be authorized to access the SQL Server instance or be a member of a user group that has access.

If you don't include the `Integrated Security = true` (or `Integrated Security = sspi`) parameter in the connection string, the connection defaults to SQL Server security, which uses a separate login and password within SQL Server.

How to Use SQL Server Security

If you really did intend to use SQL Server security because that's how your company or department has set up access to your SQL Server (perhaps because some clients are non-Microsoft), you need to specify a user name and password in the connection string, as shown here:

```
thisConnection.ConnectionString = @"server = sqlexpress; user id = sa; password = xly2z3";
```

The `sa` user name is the default system administrator account for SQL Server. If a specific user has been set up, such as `george` or `payroll`, specify that name. The password for `sa` is set when SQL Server is installed. If the user name you use has no password, you can omit the password clause entirely or specify an empty password, as follows:

```
password =;
```

However, a blank password is bad practice and should be avoided, even in a test environment.

Connection String Parameters for SqlConnection

Table 12-2 summarizes the basic parameters for the SQL Server data provider connection string.

Table 12-2. SQL Server Data Provider Connection String Parameters

Name	Alias	Default Value	Allowed Values	Description
Application Name		.Net SqlClient Data Provider	Any string	Name of application
AttachDBFileName	extended properties, Initial File Name	None	Any path	Full path of an attachable database file
Connect Timeout	Connection Timeout	15	0- 32767	Seconds to wait to connect
Data Source	Server, Address, Addr, Network Address	None	Server name or network address	Name of the target SQL Server instance
Encrypt		false	true, false, yes, no	Whether to use SSL encryption
Initial Catalog	Database	None	Any database that exists on server	Database name

Name	Alias	Default Value	Allowed Values	Description
Integrated Security	Trusted_Connection	false	true, false, yes, no, sspi	Authentication mode
Network Library	Net	dbmssocn	Dbnmpntw dbmsrpcn dbmsadsn dbmsgnet dbmslpcn dbmsspxn dbmssocn	Network .dll
Packet Size		8192	Multiple of 512	Network packet size in bytes
Password	PWD	None	Any string	Password if not using Windows Authentication
Persist Security Info		false	true, false, yes, no	Whether sensitive information should be passed back after connecting
User ID	UID		None	User name if not using Windows Authentication
Workstation ID		Local computer name	Any string	Workstation connecting to SQL Server

The Alias column in Table 12-2 gives alternate parameter names. For example, you can specify the server using any of the following:

```
data source = .\<sql instance name>
server = .\ <sql instance name>
address = .\ <sql instance name>
addr = .\ <sql instance name>
network address = .\ <sql instance name>
```

Connection Pooling

One low-level detail that's worth noting—even though you shouldn't change it—is *connection pooling*. Recall that creating connections is expensive in terms of memory and time. With pooling, a closed connection isn't immediately destroyed but is kept in memory in a pool of unused connections. If a new connection request comes in that matches the properties of one of the unused connections in the pool, the unused connection is used for the new database session.

Creating a totally new connection over the network can take seconds, whereas reusing a pooled connection can happen in milliseconds; it's much faster to use pooled connections. The connection string has parameters that can change the size of the connection pool or even turn off connection pooling. The default values (for example, connection pooling is on by default) are appropriate for the vast majority of applications.

Improving Your Use of Connection Objects

The code in the first sample program was trivial, so you could concentrate on how connections work. Let's enhance it a bit.

Using the Connection String in the Connection Constructor

In the ConnectionSql project, you created the connection and specified the connection string in separate steps. Since you always have to specify a connection string, you can use an overloaded version of the constructor that takes the connection string as an argument.

```
// create connection
SqlConnection conn = new SqlConnection(@"server = (local)\sqlexpress; integrated security =
true; ");
```

This constructor sets the ConnectionString property when creating the SqlConnection object. You will try it in the next examples and use it in later chapters.

Displaying Connection Information

Connections have several properties that provide information about the connection. Most of these properties are read-only, since their purpose is to display rather than set information. (You set connection values in the connection string.) These properties are often useful when debugging, to verify that the connection properties are what you expect them to be.

Here, we'll describe the connection properties common to most data providers.

Try It: Displaying Connection Information

In this example, you'll see how to write a program to display connection information.

1. Add a C# Console Application project named ConnectionDisplay to the Chapter12 solution.

2. Rename Program.cs to ConnectionDisplay.es. When prompted to rename all references to Program, you can click either Yes or No. Replace the code with that in Listing 12-2.

Listing 12-2. ConnectionDisplay.es

```
using System;
using System.Data;
using System.Data.SqlClient;
namespace Chapter12
{
    class ConnectionDisplay
    {
        static void Main()
        {
```

```
            // Create connection
            SqlConnection conn = new SqlConnection(@" server = .\sql2012;
              integrated  security = true; ");

            try
            {
                    // Open connection
                    conn.Open();
                    Console.WriteLine("Connection opened.");

                    // Display connection properties
                    Console.WriteLine("Connection Properties:");
                    Console.WriteLine("\tConnection String: {0}",
conn.ConnectionString);
                    Console.WriteLine( "\tDatabase: {0}", conn.Database);
                    Console.WriteLine( "\tDataSource: {0}", conn.DataSource);
                    Console.WriteLine("\tServerVersion: {0}", conn.ServerVersion);
                    Console.WriteLine( "\tState: {0}", conn.State);
                    Console.Writel_ine("\tWorkstationld: {0}", conn.Workstationld);

            }

            catch (SqlException ex)
            {
                    // Display error
                    Console.WriteLine("Error: " + ex.Message + ex.StackTrace);
            }

            finally
            {
                    // Close connection
                    conn.Close();
                    Console.WriteLine("Connection closed.");
            }

            Console.ReadLine();
        }
    }
}
```

3. To set ConnectionDisplay as the startup project, select the project in Solution
    Explorer, right-click and select Set as StartUp Project, and run it by pressing
    Ctrl+F5. If the connection is successful, you'll see output like that shown in
    Figure 12-3.

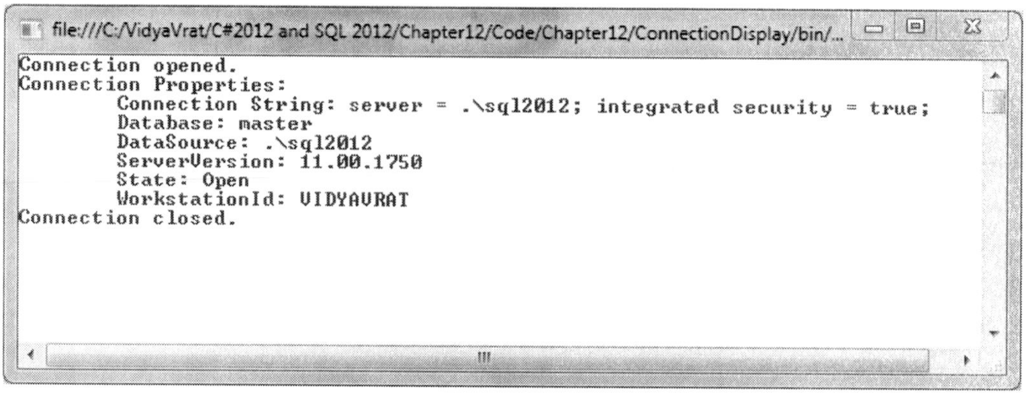

Figure 12-3. *Displaying connection information*

How It Works

The ConnectionString property can be both read and written. Here you just display it.

```
Console.WriteLine("\tConnection String: {0}", conn.ConnectionString);
```

You can see the value you assign to it, including the whitespace, in the verbatim string.

What's the point? Well, it's handy when debugging connections to verify that the connection string really contains the values you thought you assigned. For example, if you're trying different connection options, you may have different connection string parameters in the program. You may have commented out one, intending to use it later, but forgot about it. Displaying the ConnectionString property helps to see whether a parameter is missing.

The next statement displays the Database property. Since each SQL Server instance has several databases, this property shows which one you're initially using when you connect.

```
Console.WriteLine("\tDatabase: {0}",conn.Database);
```

In this program, it displays

```
Database: master
```

since you didn't specify a database in the connection string, so you were connected to the SQL Server's default database master. If you wanted to connect to the AdventureWorks or a database of your choice, you'd need to specify the Database parameter, for example:

```
// connection string
string connString = new SqlConnection(@"server = .\sqlexpress; database = northwind ";
                       integrated security = true;)
```

You can also change the default database from the master database to some other database, say, AdventureWorks, by executing the following statement:

```
exec sp_defaultdb 'sa'/adventureworks'
```

Again, this is a handy property to display for debugging purposes. If you get an error saying that a particular table doesn't exist, often the problem isn't that the table doesn't exist but that it isn't in the database to which you're connected. Displaying the Database property helps you find that kind of error quickly.

▪ **Tip** If you specify a database in the connection string that doesn't exist on the server, you may see the following error message: "System.Data.SqlClient.SqlException: Cannot open database 'database' requested by the login. The login failed."

You can change the database currently used on a connection with the ChangeDatabase method, like so:

```
Conn.ChangeDatabase("AdventureWorks");
```

The next statement displays the DataSource property, which gives the server instance name for SQL Server database connections.

```
Console.WriteLine( "\tDataSource: {0}", conn.DataSource);
```

This displays the same SQL Server instance name as per your SQL instance name; for example, in my case, it will show the following:

```
DataSource: .\sql2012
```

The utility of this, again, is mainly for debugging purposes.
The ServerVersion property displays the server version information.

```
Console.WriteLine("\tServerVersion: {0}",conn.ServerVersion);
```

It shows the version of SQL Server Express you installed in Chapter 1. (Your version may differ.)

```
ServerVersion: 11.00.1750
```

The version number is useful for debugging. This information actually comes from the server, so it indicates the connection is working.

▪ **Note** SQL Server 2008 is version 10, **and** SQL Server 2005 (and SSE) is version 9. SQL Server 2000 is version 8.

The State property indicates whether the connection is open or closed.

```
Console.WriteLine( "\tState: {0}", conn.State);
```

Since you display this property after the Open() call, it shows that the connection is open.

```
State: Open
```

You've been displaying your own message that the connection is open, but this property contains the current state. If the connection is closed, the State property would be Closed.

You then display the workstation ID, which is a string identifying the client computer. The WorkstationId property is specific to SQL Server and can be handy for debugging.

```
Console.WriteLine("\tWorkstationId: {0}",conn.WorkstationId);
```

It defaults to the computer name. My computer is named VIDYAVRAT, but yours, of course, will be different.

```
WorkstationId: <YourComputerName>
```

What makes this useful for debugging is that the SQL Server tools on the server can display which workstation ID issued a particular command. If you don't know which machine is causing a problem, you can modify your programs to display the WorkstationId property and compare them to the workstation IDs displayed on the server.

You can also set this property with the workstation ID connection string parameter as follows, so if you want all the workstations in, say, Building B to show that information on the server, you can indicate that in the program:

```
// Connection string
string connString = @" server = \sql2012; workstation id = Building B; integrated security =
true; ";
```

That completes the discussion of the fundamentals of connecting to SQL Server with SqlClient. Now let's look at connecting with another data provider.

Connecting to SQL Server with OleDbConnection

As you saw in Chapter 10, you can use the OLE DB data provider to work with any OLE DB–compatible data store. Microsoft provides OLE DB data providers for Microsoft SQL Server, Microsoft Access (Jet), Oracle, and a variety of other database and data file formats.

If a native data provider is available for a particular database or file format (such as the SqlClient data provider for SQL Server), it's generally better to use it rather than the generic OLE DB data provider. This is because OLE DB introduces an extra layer of indirection between the C# program and the data source. One common database format for which no native data provider exists is the Microsoft Access database (.mdb file) format, also known as the Jet database engine format, so in this case you need to use the OLE DB (or the ODBC) data provider.

We don't assume you have an Access database to connect to, so you'll use OLE DB with SQL Server.

Try It: Connecting to SQL Server with the OLE DB Data Provider

To connect to SSE with the OLE DB data provider, follow these steps:

1. Add a C# Console Application project named ConnectionOleDb, and rename Program.cs to ConnectionOleDb.cs.

2. Replace the code in Connection01eDb.cs with that in Listing 12-3. This is basically the same code as Connection.cs, with the changed code in bold.

Listing 12-3. Connection01eDb.cs

```csharp
using System;
using System.Data;
using System.Data.OleDb;

namespace Chapter12
{
    class ConnectionOleDb
    {
        static void Main()
        {
            // Create connection
            OleDbConnection conn = new OleDbConnection(@"provider = sqloledb;
                    data source = .\sql2012; integrated security = sspi;");

            try
            {
                // Open connection
                conn.Open();
                Console.WriteLine("Connection opened.");

                // Display connection properties
                Console.WriteLine("Connection Properties:");
                Console.WriteLine("\tConnection String: {0}",conn.ConnectionString);
                Console.WriteLine("\tDatabase: {0}",conn.Database);
                Console.WriteLine("\tDataSource: {0}",conn.DataSource);
                Console.WriteLine("\tServerVersion: {0}",conn.ServerVersion);
                Console.WriteLine("\tState: {0}",conn.State);
            }
            catch (OleDbException ex)
            {
                // Display error
                Console.WriteLine("Error: " + ex.Message + ex.StackTrace);
            }
            finally
            {
                // Close connection
                conn.Close();
                Console.WriteLine("Connection closed.");
            }

            Console.ReadLine();
        }
    }
}
```

3. Make ConnectionOleDb the startup project, and run it by pressing Ctrl+F5. If the connection is successful, you'll see output like that shown in Figure 12-4.

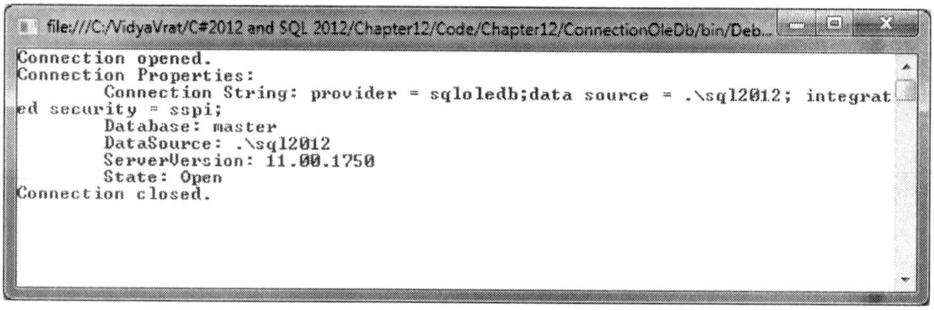

Figure 12-4. Displaying OLE DB connection information

How It Works

We'll discuss only the differences between this example and the previous one. The first step is to reference the OLE DB data provider namespace.

```
System.Data.OleDb.
using System.Data.OleDb;
```

Next, you create an `OleDbConnection` object instead of a `SqlConnection` object. Note the changes to the connection string. Instead of the `server` parameter, you use `Provider` and `Data Source`. Notice the value of the `Integrated Security` parameter must be `sspi`, not `true`.

```
// create connection
OleDbConnection conn = new O1eDbConnection(@"provider = sqloledb;data source = .\sql2012;
                                    integrated security = sspi;" );
```

Finally, note that you omit the `Workstationld` property in your display. The OLE DB data provider doesn't support it.

This is the pattern for accessing any data source with any .NET data provider. Specify the connection string with parameters specific to the data provider. Use the appropriate objects from the data provider namespace. Use only the properties and methods provided by that data provider.

Summary

In this chapter, you created, opened, and closed connections using two data providers and their appropriate connection strings, parameters, and values. You displayed information about connections after creating them using connection properties. You also saw how to handle various exceptions associated with connections.

In the next chapter, you'll look at ADO.NET commands and see how to use them to access data.

Executing ADO.NET Commands to Retrieve Data

Once you've established a connection to the database, you want to start interacting with it and getting it doing something useful for you. You may need to retrieve, add, update, or delete some data, or perhaps modify the database in some other way, usually by running a query. Whatever the task, it will inevitably involve a *command*.

In this chapter, we'll explain commands, which are objects that encapsulate the T-SQL for the action you want to perform and that provide methods for submitting it to the database. Each data provider has a command class that implements the System.Data.IDbCommand interface.

In this chapter, we'll cover the following:

- Creating commands

- Executing commands

- Executing commands with multiple results

- Executing statements

- Using stored procedures

We'll use the SQL Server data provider (System.Data.SqlClient) in our examples. Its command is named SqlCommand. The commands for the other data providers work the same way.

Creating a Command

For your commands to be executed against a database, each command must be associated with a connection to the database. You do this by setting the Connection property of the command, and in order to save resources, multiple commands can use the same connection. You can create a command by using the SqlCommand constructor. Once a command is created, then it's ready to execute the SQL statements you associated with an established connection. You will see command execution in statements in the following section.

Assigning Text to a Command

Every command has a property, CommandText, that holds the SQL statement that your created command object will execute. You can assign to this property directly or specify it when constructing the command. Let's look at these alternatives.

Try It: Setting the CommandText Property

The following Windows application shows how to use a SqlCommand to loop through a result set and retrieve rows.

1. Create a new Windows Forms Application project named Chapter13. When Solution Explorer opens, save the solution.

2. Rename the Chapter13 project to **ADO.NET_Command**. Rename the Form1.cs file to CommandText.cs.

3. Select the CommandText form by clicking the form's title bar, and set the Size property's Width to 287 and Height to 176.

4. Drag a TextBox control to the form and position it toward the center of the form. Select this TextBox control, navigate to the Properties window, and set the following properties:

   • Set the Name property to txtCommandText.

   • Set the Location property's X to 12 and Y to 12.

   • Set the Multiline property to True.

   • Set the Size property's Width to 244 and Height to 106.

   • Leave the Text property blank.

5. Now your CommandText form in the Design view should like Figure 13-1.

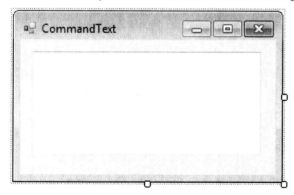

Figure 13-1. *The Design view of the CommandText form*

6. Double-click the empty surface of the CommandText.cs form, and it will open the code editor window, showing the CommandText_Load event. Modify the CommandText_Load event to look like Listing 13-1.

Listing 13-1. CommandText.cs

```
Using System.Data.SqlClient;

    private void CommandText_Load(object sender, EventArgs e)
    {
        // Create connection
        SqlConnection conn = new SqlConnection(@"server = .\sql2012;
          integrated security = true; database = AdventureWorks");

        // Create command
        SqlCommand cmd = new SqlCommand();

        try
        {
            // Open connection
            conn.Open();

            txtSQL.AppendText("Connection opened \n" );

            txtSQL.AppendText("Command created.\n");

            // Setting CommandText
            cmd.CommandText = @"select Name,ProductNumber
                         from  Production.Product";

            txtSQL.AppendText("Ready to execute SQL Statement: \n\t\t\t" +
                        cmd.CommandText);

        }
        catch (SqlException ex)
        {
            MessageBox.Show(ex.Message + ex.StackTrace,"Exception Details");
        }
        finally
        {
            conn.Close();
            txtSQL.AppendText("\nConnection Closed.");
        }
    }
```

7. Build the project, and run it by pressing Ctrl+F5. You should see the results in
   Figure 13-2.

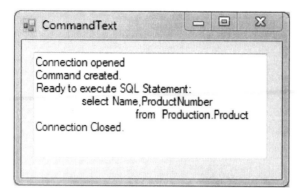

Figure 13-2. Displaying the SQL statement using CommandText

How It Works

The CommandText property returns a string, so you can display it just like any other string. The SQL statement assigned to the CommandText property will return the Name and ProductNumber values of products in the AdventureWorks Product table when you eventually execute it.

Note You must set both the Connection and CommandText properties of a command before the command can be executed.

```
// Create command
SqlCommand cmd = new SqlCommand();

 // Setting CommandText
cmd.CommandText = @"select Name,ProductNumber
                   from  Production.Product";
```

You can set both of these properties when you create the command with yet another variation of its constructor, as shown here:

```
// create command (with both text and connection)
String sql = @"select Name,ProductNumber from  Production.Product";

SqlCommand cmd = new SqlCommand(sql, thisConnection);
```

This is equivalent to the previous code that assigns each property explicitly. This is the most commonly used variation of the SqlCommand constructor, and you'll use it for the rest of the chapter.

Executing Commands

Commands aren't much use unless you can execute them, so let's look at that now. Commands have several different methods for executing SQL. The differences between these methods depend on the results you expect from the SQL. Queries return rows of data *(result sets)*, but the INSERT, UPDATE, and DELETE statements don't. You determine which method to use by considering what you expect to be returned (see Table 13-1).

Table 13-1. Command Execution Methods

If the Command Is Going to Return ...	You Should Use ...
Nothing (it isn't a query)	ExecuteNonQuery
Zero or more rows	ExecuteReader
Only one value	ExecuteScalar

The SQL you just used in the example should return one value, the number of employees. Looking at Table 13-1, you can see that you should use the ExecuteScalar() method of SqlCommand to return this one result. Let's try it.

Executing Commands with a Scalar Query

ExecuteScalar is the method that is used to execute those SQL statements that consist of scalar functions. Scalar functions are functions that return only one value from an entire set of rows in a table. For example, Min( ), Max( ), Sum( ), Count( ), and so on, are a few examples of scalar functions. If you execute a query such as Select Min(Salary) from Employee, then no matter how many rows you have in the table, only one row will be returned. Now let's see how the ExecuteScalar( ) method works with such a SQL query.

Try It: Using the ExecuteScalar Method

To use the ExecuteScalar method, follow these steps:

1. Select the ADO.NET_Command project, right-click and choose Add Windows Form. From the opened dialog, make sure Windows Form is selected, and rename Form1.cs to CommandScalar.cs. Click OK to add this form to the ADO.NET_Command project.

2. Select the CommandScalar form by clicking the form's title bar, and set the Size property's Width to 385 and Height to 126.

3. Drag a Label control to the form and position it toward the left side of the form. Select this Label control, navigate to the Properties window, and set the following properties:

   • Set the Name property to lblRowCount.

   • Set the Location property's X to 4 and Y to 35.

- Set the Size property's Width to 87 and Height to 13.

- Set the Text property to Total Row Count.

4. Drag a TextBox control to the form and position it next to the Label control. Select this TextBox control, navigate to the Properties window, and set the following properties:

- Set the Name property to txtScalar.

- Set the Location property's X to 97 and Y to 12.

- Set the Multiline property to True.

- Set the ScrollBars property to Both.

- Set the Size property's Width to 164 and Height to 65.

- Leave the Text property blank.

5. Drag a Button control to the form, and position it next to the TextBox. Select this Button control, navigate to the Properties window, and set the following properties:

- Set the Name property to btnRowCount.

- Set the Location property's X to 269 and Y to 30.

- Set the Size property'sWidth to 88 and Height to 23.

- Set the Text property to Count Rows.

6. Now your CommandScalar form in the Design view should like Figure 13-3.

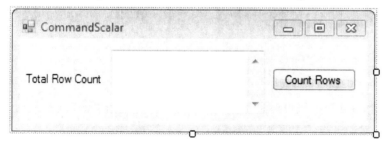

Figure 13-3. *The Design view of the CommandScalar form*

7. Double-click the Button control; it will open the code editor window, showing the btnRowCount_Click event. Place the code into the click event code template so it looks like Listing 13-2.

Listing 13-2. CommandScalar.cs

```csharp
using System.Data.SqlClient;
        private void btnRowCount_Click(object sender, EventArgs e)
        {
            // Create connection
            SqlConnection conn = new SqlConnection(@"server = .\sql2012;
                        integrated security = true; database = AdventureWorks");


            // Create Scalar query
            string sql = @"select count(*)
                    from Production.Product";

            // Create command
            SqlCommand cmd = new SqlCommand(sql, conn);
            txtScalar.AppendText("Command created and connected.\n");

            try
            {
                // Open connection
                conn.Open();

                txtScalar.AppendText("Number of Product is :");

                // Execute Scalar query with ExecuteScalar method
                txtScalar.AppendText(cmd.ExecuteScalar().ToString());
                txtScalar.AppendText("\n");
            }

            catch (SqlException ex)
            {
                MessageBox.Show(ex.ToString());
            }

            finally
            {
                conn.Close();
                txtScalar.AppendText("Connection Closed.");
            }
        }
```

8. To set the CommandScalar form as the start-up form, modify the `Program.cs` statement:

    ```csharp
    Application.Run(new CommandText ());
    ```

    to appear as:

    ```csharp
    Application.Run(new CommandScalar());
    ```

    Build the project, and run it by pressing Ctrl+F5.

9. When the form loads, click the button Count Rows. The result should look like Figure 13-4.

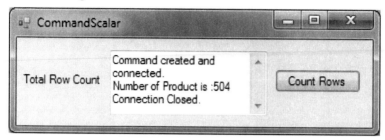

Figure 13-4. Executing a scalar command

How It Works

All you do is add a call to ExecuteScalar() within a call to the TextBox's AppendText method:

```
txtScalar.AppendText("Number of Product is :");

// Execute Scalar query with ExecuteScalar method
txtScalar.AppendText(cmd.ExecuteScalar().ToString());
```

ExecuteScalar() takes the CommandText property and sends it to the database using the command's Connection property. It returns the result as a single object, which you display with the TextBox's AppendText method.

ExecuteScalar() method's return type is object, the base class of all types in the .NET Framework, which makes perfect sense when you remember that a database can hold any type of data. So, if you want to assign the returned object to a variable of a specific type (int, for example), you must cast the object to the specific type. If the types aren't compatible, the system will generate a runtime error that indicates an invalid cast.

The following is an example that demonstrates this idea. In it, you store the result from ExecuteScalar() in the variable count, casting it to the specific type int.

```
int count = (int) cmd.ExecuteScalar();
txtScalar.AppendText ("Number of Products is: "+ count);
```

If you're sure the type of the result will always be an int (a safe bet with COUNT(*)), the previous code is safe. However, if you left the cast to int in place and changed the CommandText of the command to the following:

```
select Name
from Production.Product
where ProductNumber='BA-8327'
```

then ExecuteScalar() would return the string "Bearing Ball" instead of an integer, and you'd get this exception:

```
Unhandled Exception: System.InvalidCastException:
Specified cast is not valid.
```

because you can't cast a string to an int.

Another problem may occur if a query actually returns multiple rows where you thought it would return only one. In that case, ExecuteScalar( ) just returns the first row of the result and ignores the rest. If you use ExecuteScalar( ), make sure you not only expect but actually get a single value returned.

Executing Commands with Multiple Results

For queries where you're expecting multiple rows and columns to be returned, use the command's ExecuteReader() method.

ExecuteReader() returns a data reader, an instance of the SqlDataReader class that you'll study in the next chapter. Data readers have methods that allow you to read successive rows in result sets and retrieve individual column values.

We'll leave the details of data readers for the next chapter, but for comparison's sake, we'll give a brief example here of using the ExecuteReader() method to create a SqlDataReader from a command to display query results.

Try It: Using the ExecuteReader Method

To use the ExecuteReader method, follow these steps:

1. Select the ADO.NET_Command project, right-click, and choose Add ➤ Windows Form. From the opened dialog, make sure Windows Form is selected and rename Form1.cs to CommandReader.cs. Click OK to add this form to the ADO.NET_Command project.

2. Select the CommandReader form by clicking the form's title bar, and set the Size property's Width to 455 and Height to 283.

3. Drag a TextBox control over the form. Select this TextBox control, navigate to the Properties window, and set the following properties:

   - Set the Name property to txtReader.

   - Set the Location property's X to 12 and Y to 12.

   - Set the Multiline property to True.

   - Set the ScrollBars property to Vertical.

   - Set the Size property's Width to 415 and Height to 223.

   - Leave the Text property blank.

4. Now your CommandReader form in the Design view should like Figure 13-5.

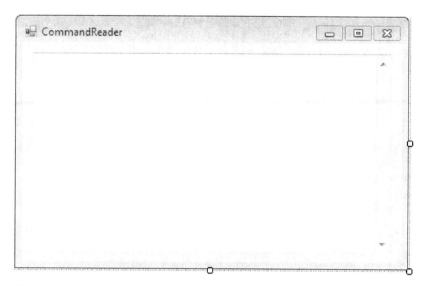

Figure 13-5. The Design view of the CommandReader form

5. Now double-click the empty surface of the CommandReader.cs form, and it will open the code editor window, showing the CommandReader_Load event. Modify the CommandReader_Load event to look like Listing 13-3.

Listing 13-3. CommandReader.cs

```
Using System.Data.SqlClient;

private void CommandReader_Load(object sender, EventArgs e)
{
    // Create connection
    SqlConnection conn = new SqlConnection(@"
                        server = .\sql2012;
                        integrated security = true;
                        database = AdventureWorks");

    // Create command
    string sql = @"select Name,ProductNumber
                from Production.Product";

    SqlCommand cmd = new SqlCommand(sql, conn);
    txtReader.AppendText("Command created and connected.\n\n");

    try
    {
        // Open connection
        conn.Open();
```

```
        // Execute query via ExecuteReader
        SqlDataReader rdr = cmd.ExecuteReader();

        while (rdr.Read())
        {
            txtReader.AppendText("\nProduct: ");
            txtReader.AppendText(rdr.GetValue(1) + "\t\t" + rdr.GetValue(0));
            txtReader.AppendText("\n");
        }
    }

    catch (SqlException ex)
    {
        MessageBox.Show(ex.Message + ex.StackTrace, "Exception Details");
    }

    finally
    {
        conn.Close();
        txtReader.AppendText("Connection Closed.");
    }
}
```

6. To set the CommandReader form as the start-up form, modify the Program.cs statement:

```
Application.Run(new CommandScalar ());
```

to appear as:

```
Application.Run(new CommandReader());
```

Build the project, and run it by pressing Ctrl+F5.

7. When the form loads, the result should look like Figure 13-6.

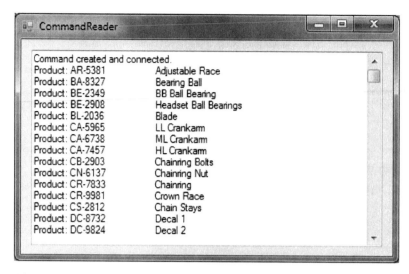

Figure 13-6. Using a data reader

How It Works

In this example, you use the ExecuteReader() method to retrieve and then output the Name and ProductNumber values of all the products in the Production.Product table. As with ExecuteScalar(), ExecuteReader() takes the CommandText property and sends it to the database using the connection from the Connection property.

When you use the ExecuteScalar method, you produce only a single scalar value. In contrast, using ExecuteReader() returns a SqlDataReader object.

```
// execute query
SqlDataReader rdr = cmd.ExecuteReader();
while (rdr.Read())
 {
        txtReader.AppendText(rdr.GetValue(1) + "\t\t" + rdr.GetValue(0));
}
```

The SqlDataReader object has a Read() method that gets each row in turn and a GetValue method that gets the value of a column in the row. The particular column whose value it retrieves is given by the integer parameter indicating the index of the column. Note that GetValue uses a zero-based index, so the first column is column 0, the second column is column 1, and so on. Since the query asked for two columns, Name and ProductNumber, these are the columns numbered 0 and 1 in this query result.

Executing Nonquery Statements

ExecuteNonQuery is the method that is used to execute SQL statements that consist of DML statements. Such statements consist of INSERT, UPDATE, and DELETE functionality of SQL Server. Hence, ExecuteNonQuery() is used to provide the DML statements to the command and execute it. As you might have noticed in previous chapters, INSERT, UPDATE, and DELETE statements do not return any records. Now let's see how the ExecuteNonQuery( ) method works with such a SQL query.

Try It: Using the ExecuteNonQuery Method

To use the ExecuteNonQuery method, follow these steps:

1. Select the ADO.NET_Command project, right-click, and choose Add ➤ Windows Form. From the opened dialog, make sure Windows Form is selected and rename Form1.cs to CommandNonQuery.cs. Click OK to add this form to the ADO.NET_Command project.

2. Select the CommandNonQuery form by clicking the form's title bar, and set the Size property's Width to 297 and Height to 277.

3. Drag a GroupBox control to the form and position it toward the left side of the form. Select the GroupBox control, navigate to the Properties window, and set the following properties:

    - Set the Name property to gbInsertCurrency.

    - Set the Location property's X to 21 and Y to 22.

    - Set the Size property's Width to 240 and Height to 201.

    - Set the Text property to Insert Currency.

4. Drag a Label control to the GroupBox named gbInsertCurrency, and position it toward the left side of the GroupBox. Select this Label control, navigate to the Properties window, and set the following properties:

    - Set the Name property to lblCurrencyCode.

    - Set the Location property's X to 16 and Y to 30.

    - Set the Size property's Width to 77 and Height to 13.

    - Set the Text property to Currency Code.

5. Drag a TextBox control to the form, and position it next to the Label control called Currency Code. Select this TextBox control, navigate to the Properties window, and set the following properties:

    - Set the Name property to txtCurrencyCode.

    - Set the Location property's X to 99 and Y to 30.

    - Set the Size property's Width to 128 and Height to 20.

    - Leave the Text property blank.

6. Drag another Label control to the GroupBox called gbInsertCurrency, and position it below the Currency Code label toward the left side of the GroupBox. Select this Label control, navigate to the Properties window, and set the following properties:

    - Set the Name property to lblName.

    - Set the Location property's X to 19 and Y to 64.

- Set the Size property's Width to 35 and Height to 13.

- Set the Text property to Name.

7. Drag a TextBox control to the form, and position it next to the Label control called Name. Select this TextBox control, navigate to the Properties window, and set the following properties:

- Set the Name property to txtName.

- Set the Location property's X to 99 and Y to 64.

- Set the Size property's Width to 128 and Height to 20.

- Leave the Text property blank.

8. Right now your CommandNonQuery form in the Design view should look like Figure 13-7.

Figure 13-7. The Design view of the CommandNonQuery form

9. Continuing with the form designing, drag another Label control over the GroupBox called gbInsertCurrency and position it below the Name label toward the left side of the GroupBox. Select this Label control, navigate to the Properties window, and set the following properties:

- Set the Name property to lblModifiedDate.

- Set the Location property's X to 19 and Y to 97.

- Set the Size property's Width to 73 and Height to 13.

- Set the Text property to Modified Date.

10. Drag a DateTimePicker control to the form and position it next to the Modified Date Label control. Select this DateTimePicker control, navigate to the Properties window, and set the following properties:

    - Set the Name property to dtpModifiedDate.

    - Set the Format property to Short.

    - Set the Location property's X to 99 and Y to 97.

    - Set the Size property's Width to 128 and Height to 20.

11. Drag a Button control to the GroupBox called gbInsertCurrency and position it below the Label and TextBox controls. Select this Button control, navigate to the Properties window, and set the following properties:

    - Set the Name property to btnInsertCurrency.

    - Set the Location property's X to 56 and Y to 133.

    - Set the Size property's Width to 128 and Height to 23.

    - Set the Text property to Insert Currency.

12. Drag another Label control to the GroupBox called gbInsertCurrency and position it below the Insert Currency button. Select this Label control, navigate to the Properties window, and set the following properties:

    - Set the Name property to lblInsertStatus.

    - Set the AutoSize property to False.

    - Set the Location property's X to 22 and Y to 168.

    - Set the Size property's Width to 205 and Height to 21.

13. Now your CommandNonQuery form in the Design view should like Figure 13-8.

14. Double-click the Insert Currency button, and it will open the code editor window, showing the btnInsertCurrency_Click event. Modify the btnInsertCurrency_Click event to look like Listing 13-4.

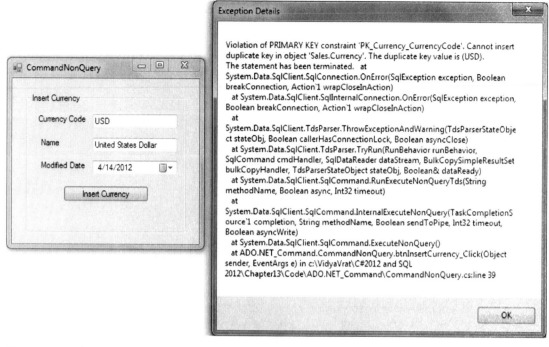

Figure 13-8. The Design view of the CommandNonQuery form

Listing 13-4. CommandNonQuery.cs

```
Using System.Data.SqlClient;

private void btnInsertCurrency_Click(object sender, EventArgs e)
{
    // Create connection
    SqlConnection conn = new SqlConnection(@"server = .\sql2012;
                                integrated security = true;
                                database = AdventureWorks");

    // Insert Query
    string sqlIns = "Insert Into Sales.Currency(CurrencyCode,Name,ModifiedDate)" +
            "Values(" + "'" + txtCurrencyCode.Text + "','" +
            txtName.Text + "','" + dtpModifiedDate.Value.ToString() + "')";

    // Create command
    SqlCommand cmd = new SqlCommand(sqlIns, conn);

    try
    {
        // Open connection
        conn.Open();
```

```
            cmd.ExecuteNonQuery();

            lblInsertStatus.Text = "New Currency Added Successfully!!";

        }

        catch (SqlException ex)
        {
            MessageBox.Show(ex.Message + ex.StackTrace, "Exception Details");
        }

        finally
        {
            conn.Close();
        }
    }
```

15. To set the CommandReader form as the start-up form, modify the `Program.cs` statement:

    ```
    Application.Run(new CommandReader ());
    ```

    to appear as:

    ```
    Application.Run(new CommandNonQuery());
    ```

    Build the project, and run it by pressing Ctrl+F5.

16. When the form loads and you are ready to enter currency details, you need to be careful because the table Sales.Currency used in the exercise has the column CurrencyCode defined as a primary key. Hence, if you try entering a currency that might already exist in the table (which will be the case when you try entering most of the well-known currencies), then you will get a primary key violation. For example, when you try to enter **USD** as the currency code, the moment you click the button Insert Currency, an exception occurs, as shown in Figure 13-9.

Figure 13-9. Insert statement showing primary key violation

17. Trying a successful entry in the table will become a possibility only when you
enter a unique key, in other words, a CurrencyCode that doesn't exist. To
access the form again, click OK in the Exception dialog. Modify the Currency
Code USD to US (I know this is not a real currency code, but for the sake of our
example, it's worth trying), and click Insert Currency button. You will see a
successful insertion, as shown in Figure 13-10.

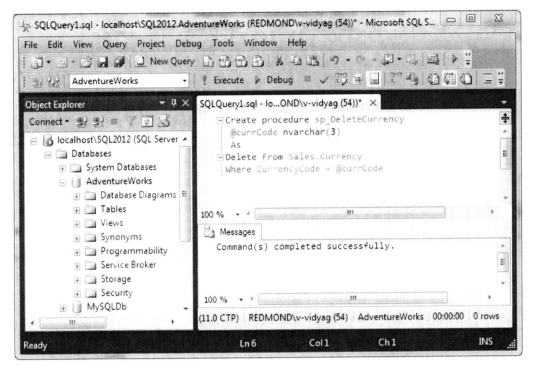

Figure 13-10. Successful insertion of currency

How It Works

In this program, you use a nonquery to insert the currency into the Sales.Currency table. As you can see in the Design view of the CommandNonQuery form, we have two TextBox controls and a DateTimePicker control, so values entered in these controls will be provided to the SQL table via the SqlCommand object. So, the INSERT query will look like this:

```
// Insert Query
            string sqlIns = "Insert Into Sales.Currency(CurrencyCode,Name,ModifiedDate)" +
                    "Values(" + "'" + txtCurrencyCode.Text + "','" +
                    txtName.Text + "','" + dtpModifiedDate.Value.ToString() + "')";
```

Then you create a command that encapsulates the INSERT query.

```
            // Create command
            SqlCommand cmd = new SqlCommand(sqlIns, conn);
   // Execute the SQL statements with a call to the following:
        cmd.ExecuteNonQuery();
ExecuteNonQuery() executes the INSERT statement, and if executed successfully, it will show
the success message in the lblResultStatus control.
            lblInsertStatus.Text = "New Currency Added Successfully!!";
```

> **Note** With ExecuteNonQuery(), you can submit virtually any SQL statement, including Data Definition Language (DDL) statements, to create and drop database objects like tables and indexes. But in industry, the most common use of ExecuteNonQuery() by developers is to insert, update, and delete the rows.

As you have seen so far, all the SQL statements to carry out tasks such as SELECT, INSERT, UPDATE, or DELETE have been hard-coded into the C# code. But most of the time, developers write stored procedures to perform SQL operations; stored procedures work just like functions and can take parameters to perform a task. One of the advantages of stored procedures is having a unified SQL statement created at the SQL Server level, because your ADO.NET code just calls it.

Working with Stored Procedures

As you learned in Chapter 6, a stored procedure is a collection of SQL statements that allows you to perform a task repeatedly. Rather than hard-coding the SQL statements in the C# code, it is an advisable practice to use stored procedures, because it takes advantage of SQL Server's compilation and offers performance-based reuse. A stored procedure simply replaces the hard-coded occurrences of code that performs actions such as inserting, updating, and deleting.

Creating a Stored Procedure to Perform a Delete Operation

In the earlier CommandNonQuery exercise, you saw an insert operation on the Sales.Currency table of the AdventureWorks2008 database. Now let's do a delete operation on the same table, but through a stored procedure.

Try It: Creating a Stored Procedure to Be Used with C#

Let's create a stored procedure using SQL Server Management Studio that will take the CurrencyCode value as a parameter to delete a currency from the Sales.Currency table in the AdventureWorks database. It requires only one input parameter.

1. Open SQL Server Management Studio. In the Connect to Server dialog, select localhost\<Your SQL Server Name> as Server name and then click Connect.

2. In the Object Explorer, expand the Databases node, select the AdventureWorks database, and click the New Query window. Enter the following query and click Execute. You should see the results shown in Figure 13-11.

```
Create procedure sp_DeleteCurrency
  @currCode nvarchar(3)
As
  Delete From Sales.Currency
  Where CurrencyCode = @currCode
```

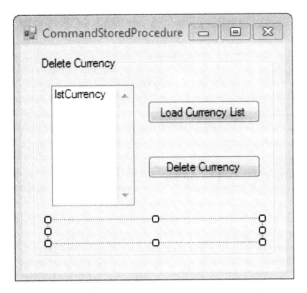

Figure 13-11. Creating a stored procedure to delete a currency

How It Works

The CREATE PROCEDURE statement created a stored procedure that has one input parameter. Parameters are specified between the procedure name and the AS keyword. Here you specified only the parameter name and data type, so by default it is an input parameter. Parameter names start with @.

```
Create procedure sp_DeleteCurrency
 @currCode nvarchar(3)
As
   Delete From Sales.Currency
```

This parameter is used in the WHERE clause of the query.

```
Where CurrencyCode = @currCode
```

Try It: Using a Stored Procedure with the ExecuteNonQuery Method

To use the ExecuteNonQuery method, follow these steps:

1. Select the ADO.NET_Command project, right-click, and choose Add ➤ Windows Form. From the opened dialog, make sure Windows Form is selected, and rename Form1.cs to CommandStoredProcedure.cs. Click OK to add this form to the ADO.NET_Command project.

2. Select the CommandStoredProcedure form by clicking the form's title bar, and set the Size property's Width to 288 and Height to 267.

3. Drag a GroupBox control to the form and position it toward the left side of the form. Select the GroupBox control, navigate to the Properties window, and set the following properties:

    - Set the Name property to gbDeleteCurrency.

    - Set the Location property's X to 12 and Y to 12.

    - Set the Size property's Width to 248 and Height to 201.

    - Set the Text property to Delete Currency.

4. Drag a ListBox control to the GroupBox called gbDeleteCurrency and position it toward the left side of the GroupBox. Select this ListBox control, navigate to the Properties window, and set the following properties:

    - Set the Name property to lblCurrencyCode.

    - Set the Location property's X to 19 and Y to 29.

    - Set the Size property's Width to 85 and Height to 121.

5. Drag a Button control over the GroupBox called gbLoadCurrency, and position it to the right side of the ListBox control. Select this Button control, navigate to the Properties window, and set the following properties:

    - Set the Name property to btnLoadCurrency.

    - Set the Location property's X to 118 and Y to 45.

    - Set the Size property's Width to 116 and Height to 23.

    - Set the Text property to Load Currency List.

6. Drag another Button control just below btnLoadCurrency. Select this Button control, navigate to the Properties window, and set the following properties:

    - Set the Name property to btnDeleteCurrency.

    - Set the Location property's X to 118 and Y to 100.

    - Set the Size property's Width to 116 and Height to 23.

    - Set the Text property to Delete Currency.

7. Drag a Label control to the GroupBox called gbDeleteCurrency, and position it below the lstCurrency ListBox. Select this Label control, navigate to the Properties window, and set the following properties:

    - Set the Name property to lblDeleteStatus.

    - Set the AutoSize property to False.

    - Set the Location property's X to 16 and Y to 165.

    - Set the Size property's Width to 218 and Height to 21.

    - Leave the Text property to Blank.

8. Now your CommandStoredProcedure form in the Design view should like
    Figure 13-12.

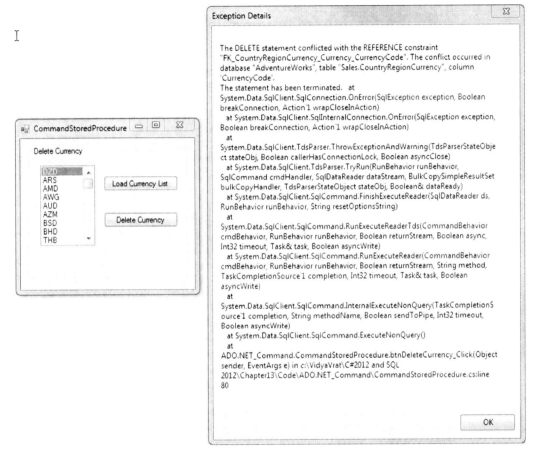

Figure 13-12. *The Design view of the CommandStoredProcedure form*

9. Double-click the Load Currency List button, and it will open the code editior
    window, showing the btnLoadCurrency_Click event. Modify the
    btnLoadCurrency_Click event to look like Listing 13-5.

Listing 13-5. *CommandStoredProcedure.cs*

```
Using System.Data.SqlClient;

private void btnLoadCurrency_Click(object sender, EventArgs e)
{
    // Create connection
    SqlConnection conn = new SqlConnection(@"server = .\sql2012;
                            integrated security = true;
```

```csharp
                                            database = AdventureWorks");

        // Select query
        string sqlSelect = @"select CurrencyCode
                        from Sales.Currency";

        SqlCommand cmd = new SqlCommand(sqlSelect, conn);

        try
        {
            // Open connection
            conn.Open();
            // Execute query via ExecuteReader
            SqlDataReader rdr = cmd.ExecuteReader();

            while (rdr.Read())
            {
                lstCurrency.Items.Add(rdr[0]);
            }
        }

        catch (SqlException ex)
        {
            MessageBox.Show(ex.Message + ex.StackTrace, "Exception Details");
        }
        finally
        {
            conn.Close();
        }
    }
```

10. Now it's time to add functionality for the Delete Currency button. Double-click
    the Delete Currency button, and it will open the code editior window, showing
    the btndeleteCurrency_Click event. Modify the btnDeleteCurrency_Click
    event to look like Listing 13-6.

Listing 13-6. CommandStoredProcedure.cs

```csharp
    private void btnDeleteCurrency_Click(object sender, EventArgs e)
    {
        // Create connection
        SqlConnection conn = new SqlConnection(@"server = .\sql2012;
                                        integrated security = true;
                                        database = AdventureWorks");

        // Create command object with Stored Procedure name
        SqlCommand cmd = new SqlCommand("sp_DeleteCurrency", conn);

        //Set command object for Stored Procedure execution
        cmd.CommandType = CommandType.StoredProcedure;
```

```
            cmd.Parameters.Add(new SqlParameter("currCode", SqlDbType.NVarChar, 3));
            cmd.Parameters["currCode"].Value = lstCurrency.SelectedItem.ToString();
            try
            {
                // Open connection
                conn.Open();
                // Delete Query
                if (lstCurrency.SelectedIndex == -1)
                {
                    MessageBox.Show("Please Select a Currency before performing Delete
action",
                                    "Information");
                }
                else
                {
                    cmd.ExecuteNonQuery();
                    lblDeleteStatus.Text = "Currency is Deleted Successfully!!";
                }

            }
            catch (SqlException ex)
            {
                MessageBox.Show(ex.Message + ex.StackTrace, "Exception Details");
            }

            catch (NullReferenceException ex)
            {
              MessageBox.Show("Load the Currency List first" + ex.StackTrace, "Exception
                        Details");
            }

            finally
            {
                conn.Close();
            }
        }
```

11. To set the CommandStoredProcedure form as the start-up form, modify the
    Program.cs statement.

    ```
    Application.Run(new CommandNonQuery ());
    ```

    to appear as:

    ```
    Application.Run(new CommandStoredProcedure());
    ```

    Build the project, and run it by pressing Ctrl+F5.

12. When the form loads, click the Button control called Load Currency List first;
    this will load the currencies from the Sales.Currency table.

13. Now, select a currency (the one that you have *not* added), and click the Delete
    Currency button. As you may remember, the Sales.Currency table uses
    CurrencyCode as a primary key, so this key column is referenced by the

Sales.CountryRegionCurrency table, and so a reference constraint–related exception will occur, as shown in Figure 13-13.

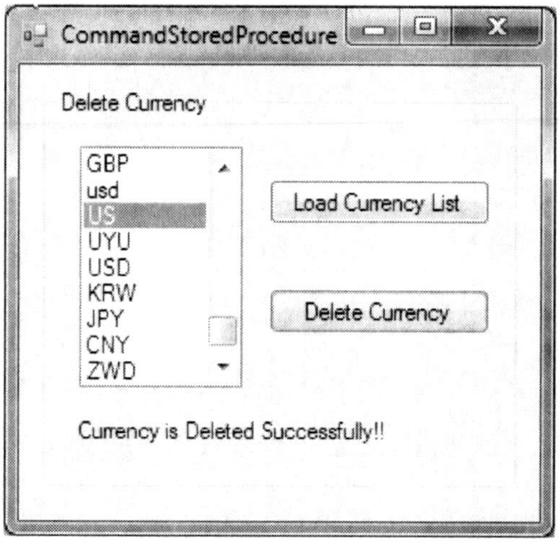

Figure 13-13. *Delete statement showing reference constraint conflict*

14. Click OK. As you have seen, you can't delete the currencies that have referenced entries in the Sales.CountryCurrencyRegion table. Hence, you can only delete the entry that is not related to this referencing table. In the CommandNonQuery exercise, you inserted a CurrencyCode called US, as shown in Figure 13-9. Scroll the currency list until you see US, and then click the Delete Currency button. You will see the successful deletion of the currency, as shown in Figure 13-14.

Figure 13-14. *Successful deletion of the currency*

15. If you will click the Load Currency List again, you will see that the currency code US is not listed, because it has been deleted.

How It Works

In this program, you use a stored procedure to delete the currency from the Sales.Currency table. As you can see in the Design view of the CommandStoredProcedure form, you have a ListBox and two Button controls. The value selected in the ListBox will be passed to a stored procedure, which has a delete query. So, the preparation for passing the value to a stored procedure takes place through these statements:

```
// Create command object with Stored Procedure name
SqlCommand cmd = new SqlCommand("sp_DeleteCurrency", conn);

//Set command object for Stored Procedure execution
cmd.CommandType = CommandType.StoredProcedure;
```

Once you have specified that the command object is going to use a stored procedure, it's time to prepare the parameter(s) required by the stored procedure for execution.

```
cmd.Parameters.Add(new SqlParameter("currCode", SqlDbType.NVarChar, 3));
```

As you can see, we want the ListBox's selection to be deleted, so we are passing the data to the stored procedure parameter as ListBox.SelectedItem.

```
cmd.Parameters["currCode"].Value = lstCurrency.SelectedItem.ToString();
```

Once the parameter is ready, we open the connection and execute the stored procedure by using ExecuteNonQuery.

```
// Open connection
conn.Open();

// Execute command associated with StoredProcedure
cmd.ExecuteNonQuery();
```

Summary

In this chapter, I covered what an ADO.NET command is and how to create a Command object. I also discussed associating a command with a connection, setting command text, and using ExecuteScalar(), ExecuteReader(), and ExecuteNonQuery() statements. You also learned how to use stored procedures with C# code to perform DML operations. In the next chapter, you'll look at data readers.

CHAPTER 14

Using Data Readers

In Chapter 13, you used data readers to retrieve data from a multirow result set. In this chapter, we'll look at data readers in more detail. You'll see how they're used and their importance in ADO.NET programming.

In this chapter, we'll cover the following:

- Understanding data readers in general
- Getting data about data
- Getting data about tables
- Using multiple result sets with a data reader

Understanding Data Readers in General

The third component of a data provider, after connections and commands, is the *data reader*. Once you've connected to a database and queried it, you need some way to access the result set. This is where the data reader comes in.

Data readers are objects that implement the System.Data.IDataReader interface. A data reader is a fast, unbuffered, forward-only, read-only *connected* stream that retrieves data on a per-row basis. It reads one row at a time as it loops through a result set.

You can't directly instantiate a data reader; instead, you create one with the ExecuteReader method of a command. For example, assuming cmd is a SqlClient command object for a query, here's how to create a SqlClient data reader:

```
SqlDataReader rdr = cmd.ExecuteReader();
```

You can now use this data reader to access the query's result set.

Tip One point that we'll discuss further in the next chapter is choosing a data reader vs. a data set. The general rule is to always use a data reader for simply retrieving data. If all you need to do is display data, all you need to use in most cases is a data reader.

We'll demonstrate basic data reader usage with a few examples. The first example is the most basic; it simply uses a data reader to loop through a result set.

Let's say you've successfully established a connection with the database, a query has been executed, and everything seems to be going fine—what now? The next sensible thing to do would be to retrieve the rows and process them.

Try It: Looping Through a Result Set

The following Windows application shows how to use a SqlDataReader to loop through a result set and retrieve rows:

1. Create a new Windows Forms Application project named Chapter14. When Solution Explorer opens, save the solution.

2. Rename the Chapter14 project to DataReader. Rename the Form1.cs file to DataLooper.cs.

3. Select the DataLooper form by clicking the form's title bar, and set the Size property's Width to 346 and Height to 476.

4. Drag a ListBox control onto the form, and position it toward the center of the form. Select this ListBox, navigate to the Properties window, and set the following properties:

    •   Set the Name property to lbxProduct.

    •   Set the Location property's X to 21 and Y to 22.

    •   Set the Size property's Width to 281 and Height to 394.

5. Now your DataLooper form in the Design view should like Figure 14-1.

Figure 14-1. The Design view of the DataLooper form

6.   Double-click the empty surface of the DataLooper.cs form, and it will open the code editor window, showing the DataLooper_Load event. Modify the DataLooper_Load event to look like Listing 14-1.

Listing 14-1. DataLooper.cs

```
Using System.Data.SqlClient;

        private void DataLooper_Load(object sender, EventArgs e)
        {
            // Connection string
            string connString = @"server=.\sql2012;database=AdventureWorks;
                            Integrated Security=SSPI";

            // Query
            string sql = @"select Name from Production.Product";
```

```csharp
        // Create connection
        SqlConnection conn = new SqlConnection(connString);

        try
        {
            // Open connection
            conn.Open();

            // Create command
            SqlCommand cmd = new SqlCommand(sql, conn);

            // Create data reader
            SqlDataReader rdr = cmd.ExecuteReader();

            // Loop through result set
            while (rdr.Read())
            {
                // Add to listbox - one row at a time
                lbxProduct.Items.Add(rdr[0]);
            }

            // Close data reader
            rdr.Close();
        }

        catch (SqlException ex)
        {
            MessageBox.Show(ex.Message + ex.StackTrace);
        }

        finally
        {
            conn.Close();
        }
    }
```

7. Build the project, and run the DataLooper form by pressing Ctrl+F5. Your results should look like Figure 14-2.

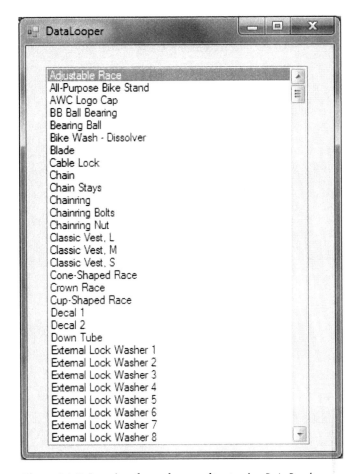

Figure 14-2. Looping through a result set using DataReader

How It Works

SqlDataReader is an abstract class and can't be instantiated explicitly. For this reason, you obtain an instance of a SqlDataReader by executing the ExecuteReader method of SqlCommand.

```
// Create data reader
SqlDataReader rdr = cmd.ExecuteReader();
```

ExecuteReader() doesn't just create a data reader; it sends the SQL to the connection for execution, so when it returns, you can loop through each row of the result set and retrieve values column by column. To do this, you call the Read method of SqlDataReader, which returns true if a row is available and advances the *cursor* (the internal pointer to the next row in the result set) or returns false if another row isn't available. Since Read() advances the cursor to the next available row, you have to call it for all the rows in the result set, so you call it as the condition in a while loop.

```
// Loop through result set
while (rdr.Read())
{
        // Add to listbox - one row at a time
        lbxProduct.Items.Add(rdr[0]);
}
```

Once you call the Read method, the next row is returned as a collection and stored in the SqlDataReader object. To access data from a specific column, you can use a number of methods (we'll cover these in the next section), but for this application you use the ordinal indexer lookup method, giving the column number to the reader to retrieve values (just as you'd specify an index for an array). Since in this case you choose a single column from the Customers table while querying the database, only the "zeroth" indexer is accessible, so you hard-code the index as rdr[0].

To use the *connection* for another purpose or to run another query on the database, it's important to call the Close method of SqlDataReader to close the reader explicitly. Once a reader is attached to an active connection, the connection remains busy fetching data for the reader and remains unavailable for other uses until the reader has been detached from it. That's why you close the reader in the try block rather than in the finally block (even though this simple program doesn't need to use the connection for another purpose).

```
// Close data reader
rdr.Close();
```

Using Ordinal Indexers

You use an ordinal indexer to retrieve column data from the result set. Let's learn more about ordinal indexers. The following code:

```
rdr[0]
```

is a reference to the data reader's Item property and returns the value in the column specified for the current row. The value is returned as an object.

Try It: Using Ordinal Indexers

In this example, you'll add a Windows form to the DataReader project, and then you will use an ordinal indexer.

1. Select the DataReader project, right-click, and choose Add ➤ Windows Form. From the opened dialog, make sure the Windows form is selected and rename Form1.cs to OrdinalIndexer.cs; then click OK to add this form to the DataReader project.

2. Select the OrdinalIndexer form by clicking the form's title bar, and set the Size property's Width to 289 and Height to 351.

3. Drag a TextBox control to the form, and position it toward the center of the form. Select this TextBox control, navigate to the Properties window, and set the following properties:

    •   Set the Name property to txtValues.

    •   Set the Location property's X to 12 and Y to 12.

- Set the Multiline property to True.

- Set the ScrollBars property to Vertical.

- Set the Size property's Width to 249 and Height to 287.

- Leave the Text property blank.

4.   Now your OrdinalIndexer form in the Design view should like Figure 14-3.

Figure 14-3. The Design view of OrdinalIndexer form

5.   Double-click the empty surface of the DataLooper.cs form, and it will open the code editor window, showing the DataLooper_Load event. Modify the DataLooper_Load event to look like Listing 14-2.

Listing 14-2. OrdinalIndexer.cs

```
Using System.Data.SqlClient;

    private void OrdinalIndexer_Load(object sender, EventArgs e)
    {
        // Connection string
        string connString = @"server=.\sql2012;database=AdventureWorks;
                        Integrated Security=SSPI";
```

```csharp
// Query
string sql = @" select FirstName,LastName
                from  Person.Contact
                where FirstName like 'M%'";

// Create connection
SqlConnection conn = new SqlConnection(connString);

try
{
    // Open connection
    conn.Open();

    // Create command
    SqlCommand cmd = new SqlCommand(sql, conn);

    // Create data reader
    SqlDataReader rdr = cmd.ExecuteReader();

    // Print headings
    StringBuilder sb=new StringBuilder();
    txtValues.AppendText("First Name".PadRight(25));
    txtValues.AppendText("Last Name".PadLeft(20));
    txtValues.AppendText(Environment.NewLine);
    txtValues.AppendText("-----------------------------------------
                         --------------------------");
    txtValues.AppendText(Environment.NewLine);

    // Loop through result set
    while (rdr.Read())
    {
        txtValues.AppendText(rdr[0].ToString());
        txtValues.AppendText("\t\t\t");
        txtValues.AppendText(rdr[1].ToString());
        txtValues.AppendText(Environment.NewLine);
    }

    // Close reader
    rdr.Close();
}

catch (SqlException ex)
{
    MessageBox.Show(ex.Message + ex.StackTrace,"Exception Details");
}

finally
{
    // Close connection
    conn.Close();
}
```

```
    }
```

6. To set the OrdinalIndexer form as the start-up form, modify the Program.cs
    statement:

```
Application.Run(new DataLooper());
```

to appear as:

```
Application.Run(new OrdinalIndexer());
```

7. Build the project, and run it by pressing Ctrl+F5. You should see the results in
    Figure 14-4.

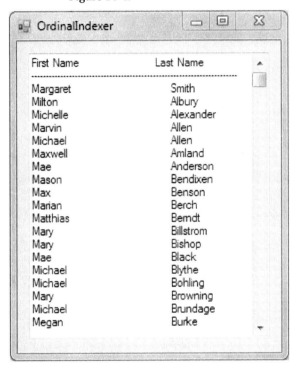

Figure 14-4. Displaying multiple columns using OrdinalIndexer

How It Works

You query the Person.Contact table for the columns FirstName and LastName, where contact names
begin with the letter *M*.

```
// Query
string sql = @" select FirstName,LastName
        from  Person.Contact
        where FirstName like 'M%'";
```

Since two columns are selected by your query, the returned data also comprises a collection of rows from only these two columns, thus allowing access to only two possible ordinal indexers, 0 and 1.

For formatting purposes, we want to show the column headings FirstName and LastName as the first header row, and then we want all other value rows to be added below it. So, you can use the PadeRight and PadLeft methods to format the output in such a way that all the characters will be left- and right-aligned by padding with spaces on the left/right for a specified total length.

```
// Print headings
StringBuilder sb=new StringBuilder();
txtValues.AppendText("First Name".PadRight(25));
txtValues.AppendText("Last Name".PadLeft(20));
txtValues.AppendText(Environment.NewLine);
txtValues.AppendText("---------------------------------------------
--------------------");
txtValues.AppendText(Environment.NewLine);
```

Now you read each row in a while loop, fetching values of the two columns with their indexers and appending these two the TextBox so all the names appear as a list, like shown in Figure 14-2.

```
// Loop through result set
while (rdr.Read())
{
    txtValues.AppendText(rdr[0].ToString());
    txtValues.AppendText("\t\t\t");
    txtValues.AppendText(rdr[1].ToString());
    txtValues.AppendText(Environment.NewLine);
}
```

After processing all rows in the result set, you explicitly close the reader to free the connection.

```
// Close reader
rdr.Close();
```

Using Column Name Indexers

Most of the time, we don't really keep track of column numbers and prefer retrieving values by their respective column names, simply because it's much easier to remember them by their names, which also makes the code more self-documenting.

You use column name indexing by specifying column names instead of ordinal index numbers. This has its advantages. For example, a table may be changed by the addition or deletion of one or more columns, upsetting column ordering and raising exceptions in older code that uses ordinal indexers. Using column name indexers would avoid this issue, but ordinal indexers are faster, since they directly reference columns rather than look them up by name.

The following code snippet retrieves the same columns (FirstName and LastName) that the previous example did, using column name indexers.

```
// Loop through result set
while (rdr.Read())
{
    txtValues.AppendText(rdr["FirstName"].ToString());
    txtValues.AppendText(rdr["LastName"].ToString());
}
```

Replace the ordinal indexers in `OrdinalIndexer.cs` with column name indexers, and rerun the project; you'll get the same results as in Figure 14-2. The next section discusses a better approach for most cases.

Using Typed Accessor Methods

When a data reader returns a value from a data source, the resulting value is retrieved and stored locally in a .NET type rather than the original data source type. This in-place type conversion feature is a trade-off between consistency and speed, so to give some control over the data being retrieved, the data reader exposes typed accessor methods that you can use if you know the specific type of the value being returned.

Typed accessor methods all begin with `Get`, take an ordinal index for data retrieval, and are type safe; C# won't allow you to get away with unsafe casts. These methods turn out to be faster than both the ordinal and the column name indexer methods. Being faster than column name indexing seems only logical, because the typed accessor methods take ordinals for referencing; however, we need to explain how it's faster than ordinal indexing. This is because even though both techniques take in a column number, the conventional ordinal indexing method needs to look up the data source data type of the result and then go through a type conversion. This overhead of looking up the schema is avoided with typed accessors.

.NET types and typed accessor methods are available for almost all data types supported by SQL Server and OLE DB databases.

Table 14-1 should give you a brief idea of when to use typed accessors and with what data type. It lists SQL Server data types, their corresponding .NET types, .NET typed accessors, and special SQL Server–specific typed accessors designed particularly for returning objects of type `System.Data.SqlTypes`.

Table 14-1. *SQL Server Typed Accessors*

SQL Server Data Types	.NET Type	.NET Typed Accessor
bigint	Int64	GetInt64
binary	Byte[]	GetBytes
bit	Boolean	GetBoolean
char	String or Char[]	GetString or GetChars
datetime	DateTime	GetDateTime
decimal	Decimal	GetDecimal
float	Double	GetDouble
image or long varbinary	Byte[]	GetBytes
int	Int32	GetInt32

SQL Server Data Types	.NET Type	.NET Typed Accessor
money	Decimal	GetDecimal
nchar	String or Char[]	GetString or GetChars
ntext	String or Char[]	GetString or GetChars
numeric	Decimal	GetDecimal
nvarchar	String or Char[]	GetString or GetChars
real	Single	GetFloat
smalldatetime	DateTime	GetDateTime
smallint	Int16	GetInt16
smallmoney	Decimal	GetDecimal
sql variant	Object	GetValue
long varchar	String or Char[]	GetString or GetChars
timestamp	Byte[]	GetBytes
tinyint	Byte	GetByte
uniqueidentifier	Guid	GetGuid
varbinary	Byte[]	GetBytes
varchar	String or Char[]	GetString or GetChars

Table 14-2 lists some available OLE DB data types, their corresponding .NET types, and their .NET typed accessors.

Table 14-2. OLE DB Typed Accessors

OLE DB Type	.NET Type	.NET Typed Accessor
DBTYPE_I8	Int64	GetInt64
DBTYPE_BYTES	Byte[]	GetBytes
DBTYPE_BOOL	Boolean	GetBoolean

OLE DB Type	.NET Type	.NET Typed Accessor
DBTYPE_BSTR	String	GetString
DBTYPE_STR	String	GetString
DBTYPE_CY	Decimal	GetDecimal
DBTYPE_DATE	DateTime	GetDateTime
DBTYPE_DBDATE	DateTime	GetDateTime
DBTYPE_DBTIME	DateTime	GetDateTime
DBTYPE_DBTIMESTAMP	DateTime	GetDateTime
DBTYPE_DECIMAL	Decimal	GetDecimal
DBTYPE_R8	Double	GetDouble
DBTYPE_ERROR	ExternalException	GetValue
DBTYPE_FILETIME	DateTime	GetDateTime
DBTYPE_GUID	Guid	GetGuid
DBTYPE_I4	Int32	GetInt32
DBTYPE_LONGVARCHAR	String	GetString
DBTYPE_NUMERIC	Decimal	GetDecimal
DBTYPE_R4	Single	GetFloat
DBTYPE_I2	Int16	GetInt16
DBTYPE_I1	Byte	GetByte
DBTYPE_UI8	UInt64	GetValue
DBTYPE_UI4	UInt32	GetValue
DBTYPE_UI2	UInt16	GetValue
DBTYPE_VARCHAR	String	GetString

OLE DB Type	.NET Type	.NET Typed Accessor
DBTYPE_VARIANT	Object	GetValue
DBTYPE_WVARCHAR	String	GetString
DBTYPE_WSRT	String	GetString

To see typed accessors in action, you'll build a console application that uses them. For this example, you'll use the Products table from the Northwind database.

Table 14-3 shows the data design of the table. Note that the data types given in the table will be looked up for their corresponding typed accessor methods in Table 14-1 so you can use them correctly in your application.

Table 14-3. AdventureWorks Sales.CreditCard Table Data Types

Column Name	Data Type	Length	Allow Nulls?
CreditCardID (unique)	int	4	No
CardType	nvarchar	50	No
CardNumber	nvarchar	25	No
ExpMonth	tinyint	1	No
ExpYear	smallint	2	No
ModifiedDate	datetime	8	No

Try It: Using Typed Accessor Methods

In this example, you'll add a Windows form to the DataReader project, and then you will use typed accessor methods.

1. Select the DataReader project, right-click, and choose Add ➤ Windows Form. From the opened dialog, make sure the Windows form is selected and rename Form1.cs to TypedAccessor.cs; click OK to add this form to the DataReader project.

2. Select the TypedAccessor form, and set the Size property's Width to 476 and Height to 353.

3. Drag a TextBox control to the form and position it toward center of the form. Select this TextBox control, navigate to the Properties window, and set the following properties:

   • Set the Name property to txtTypeAccess.

- Set the Location property's X to 12 and Y to 12.

- Set the ScrollBars property to Vertical.

- Set the Size property's Width to 437 and Height to 290.

- Set the Multiline property to True.

4. Now your TypedAccessor form in the Design view should look like Figure 14-5.

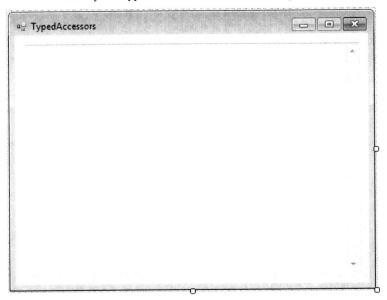

Figure 14-5. The Design view of the TypedAccessor form

5. Now double-click the empty surface of the TypedAccessor.cs form, and it will open the code editor window, showing the TypedAccessor_Load event. Modify the TypedAccessor _Load event to look like Listing 14-3.

Listing 14-3. TypedAccessors.cs

```
Using System.Data.SqlClient;
private void TypedAccessors_Load(object sender, EventArgs e)
{
    // Connection string
    string connString = @"server=.\sql2012;database=AdventureWorks;
                    Integrated Security=SSPI";

    // Query
    string sql = @"select CardType, CardNumber,ExpMonth,ExpYear from
Sales.CreditCard";
```

```
        // Create connection
        SqlConnection conn = new SqlConnection(connString);

        try
        {
            // Open connection
            conn.Open();

            // Create command
            SqlCommand cmd = new SqlCommand(sql, conn);

            // Create data reader

            SqlDataReader rdr = cmd.ExecuteReader();

            // Fetch data
            while (rdr.Read())
            {

                // CardType
                txtTypeAccess.AppendText(rdr.GetString(0).PadRight(30));
                txtTypeAccess.AppendText("\t");
                // CardNumber
                txtTypeAccess.AppendText(rdr.GetString(1));
                txtTypeAccess.AppendText("\t\t");
                // ExpMonth
                txtTypeAccess.AppendText(rdr.GetByte(2).ToString());
                txtTypeAccess.AppendText("\t\t");
                // ExpYear
                txtTypeAccess.AppendText(rdr.GetInt16(3).ToString());
                txtTypeAccess.AppendText("\n");
            }
            // Close data reader
            rdr.Close();
        }
        catch (SqlException ex)
        {
            MessageBox.Show(ex.Message + ex.StackTrace,"Exception Details");
        }

        finally
        {

            // Close connection
            conn.Close();
        }
    }
```

6. To set the TypedAccessor form as the start-up form, modify the Program.cs statement.

```
Application.Run(new OrdinalIndexer ());
```

to appear as:

```
Application.Run(new TypedAccessor());
```

7. Build the project, and run it by pressing Ctrl+F5. You should see the results in
   Figure 14-6.

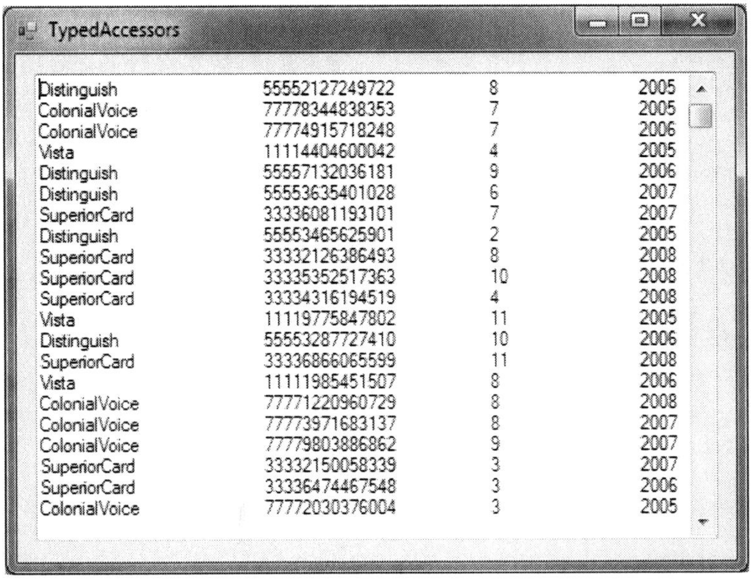

Figure 14-6. Using typed accessors

How It Works

You query the Sales.CreditCard table for CardType, CardNumber, ExpMonth, and ExpYear.

```
// Query
string sql = @"select CardType, CardNumber,ExpMonth,ExpYear from
Sales.CreditCard";
```

The reason we have you choose these columns is to deal with different kinds of data types and show
how to use relevant typed accessors to obtain the correct results.

```
// Fetch data
while (rdr.Read())
{

    // CardType
    txtTypeAccess.AppendText(rdr.GetString(0).PadRight(30));
    txtTypeAccess.AppendText("\t");
    // CardNumber
    txtTypeAccess.AppendText(rdr.GetString(1));
    txtTypeAccess.AppendText("\t\t");
```

```
        // ExpMonth
        txtTypeAccess.AppendText(rdr.GetByte(2).ToString());
        txtTypeAccess.AppendText("\t\t");
        // ExpYear
        txtTypeAccess.AppendText(rdr.GetInt16(3).ToString());
        txtTypeAccess.AppendText("\n");
    }
```

Looking at Table 14-1, you can see that you can access nvarchar, tinyint, and smallint data types in SQL Server with the GetString, GetByte, and GetInt16 accessor methods, respectively.

This technique is fast and completely type safe. By this, we mean that if implicit conversions from native data types to .NET types fail, an exception is thrown for invalid casts. For instance, if you try using the GetString method on a bit data type instead of using the GetBoolean method, a "Specified cast is not valid" exception will be thrown.

Getting Data About Data

So far, all you've done is retrieve data from a data source. Once you have a populated data reader in your hands, you can do a lot more. There are a number of useful methods for retrieving schema information or retrieving information directly related to a result set. Table 14-4 describes some of the metadata methods and properties of a data reader.

Table 14-4. Data Reader Metadata Properties and Methods

Method or Property Name	Description
Depth	A property that gets the depth of nesting for the current row
FieldCount	A property that holds the number of columns in the current row
GetDataTypeName	A method that accepts an index and returns a string containing the name of the column data type
GetFieldType	A method that accepts an index and returns the .NET Framework type of the object
GetName	A method that accepts an index and returns the name of the specified column
GetOrdinal	A method that accepts a column name and returns the column index
GetSchemaTable	A method that returns column metadata
HasRows	A property that indicates whether the data reader has any rows
RecordsAffected	A property that gets the number of rows changed, inserted, or deleted

Try It: Getting Information About a Result Set with a Data Reader

In this exercise, you'll use some of these methods and properties.

1. Select the DataReader project, right-click, and choose Add ➤ Windows Form. From the opened dialog, make sure Windows Form is selected and rename Form1.cs to ResultSetInfo.cs; then click OK to add this form to the DataReader project.

2. Select the ResultSetInfo form, and set the Size property's Width to 462 and Height to 460.

    *   Drag a Label control to the form, select this control, navigate to the Properties window, and set the following properties:

    *   Set the Name property to lblDataType.

    *   Set the AutoSize property to false.

    *   Set the Location property's X to 3 and Y to 31.

    *   Set the Size property's X to 57 and Y to 13.

    *   Set the Text property to Data Type.

3. Drag a Label control to the form. Select this control, navigate to the Properties window, and set the following properties:

    *   Set the Name property to lblType1.

    *   Set the AutoSize property to false.

    *   Set the Location property's X to 80 and Y to 21.

    *   Set the Size property's X to 101 and Y to 34.

    *   Leave the Text property blank.

    *   Drag a Label control to the form. Select this control, navigate to the Properties window, and set the following properties:

    *   Set the Name property to lblType2.

    *   Set the AutoSize property to false.

    *   Set the Location property's X to 222 and Y to 21.

    *   Set the Size property's X to 101 and Y to 34.

    *   Leave the Text property blank.

    *   Drag a TextBox control below the Label controls, and navigate to the Properties windows to configure the following properties:

    *   Set the Name property to txtResultSet.

    *   Set the Multiline property to True.

- Set the Location property's X to 32 and Y to 58.

- Set the ScrollBars property to Vertical.

- Set the Size property's Width to 341 and Height to 234.

- Drag a Label control below the TextBox, navigate to the Properties window, and set the following properties:

- Set the Name property to lblType3.

- Set the AutoSize property to false.

- Set the Location property's X to 38 and Y to 317.

- Set the Size property's Width to 335 and Height to 13.

- Leave the Text property blank.

- Drag another Label control below the label you just added. Select this control, navigate to the Properties window, and set the following properties:

- Set the Name property to lblType4.

- Set the AutoSize property to false.

- Set the Location property's X to 38 and Y to 352.

- Set the Size property's Width to 335 and Height to 13.

- Leave the Text property blank.

- Drag another Label control below the label you just added. Select this control, navigate to the Properties window, and set the following properties:

- Set the Name property to lblType5.

- Set the AutoSize property to false.

- Set the Location property's X to 38 and Y to 381.

- Set the Size property's Width to 335 and Height to 13.

- Leave the Text property blank.

4. Now your ResultSetInfo form in the Design view should like Figure 14-7.

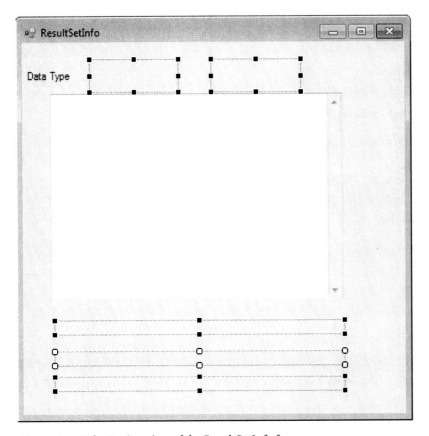

Figure 14-7. The Design view of the ResultSetInfo form

5. Double-click the empty surface of the TypedAccessor.cs form, and it will open the code editor window, showing the TypedAccessor_Load event. Modify the TypedAccessor_Load event to look like Listing 14-4.

Listing 14-4. ResultSetInfo.cs

```
Using System.Data.SqlClient;

private void ResultSetInfo_Load(object sender, EventArgs e)
{
    // Connection string
    string connString = @"server=.\sql2012;database=AdventureWorks;
                Integrated Security=SSPI";

    // Query
    string sql = @" select FirstName,LastName from Person.Contact
                order by LastName";
```

```
// Create connection
SqlConnection conn = new SqlConnection(connString);

try
{
    conn.Open();

    SqlCommand cmd = new SqlCommand(sql, conn);

    SqlDataReader rdr = cmd.ExecuteReader();

    // Get column names
    lbltype1.Text = rdr.GetName(0);
    lblType2.Text = rdr.GetName(1);

    //Get column data types
    lbltype1.Text += "\n"+ rdr.GetDataTypeName(0).ToString();
    lblType2.Text += "\n"+ rdr.GetDataTypeName(1).ToString();

    // Get number of columns
    lblType3.Text = "Number of columns in a row::" + rdr.FieldCount.ToString();

    // Get info about each column
    lblType4.Text = rdr.GetName(0).ToString() + " is at index::" +
                    rdr.GetOrdinal("FirstName").ToString()   +
                    " and its type is::" + rdr.GetFieldType(0).ToString();

    lblType5.Text = rdr.GetName(1).ToString() + " is at index:: "+
                    rdr.GetOrdinal("LastName").ToString()   +
                    " and its type is::" + rdr.GetFieldType(1).ToString();

    while (rdr.Read())
    {
      // Get column values for all rows
        txtResultSet.AppendText("\t");
        txtResultSet.AppendText(rdr[0].ToString());
        txtResultSet.AppendText("\t\t\t");
        txtResultSet.AppendText(rdr[1].ToString() );
        txtResultSet.AppendText("\n");
    }

    //Close reader
    rdr.Close();

}
catch (SqlException ex)
{
    MessageBox.Show(ex.Message + ex.StackTrace,"Exception Details");
}

finally
{
```

```
            //Clsoe connection
            conn.Close();
        }
    }
```

6. To set the ResultSetInfo form as the start-up form, modify the Program.cs statement.

```
Application.Run(new TypedAccessor ());
```

to appear as:

```
Application.Run(new ResultSetInfo());
```

7. Build the project, and run it by pressing Ctrl+F5. Your results should look like Figure 14-8.

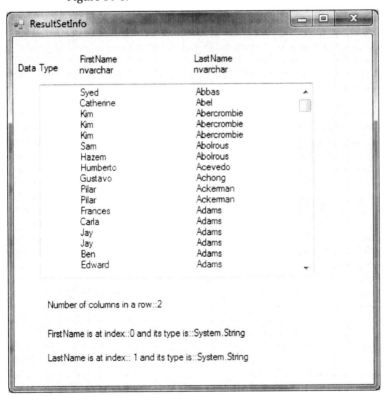

Figure 14-8. Displaying result set metadata

How It Works

The GetName method gets a column name by its index. This method returns information *about* the result set, so it can be called before the first call to Read().

```
// Get column names
lbltype1.Text = rdr.GetName(0);
lblType2.Text = rdr.GetName(1);
```

The GetDataTypeName method returns the database data type of a column. It too can be called before the first call to Read().

```
//Get column data types
lbltype1.Text += "\n"+ rdr.GetDataTypeName(0).ToString();
lblType2.Text += "\n"+ rdr.GetDataTypeName(1).ToString();
```

The FieldCount property of the data reader contains the number of columns in the result set. This is useful for looping through columns without knowing their names or other attributes.

```
// Get number of columns
lblType3.Text = "Number of columns in a row::" + rdr.FieldCount.ToString();
```

Finally, you see how the GetOrdinal and GetFieldType methods are used. The former returns a column index based on its name; the latter returns the C# type. These are the countertypes of GetName() and GetDataTypeName(), respectively.

```
// Get info about each column
lblType4.Text = rdr.GetName(0).ToString() + " is at index::" +
                rdr.GetOrdinal("FirstName").ToString()  +
                " and its type is::" + rdr.GetFieldType(0).ToString();

lblType5.Text = rdr.GetName(1).ToString() + " is at index:: "+
                rdr.GetOrdinal("LastName").ToString()  +
                " and its type is::" + rdr.GetFieldType(1).ToString();
```

So much for obtaining information about result sets. You'll now learn how to get information about schemas.

Getting Data About Tables

The term *schema* has several meanings in regard to relational databases. Here, we use it to refer to the design of a data structure, particularly a database table. A table consists of rows and columns, and each column can have a different data type. The columns and their attributes (data type, length, and so on) make up the table's schema.

To retrieve schema information easily, you can call the GetSchemaTable method on a data reader. As the name suggests, this method returns a System.Data.DataTable object, which is a representation (schema) of the table queried and contains a collection of rows and columns in the form of DataRow and DataColumn objects. These rows and columns are returned as collection objects by the properties Rows and Columns of the DataTable class.

However, here's where a slight confusion usually occurs. Data column objects aren't column values; rather, they are column definitions that represent and control the behavior of individual columns. They can be looped through by using a column name indexer, and they can tell you a lot about the data set.

Try It: Getting Schema Information

Here you'll see a practical demonstration of the GetSchemaTable method.

1. Select the DataReader project, right-click, and choose Add ➤ Windows Form. From the opened dialog, make sure the Windows form is selected and rename Form1.cs to SchemaTable.cs, and click OK to add this form to the DataReader project.

2. Select the SchemaTable form, and set the Size property's Width to 378 and Height to 459.

3. Drag a TextBox control to the form, and position it toward the middle of the form. Select this TextBox control, navigate to the Properties window, and set the following properties:

    - Set the Name property to txtSchema.

    - Set the Location property's X to 12 and Y to 12.

    - Set the Multiline property to True.

    - Set the ScrollBars property to Vertical.

    - Set the Size property's Width to 392 and Height to 333.

4. Now your SchemaTable form in the Design view should look like Figure 14-9.

Figure 14-9. The Design view of the SchemaTable form

5. Double-click the empty surface of the SchemaTable.cs form, and it will open the code editor window, showing the SchemaTable_Load event. Modify the SchemaTable _Load event to look like Listing 14-5.

Listing 14-5. SchemaTable.cs

```
Using System.Data.SqlClient
        private void SchemaTable_Load(object sender, EventArgs e)
        {
            // Connection string
            string connString = @"server=.\sql2012;
            database=AdventureWorks;Integrated Security=SSPI";

            // Query
            string sql = @"select * from  Person.Address";

            // Create connection
            SqlConnection conn = new SqlConnection(connString);

            try
            {
                conn.Open();

                SqlCommand cmd = new SqlCommand(sql, conn);
                SqlDataReader rdr = cmd.ExecuteReader();

                // Store Employees schema in a data table
                DataTable schema = rdr.GetSchemaTable();

                // Display info from each row in the data table.
                // Each row describes a column in the database table.

                foreach (DataRow row in schema.Rows)
                {
                    foreach (DataColumn col in schema.Columns)
                    {
                        txtSchema.AppendText(col.ColumnName + " = " + row[col]);
                        txtSchema.AppendText("\n");
                    }
                    txtSchema.AppendText("----------------");
                }

                //Close reader
                rdr.Close();

            }
            catch (Exception err)
            {
                MessageBox.Show(err.ToString() );
            }
            finally
            {
```

```
                //connection close
                conn.Close();
        }
}
```

6. To set the SchemaTable form as the start-up form, modify the Program.cs statement.

```
Application.Run(new ResultSetInfo ());
```

to appear as

```
Application.Run(new SchemaTable());
```

7. Build the project, and run it by pressing Ctrl+F5. You should see the results in Figure 14-10.

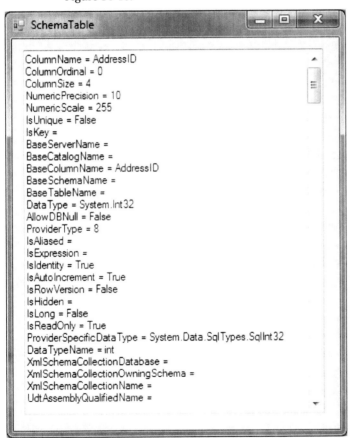

Figure 14-10. Displaying schema metadata

How It Works

This code is a bit different from what you've written earlier. When the call to the GetSchemaTable method is made, a populated instance of a data table is returned.

```
// Store Person's schema in a data table
DataTable schema = rdr.GetSchemaTable();
```

You can use a data table to represent a complete table in a database, either in the form of a table that represents its schema or in the form of a table that holds all its original data for offline use.

In this example, once you grab hold of a schema table, you retrieve a collection of rows through the Rows property of DataTable and a collection of columns through the Columns property of DataTable. (You can use the Rows property to add a new row into the table altogether or remove one, and you can use the Columns property for adding or deleting an existing column—we'll cover this in Chapter 15.) Each row returned by the table describes one column in the original table, so for each of these rows, you traverse through the column's schema information one by one, using a nested foreach loop.

```
// Display info from each row in the data table.
// Each row describes a column in the database table.
foreach (DataRow row in schema.Rows)
{
    foreach (DataColumn col in schema.Columns)
    {
        txtSchema.AppendText(col.ColumnName + " = " + row[col]);
        txtSchema.AppendText("\n");
    }
        txtSchema.AppendText("----------------");
}
```

Notice how you use the ColumnName property of the DataColumn object to retrieve the current schema column name in the loop, and then you retrieve the value related to that column's definition by using the familiar indexer-style method that uses a DataRow object. DataRow has a number of overloaded indexers, and this is only one of several ways of doing it.

Using Multiple Result Sets with a Data Reader

Sometimes you may really want to get a job done quickly and also want to query the database with two or more queries at the same time. And, you wouldn't want the overall application performance to suffer in any way either by instantiating more than one command or data reader or by exhaustively using the same objects over and over again, adding to the code as you go.

So, is there a way you can get a single data reader to loop through multiple result sets? Yes, data readers have a method, NextResult(), that advances the reader to the next result set.

Try It: Handling Multiple Result Sets

In this example, you'll use NextResult() to process multiple result sets.

1. Select the DataReader project, right-click, and choose Add ➤ Windows Form. From the opened dialog, make sure the Windows form is selected, and rename Form1.cs to MultipleResults.cs. Click OK to add this form to the DataReader project.

2. Select the MultipleResults form, and set the Size property's Width to 358 and Height to 516.

3. Drag a TextBox control onto the form, and position it toward the middle of the form. Select this TextBox, navigate to the Properties window, and set the following properties:

   - Set the Name property to txtResult.

   - Set the Location property's X to 12 and Y to 12.

   - Set the Multiline property to True.

   - Set the ScrollBars property to Vertical.

   - Set the Size property's Width to 318 and Height to 454.

4. Now your MultipleResults form in the Design view should like Figure 14-11.

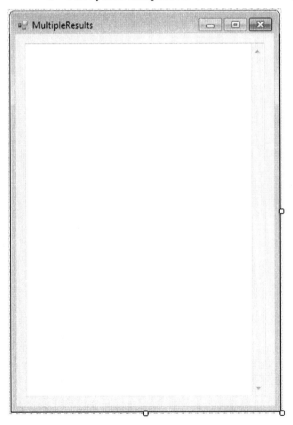

Figure 14-11. The Design view of the MultipleResults form

5. Now double-click the empty surface of the MultipleResults.cs form, and it will open the code editor window, showing the SchemaTable_Load event. Modify the MultipleResults_Load event to look like Listing 14-6.

Listing 14-6. MultipleResults.cs

```csharp
using System.Data.SqlClient;

private void MultipleResults_Load(object sender, EventArgs e)
{
    // Connection string
    string connString = @"server=.\sql2012;database=AdventureWorks;
                        Integrated Security=SSPI";

    // Query1
    string sql1 = @"select CountryRegionCode,Name
                    from Person.CountryRegion
                    where Name like 'A%' ";

    //Query2
    string sql2 = @"select FirstName, LastName
                    from Person.Contact";

    //Combining queries to produce multiple result set
    string sql = sql1 + sql2;

    // Create connection
    SqlConnection conn = new SqlConnection(connString);
    try
    {
        // Open connection
        conn.Open();

        // Create command
        SqlCommand cmd = new SqlCommand(sql, conn);

        // Create data reader
        SqlDataReader rdr = cmd.ExecuteReader();

        // Loop through result sets
        do
        {
            txtResult.AppendText(rdr.GetName(0));
            txtResult.AppendText("\t\t");
            txtResult.AppendText(rdr.GetName(1));
            txtResult.AppendText("\n");
            txtResult.AppendText("".PadLeft(30, '='));
            txtResult.AppendText("\n");

            while (rdr.Read())
            {
                // Print one row at a time
```

```
            txtResult.AppendText(rdr[0].ToString());
            txtResult.AppendText("\t\t\t");
            txtResult.AppendText(rdr[1].ToString());
            txtResult.AppendText("\n");
        }
    }
    while (rdr.NextResult());

    // Close data reader
    rdr.Close();
}
catch (SqlException ex)
{
    MessageBox.Show(ex.Message + ex.StackTrace,"Exception Details");
}
finally
{
    // Close connection
    conn.Close();
}
```

6. To set the MultipleResults form as the start-up form, modify the Program.cs statement.

```
Application.Run(new SchemaTable ());
```

to appear as:

```
Application.Run(new MultipleResults());
```

7. Build the project, and run it by pressing Ctrl+F5. You should see the results in Figure 14-12.

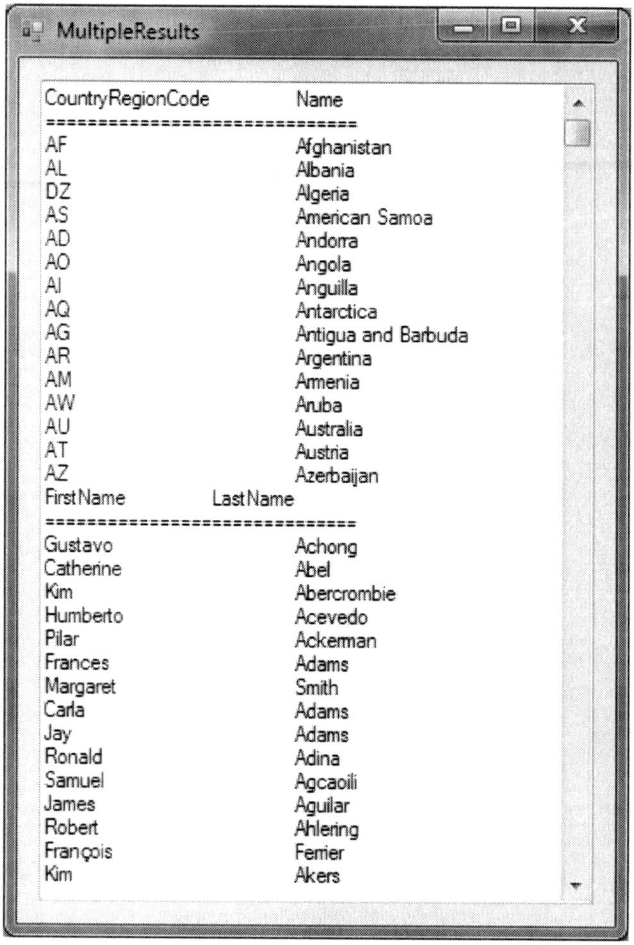

Figure 14-12. Handling multiple result sets

How It Works

This program is essentially the same as the first, DataLooper.cs (Listing 14-1). Here, you define two separate queries and then combine them.

```
// Query1
string sql1 = @"select CountryRegionCode,Name
                from Person.CountryRegion
                where Name like 'A%' ";

//Query2
string sql2 = @"select FirstName, LastName
                from Person.Contact";
```

```
//Combining queries to produce multiple result set
string sql = sql1 + sql2;
```

The only other change is that you loop through result sets. You nest the loop that retrieves rows inside one that loops through result sets.

```
// Loop through result sets
do
{
    txtResult.AppendText(rdr.GetName(0));
    txtResult.AppendText("\t\t");
    txtResult.AppendText(rdr.GetName(1));
    txtResult.AppendText("\n");
    txtResult.AppendText("".PadLeft(30, '='));
    txtResult.AppendText("\n");

    while (rdr.Read())
    {
        // Print one row at a time
        txtResult.AppendText(rdr[0].ToString());
        txtResult.AppendText("\t\t\t");
        txtResult.AppendText(rdr[1].ToString());
        txtResult.AppendText("\n");
    }
}
while (rdr.NextResult());
```

We have you choose only two character-string columns per query to simplify things. Extending this to handle result tables with different numbers of columns and column data types is straightforward.

Summary

In this chapter, you used data readers to perform a variety of common tasks, from simply looping through single result sets to handling multiple result sets. You learned how to retrieve values for columns by column name and index and learned about methods available for handling values of different data types. You also learned how to get information about result sets and get schema information.

In the next chapter, we'll cover the really interesting aspects of ADO.NET: handling database data while disconnected from the database using DataSets and DataAdapters.

Working with Advanced ADO.NET Related Features

Using Data Sets and Data Adapters

In Chapter 14, you saw how to use data readers to access database data in a connected, forward-only, read-only fashion. Often, this is all you want to do, and a data reader suits your purposes perfectly.

In this chapter, you'll look at a new object for accessing data, the *data set*. Unlike data readers, which are objects of data provider–specific classes that implement the `System.Data.IDataReader` interface, data sets are objects of the class `System.Data.DataSet`, a distinct ADO.NET component used by all data providers. Data sets are completely independent of and can be used either connected to or disconnected from data sources. Their fundamental purpose is to provide a relational view of data stored in an in-memory cache.

Note In yet another somewhat confusing bit of terminology, the class is named `DataSet`, but the generic term is spelled *data set*

So, if a data set doesn't have to be connected to a database, how do you populate it with data and save its data to the database? This is where *data adapters* come in. Think of data adapters as bridges between data sets and data sources. Without a data adapter, a data set can't access any kind of data source. The data adapter takes care of all connection details for the data set, populates it with data, and updates the data source.

In this chapter, we'll cover the following:

- Understanding the object model

- Working with data sets and data adapters

- Propagating changes to a data source

- Concurrency

- Using data sets and XML

- Understanding typed and untyped data sets

Understanding the Object Model

We'll start this chapter with a quick presentation of all the new objects you'll need to understand in order to work with data sets and data adapters. You'll start by looking at the difference between data sets and data readers and then move on to look in more detail at how data is structured within a data set and how a data set works in collaboration with a data adapter.

Data Sets vs. Data Readers

If you simply want to read and display data, then you need to use only a data reader, as you saw in the previous chapter, particularly if you're working with large quantities of data. In situations where you need to loop through thousands or millions of rows, you want a fast sequential reader (reading rows from the result set one at a time), and the data reader does this job in an efficient way.

If you need to manipulate the data in any way and then update the database, you need to use a data set. A data adapter fills a data set by using a data reader; additional resources are needed to save data for disconnected use. You need to think about whether you really need a data set; otherwise, you'll just be wasting resources. Unless you need to update the data source or use other data set features such as reading and writing to XML files, exporting database schemas, and creating XML views of a database, you should use a data reader.

A Brief Introduction to Data Sets

The notion of a data set in ADO.NET is a big step in the world of multitiered database application development. When retrieving or modifying large amounts of data, maintaining an open connection to a data source while waiting for users to make requests is an enormous waste of precious resources.

Data sets help tremendously here, because they enable you to store and modify large amounts of data in a local cache, view the data as tables, and process the data in an *offline* mode (in other words, disconnected from the database).

Let's look at an example. Imagine you're trying to connect to a remote database server over the Internet for detailed information about some business transactions. You search on a particular date for all available transactions, and the results are displayed. Behind the scenes, your application creates a connection with the data source, joins a couple of tables, and retrieves the results. Suppose you now want to edit this information and add or remove details. Whatever the reason, your application will go through the same cycle over and over again: creating a new connection, joining tables, and retrieving data. Not only is there overhead in creating a new connection each time, but you may be doing a lot of other redundant work, especially if you're dealing with the same data. Wouldn't it be better if you could connect to the data source once, store the data locally in a structure that resembles a relational database, close the connection, modify the local data, and then propagate the changes to the data source when the time is right?

This is exactly what the data set is designed to do. A data set stores relational data as collections of *data tables*. You met data tables briefly in the previous chapter when a System.Data.DataTable object was to hold schema information. In that instance, however, the data table contained only schema information, but in a data set, the data tables contain both metadata describing the structure of the data and the data itself.

Figure 15-1 shows the data set architecture.

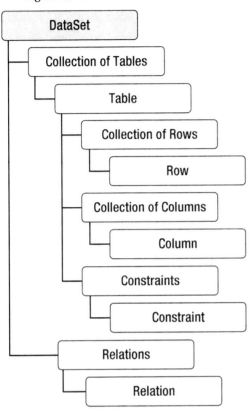

Figure 15-1. Data set architecture

The architecture mirrors the logical design of a relational database. You'll see how to use data tables, data rows, and data columns in this chapter.

A Brief Introduction to Data Adapters

When you first instantiate a data set, it contains no data. You obtain a populated data set by passing it to a data adapter, which takes care of connection details and is a component of a data provider. A data set isn't part of a data provider. It's like a bucket, ready to be filled with water, but it needs an external pipe to let the water in. In other words, the data set needs a data adapter to populate it with data and to support access to the data source.

Each data provider has its own data adapter in the same way that it has its own connection, command, and data reader. Figure 15-2 depicts the interactions between the data set, data adapter, and data source.

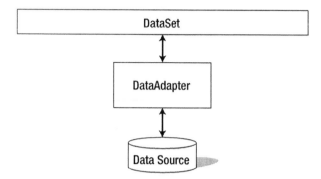

Figure 15-2. *Dataset, data adapter, and data source interaction*

The data adapter constructor is overloaded. You can use any of the following to get a new data adapter. We're using the SQL Server data provider, but the constructors for the other data providers are analogous.

```
SqlDataAdapter  da  =  new   SqlDataAdapter();
SqlDataAdapter  da  =  new   SqlDataAdapter(cmd);
SqlDataAdapter  da  =  new   SqlDataAdapter(sql, conn);
SqlDataAdapter  da  =  new   SqlDataAdapter(sql, connString);
```

So, you can create a data adapter in four ways:

- You can use its parameterless constructor (assigning SQL and the connection later).

- You can pass its constructor a command (here, cmd is a SqlCommand object).

- You can pass a SQL string and a connection.

- You can pass a SQL string and a connection string.

You'll see all this working in action shortly. For now, we'll move on and show how to use data tables, data columns, and data rows. You'll use these in upcoming sections.

A Brief Introduction to Data Tables, Data Columns, and Data Rows

A data table is an instance of the class System.Data.DataTable. It's conceptually analogous to a relational table. As shown in Figure 15-1, a data table has collections of data rows and data columns. You can access these nested collections via the Rows and Columns properties of the data table.

A data table can represent a stand-alone independent table, either inside a data set, as you'll see in this chapter, or as an object created by another method, as you saw in the previous chapter when a data table was returned by calling the GetSchemaTable method on a data reader.

A data column represents the schema of a column within a data table and can then be used to set or get column properties. For example, you could use it to set the default value of a column by assigning a value to the DefaultValue property of the data column.

You obtain the collection of data columns using the data table's Columns property, whose indexer accepts either a column name or a zero-based index, for example (where dt is a data table):

```
DataColumn col = dt.Columns["ContactName"];
```

```
DataColumn col = dt.Columns[2];
```

A data row represents the data in a row. You can programmatically add, update, or delete rows in a data table. To access rows in a data table, you use its Rows property, whose indexer accepts a zero-based index, for example (where dt is a data table):

```
DataRow row = dt.Rows[2];
```

That's enough theory for now. It's time to do some coding and see how these objects work together in practice!

Working with Data Sets and Data Adapters

The data set constructor is overloaded.

```
DataSet ds = new DataSet();
DataSet ds = new DataSet("MyDataSet");
```

If you use the parameterless constructor, the data set name defaults to NewDataSet. If you need more than one data set, it's good practice to use the other constructor and name it explicitly. However, you can always change the data set name by setting its DataSetName property.

You can populate a data set in several ways, including the following:

- Using a data adapter

- Reading from an XML document

In this chapter, we'll use data adapters. However, in the "Using Datasets and XML" section, you'll take a quick peek at the converse of the second method, and you'll write from a data set to an XML document.

Try It: Populating a DataSet with a Data Adapter

In this example, you'll create a data set, populate it with a data adapter, and then display its contents.

1. Create a new Windows Forms Application project named Chapter15. When Solution Explorer opens, save the solution.

2. Rename the Chapter15 project to DataSetandDataAdapter.

3. Rename the Form1.cs file to PopDataSet.cs.

4. Select the PopDataSet form by clicking the form's title bar, and set the Size property's Width to 301 and Height to 342.

5. Drag a GridView control onto the form, and position it toward the top-left corner of the form. Select this GridView, navigate to the Properties window, and set the following properties:

   - Set the Name property to gvProduct.

   - For the Location property, set X to 12 and Y to 12.

   - Set the ScrollBars property to Both.

281

- For the Size property, set Width to 263 and Height to 282.

6. Now your PopDataSet form in the Design view should look like Figure 15-3.

Figure 15-3. *The Design view of the PopDataSet form*

7. Double-click the empty surface of the PopDataSet.cs form, and it will open the code editor window, showing the PopDataSet_Load event. Modify the PopDataSet_Load event to look like Listing 15-1.

Listing 15-1. PopDataSet.cs

```
Using System.Data.SqlClient;

private void PopDataSet_Load(object sender, EventArgs e)
{
    // Connection string
    string connString = @" server=.\sql2012;database=AdventureWorks;
                Integrated Security=true";

    // Query
    string sql = @"select Name,ProductNumber
                from Production.Product
                where SafetyStockLevel > 600";

    // Create connection
    SqlConnection conn = new SqlConnection(connString);
```

```
        try
        {
            // Open connection
            conn.Open();

            // Create Data Adapter
            SqlDataAdapter da = new SqlDataAdapter(sql, conn);

            // Create Dataset
            DataSet ds = new DataSet();

            // Fill Dataset
            da.Fill(ds, "Production.Product");


            // Display data
            gvProduct.DataSource = ds.Tables["Production.Product"];
        }
        catch (Exception ex)
        {
            MessageBox.Show(ex.Message + ex.StackTrace);
        }
        finally
        {
            //Connection close
            conn.Close();
        }
    }
```

8. Build the project, and run the DataLooper form by pressing Ctrl+F5. Your results should look like 15-4.

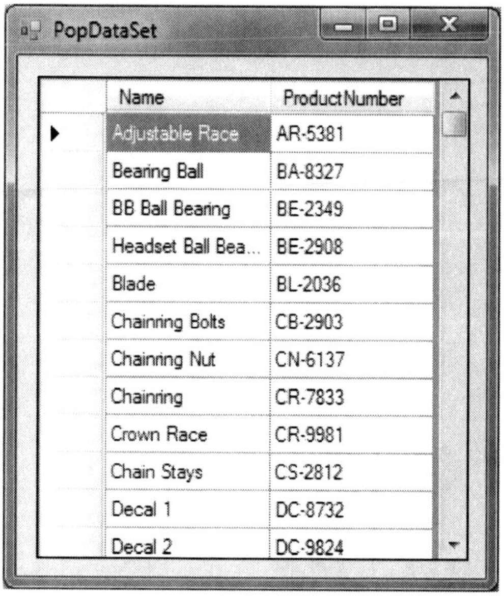

Figure 15-4. Populating a data set

How It Works

After defining a query and opening a connection, you create and initialize a data adapter.

```
// Create Data Adapter
SqlDataAdapter da = new SqlDataAdapter(sql, conn);
```

Then you create a data set.

```
// Create Dataset
DataSet ds = new DataSet();
```

At this stage, all you have is an empty data set. The key line is where you use the Fill method on the data adapter to execute the query, retrieve the data, and populate the data set.

```
// Fill Dataset
da.Fill(ds, "Production.Product");
```

The Fill method uses a data reader internally to access the table schema and data and then uses them to populate the data set.

Note that this method isn't just used for filling data sets. It has a number of overloads and can also be used for filling an individual data table without a data set, if needed.

If you don't provide a name for the table to the Fill method, it will automatically be named TableN, where N starts as an empty string (the first table name is simply Table) and increments every time a new table is inserted into the data set. It's better practice to explicitly name data tables, but here it doesn't really matter.

If the same query is run more than once on the data set that already contains data, Fill() updates the data, skipping the process of redefining the table based on the schema.

It's worth mentioning here that the following code would have produced the same result. Instead of passing the SQL and connection to the data adapter's constructor, you could have set its SelectCommand property with a command that you create with the appropriate SQL and connection.

```
// Create data adapter
SqlDataAdapter da = new SqlDataAdapter();
da.SelectCommand = new SqlCommand(sql, conn);
```

With a populated data set at your disposal, you can now access the data in individual data tables. (This data set contains only one data table.)

```
// get data table
DataTable dt = ds.Tables["Production.Product"];
```

Finally, you use nested foreach loops to access the columns in each row and output their data values to the screen.

```
// display data
gvProduct.DataSource = ds.Tables["Production.Product"];
```

Filtering and Sorting in a Data Set

In the previous example, you saw how to extract data from a data set. However, if you're working with data sets, chances are that you're going to want to do more with the data than merely display it. Often, you'll want to dynamically filter or sort the data. In the following example, you'll see how you can use data rows to do this.

Try It: Dynamically Filtering and Sorting Data in a Data Set

We'll get all the rows and columns from the Customers table, filter the result for only German customers, and sort it by company. We'll use a separate query to find products and fill two data tables in the same data set.

1. Select the DataSetandDataAdapter project, right-click, and choose Add ➤ Windows Form. From the opened dialog, make sure the Windows form is selected, and rename Form1.cs to FilterSort.cs. Click OK to add this form to the DataSetandDataAdapter project.

2. Select the FilterSort form by clicking the form's title bar, and set the Size property's Width to 350 and Height to 489.

3. Drag a Text Box control to the form, and position it toward the center of the form. Select this TextBox control, navigate to the Properties window, and set the following properties:

   - Set the Name property to txtSort.
   - For the Location property, set X to 12 and Y to 8.
   - Set the Multiline property to True.
   - Set the ScrollBars property to Vertical.
   - For the Size Property, set Width to 312 and Height to 435.

- Leave the Text property blank.

4. Now your FilterSort form in the Design view should look like Figure 15-5.

Figure 15-5. The Design view of the FilterSort form

5. Double-click the empty surface of the FilterSort.cs form, and it will open the code editor window, showing the FilterSort_Load event. Modify the FilterSort_Load event to look like Listing 15-2.

Listing 15-2. FilterSort.cs

```
Using System.Data.SqlClient;
private void FilterSort_Load(object sender, EventArgs e)
{
    // Connection string
    string connString = @"server=.\sql2012; database=AdventureWorks;
                Integrated Security=true";

    // Query
    string sql1 = @" select *
                from Production.Product
                where Name Like 'Mountain%'";

    string sql2 = @" select *
                from Production.Location
```

```
                    where CostRate > 10.0 ";

// Combine queries
string sql = sql1 + sql2;

// Create connection
SqlConnection conn = new SqlConnection(connString);

try
{
    // Create Data Adapter
    SqlDataAdapter da = new SqlDataAdapter();
    da.SelectCommand = new SqlCommand(sql, conn);

    // Create and Fill Data Set
    DataSet ds = new DataSet();
    da.Fill(ds, "Production.Product");

    // Get the data tables collection
    DataTableCollection dtc = ds.Tables;

    // Display data from first data table
    //
    // Display output header
    txtSort.AppendText("Results from Product table:\n");
    txtSort.AppendText("*****************************\n");
    txtSort.AppendText("Name\t\t\t\tProductNumber\n");

    txtSort.AppendText("_____\n");

    // set display filter
    string fl = "Color = 'Black'";

    // Set sort
    string srt = "ProductNumber asc";

    // display filtered and sorted data
    foreach (DataRow row in dtc["Production.Product"].Select(fl, srt))
    {
        txtSort.AppendText(row["Name"].ToString().PadRight(25));
        txtSort.AppendText("\t\t");
        txtSort.AppendText(row["ProductNumber"].ToString());
        txtSort.AppendText(Environment.NewLine);
    }

    txtSort.AppendText("============================================\n");
    // Display data from second data table

    // Display output header

    txtSort.AppendText("Results from Location table:\n");
    txtSort.AppendText("*********************************\n");
```

```
            txtSort.AppendText("Name\t\t\tCostRate\n");
            txtSort.AppendText("_____\n");

        // Display data
        foreach (DataRow row in dtc[1].Rows)
        {
            txtSort.AppendText(row["Name"].ToString().PadRight(25));
            txtSort.AppendText("\t");
            txtSort.AppendText(row["CostRate"].ToString() );
            txtSort.AppendText(Environment.NewLine);
        }
    }

    catch (Exception ex)
    {
        MessageBox.Show(ex.Message + ex.StackTrace);
    }

    finally
    {
        // Connection close
        conn.Close();
    }
}
```

6. To set the FilterSort form as the start-up form, modify the Program.cs statement.

```
Application.Run(new PopDataSet());
```

to appear as:

```
Application.Run(new FilterSort());
```

Build the project, and run it by pressing Ctrl+F5. Your results should look like Figure 15-6.

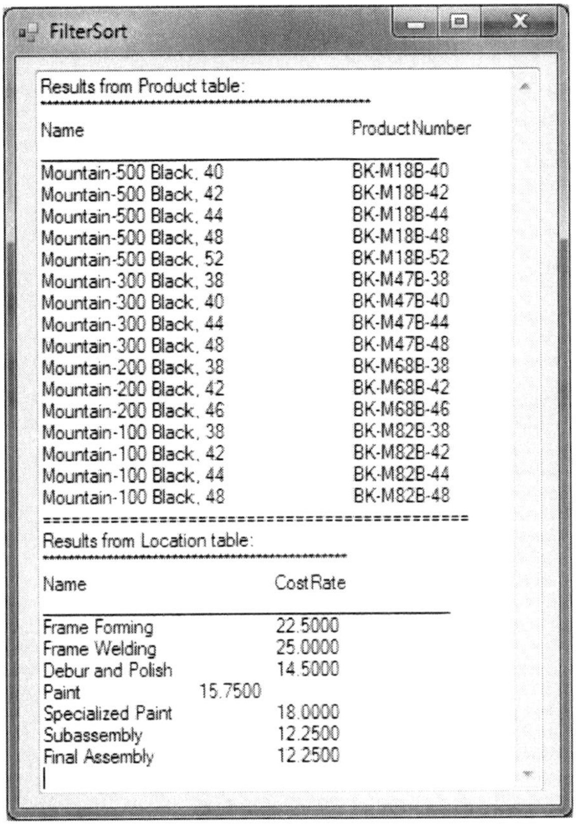

Figure 15-6. Filtering and sorting a data table

How It Works

You code and combine two queries for execution on the same connection.

```
            // Query1
            string sql1 = @" select *
                        from Production.Product
                        where Name Like 'Mountain%'";

            // Query2
            string sql2 = @" select *
                        from Production.Location
                        where CostRate > 10.0 ";

// Combine queries
string sql = sql1 + sql2;
```

```
// Create connection
SqlConnection conn = new SqlConnection(connString);
```

You create a data adapter, assigning to its SelectCommand property a command that encapsulates the query and connection (for internal use by the data adapter's Fill method).

```
// Create Data Adapter
SqlDataAdapter da = new SqlDataAdapter();
da.SelectCommand = new SqlCommand(sql, conn);
```

You then create and fill a data set.

```
// Create and Fill Data Set
DataSet ds = new DataSet();
da.Fill(ds, "Production.Product");
```

Each query returns a separate result set, and each result set is stored in a separate data table (in the order in which the queries were specified). The first table is explicitly named Product; the second is given the default name Location.

You get the data table collection from the data set's Tables property for ease of reference later.

```
// get the data tables collection
DataTableCollection dtc = ds.Tables;
```

As part of displaying the first data table, you declare two strings.

```
// Set display filter
string fl = "Color = 'Black'";
// Set sort
string srt = "ProductNumber asc";
```

The first string is a *filter expression* that specifies row selection criteria. It's syntactically the same as a SQL WHERE clause predicate. You want only those rows where the Color column equals Black. The second string specifies your sort criteria and is syntactically the same as a SQL ORDER BY clause, giving a data column name and sort sequence.

You use a foreach loop to display the rows selected from the data table, passing the filter and sort strings to the Select method of the data table. This particular data table is the one named Product in the data table collection.

```
            // display filtered and sorted data
            foreach (DataRow row in dtc["Production.Product"].Select(fl, srt))
            {
                txtSort.AppendText(row["Name"].ToString().PadRight(25));
                txtSort.AppendText("\t\t");
                txtSort.AppendText(row["ProductNumber"].ToString());
                txtSort.AppendText(Environment.NewLine);
            }
```

You obtain a reference to a single data table from the data table collection (the dtc object) using the table name that you specify when creating the data set. The overloaded Select method does an internal search on the data table, filters out rows not satisfying the selection criterion, sorts the result as prescribed, and finally returns an array of data rows. You access each column in the row, using the column name in the indexer.

It's important to note that you can achieve the same result—much more efficiently—if you simply use a different query for the customer data.

```
Select *
From Production.Productionwhere Color= 'Black'
order by ProductNumber asc
```

This would be ideal in terms of performance, but it'd be feasible only if the data you needed was limited to these specific rows in this particular sequence. However, if you were building a more elaborate system, it might be better to pull all the data once from the database (as you do here) and then filter and sort it in different ways. ADO.NET's rich suite of methods for manipulating data sets and their components gives you a broad range of techniques for meeting specific needs in an optimal way.

Tip In general, try to exploit SQL, rather than code C# procedures, to get the data you need from the database. Database servers are optimized to perform selections and sorts, as well as other things. Queries can be far more sophisticated and powerful than the ones you've been playing with in this book. By carefully (and creatively) coding queries to return *exactly* what you need, you not only minimize resource demands (on memory, network bandwidth, and so on) but also reduce the code you must write to manipulate and format result set data.

The loop through the second data table is interesting mainly for its first line, which uses an ordinal index:

```
foreach (DataRow row in dtc[1].Rows)
```

You don't rename the second data table (you could do so with its TableName property), it is better to use the index rather than the name Location), since a change to the name in the Fill() call would require you to change it here, an unlikely thing to remember to do, if the case ever arises.

Comparing FilterSort to PopDataSet

In the first example, PopDataSet (Listing 15-1), you saw how simple it is to get data into a data set. The second example, FilterSort (Listing 15-2), was just a variation, demonstrating how multiple result sets are handled and how to filter and sort data tables. However, the two programs have one major difference. Did you notice it?

FilterSort doesn't explicitly open a connection! In fact, it's the first (but won't be the last) program you've written that doesn't. Why doesn't it?

The answer is simple but *very* important. The Fill method *automatically* opens a connection if it's not open when Fill() is called. It then closes the connection after filling the data set. However, if a connection is open when Fill() is called, it uses that connection and *doesn't* close it afterward.

So, although data sets are completely independent of databases (and connections), just because you're using a data set doesn't mean you're running disconnected from a database. If you want to run disconnected, use data sets, but don't open connections before filling them (or, if a connection is open, close it first). In other words, data sets are inherently disconnected from the database. However, that does not mean the application using DataSet is disconnected.

You leave the standard conn.Close(); in the finally block. Since Close() can be called without error on a closed connection, it presents no problems if called unnecessarily, but it definitely guarantees that the connection will be closed, whatever may happen in the try block.

Note If you want to prove this for yourself, simply open the connection in `FilterSort` before calling `Fill()` and then display the value of the connection's `State` property. It will be `Open`. Comment out the `Open()` call, and run it again. `State` will be closed.

Using Data Views

In the previous example, you saw how to dynamically filter and sort data in a data table using the `Select` method. However, ADO.NET has another approach for doing much the same thing and more: *data views*. A data view (an instance of the class `System.Data.DataView`) enables you to create dynamic views of the data stored in an underlying data table, reflecting all the changes made to its content and its ordering. This differs from the `Select` method, which returns an array of data rows whose contents reflect the changes to data values but not the data ordering.

Note A data view is a dynamic representation of the contents of a data table. Like a SQL view, it doesn't actually hold data.

Try It: Refining Data with a Data View

We won't cover all aspects of data views here, because they're beyond the scope of this book. However, to show how they can be used, we'll present a short example that uses a data view to dynamically sort and filter an underlying data table.

1. Select the DataSetandDataAdapter project, right-click, and choose Add ➤ Windows Form. From the opened dialog, make sure the Windows form is selected and rename `Form1.cs` to `DataViews.cs`. Click OK to add this form to the DataSetandDataAdapter project.

2. Select the DataViews form by clicking the form's title bar, and set the Size property's Width to 304 and Height to 359.

3. Drag a GridView control to the form, and position it toward the center of the form. Select this GridView control, navigate to the Properties window, and set the following properties:

    - Set the Name property to gvContact.

    - For the Location property, set X to 12 and Y to 12.

    - Set the ScrollBars property to Vertical.

    - For the Size property, set Width to 262 and Height to 298.

4. Now your FilterSort form in the Design view should look like Figure 15-7.

Figure 15-7. *The Design view of the DataViews form*

5.   Double-click the empty surface of the DataViews.cs form, and it will open the code editor window, showing the DataViews_Load event. Modify the DataViews_Load event to look like Listing 15-3.

Listing 15-3. DataViews.cs

```
Using System.Data.SqlClient;
private void DataViews_Load(object sender, EventArgs e)
{
    // Connection string
    string connString = @"server=.\sql2012;database=AdventureWorks;Integrated
Security=true";

    // Query
    string sql = @"select FirstName, MiddleName
                from Person.Contact";

    // Create connection
    SqlConnection conn = new SqlConnection(connString);

    try
    {
        // Create Data Adapter
        SqlDataAdapter da = new SqlDataAdapter();
```

```
            da.SelectCommand = new SqlCommand(sql, conn);

            // Create and Fill Dataset
            DataSet ds = new DataSet();

            da.Fill(ds, "Person.Contact");

            // Get Data Table reference
            DataTable dt = ds.Tables["Person.Contact"];

            // Create Data View
            DataView dv = new DataView(dt,
                "MiddleName = 'J.'",
                "MiddleName",
                DataViewRowState.CurrentRows);

            // Display data from data view
            gvContact.DataSource = dv;
        }

        catch (Exception ex)
        {
            MessageBox.Show(ex.Message + ex.StackTrace);
        }

        finally
        {
            //Connection close
            conn.Close();
        }
    }
```

6. To set the FilterSort form as the start-up form, modify the `Program.cs` statement.

    ```
    Application.Run(new FilterSort());
    ```

    to appear as:

    ```
    Application.Run(new DataView());
    ```

    Build the project, and run it by pressing Ctrl+F5. You should see the results in Figure 15-8.

Figure 15-8. *Using a data view*

How It Works

This program is basically the same as the other examples, so we'll focus on its use of a data view. You create a new data view and initialize it by passing four parameters to its constructor.

```
// Create Data View
DataView dv = new DataView(dt,
                "MiddleName = 'J.'",
                "MiddleName",
                DataViewRowState.CurrentRows);
```

The first parameter is a data table, the second is a filter for the contents of the data table, the third is the sort column, and the fourth specifies the types of rows to include in the data view.

System.Data.DataViewRowState is an enumeration of states that rows can have in a data view's underlying data table. Table 15-1 summarizes the states.

Table 15-1. Data View Row States

DataViewRowState Members	Description
Added	A new row
CurrentRows	Current rows including unchanged, new, and modified ones
Deleted	A deleted row
ModifiedCurrent	The current version of a modified row
ModifiedOriginal	The original version of a modified row
None	None of the rows
OriginalRows	Original rows, including unchanged and deleted rows
Unchanged	A row that hasn't been modified

Every time a row is added, modified, or deleted, its row state changes to the appropriate one in Table 15-1. This is useful if you're interested in retrieving, sorting, or filtering specific rows based on their state (for example, all new rows in the data table or all rows that have been modified).

You then bind the data view to the grid view as a data source.

```
// display data from data view
gvContact.DataSource = dv;
```

Just as a data row represents a single row in a data table, a *data row view* (perhaps it would have been better to call it a *data view row*) represents a single row in a data view. You retrieve the filtered and the sorted column data for each data row view and output it to the console.

As this simple example suggests, data views offer a powerful and flexible means of dynamically changing what data works within a data table.

Modifying Data in a Dataset

In the following sections, you'll work through a practical example showing a number of ways to update data in data tables programmatically. Note that here you'll just modify the data in the data set but not update the data in the database. You'll see in the "Propagating Changes to a Data Source" section how to persist the original data source changes made to a data set.

■ **Note** Changes you make to a data set aren't automatically propagated to a database. To save the changes in a database, you need to connect to the database again and explicitly perform the necessary updates.

Try It: Modifying a Data Table in a Data Set

Let's update a row and add a row in a data table.

1. Select the DataSetandDataAdapter project, right-click, and choose Add ➤ Windows Form. From the opened dialog, make sure the Windows form is selected and rename `Form1.cs` to `ModifyDataTable.cs`. Click OK to add this form to the DataSetandDataAdapter project.

2. Select the ModifyDataTable form by clicking the form's title bar, and set the Size property's Width to 371 and Height to 348.

3. Drag a GridView control to the form, and position it toward the center of the form. Select this GridView control, navigate to the Properties window, and set the following properties:

    - Set the Name property to gvAddress.

    - For the Location property, set X to 12 and Y to 12.

    - Set the ScrollBars property to Vertical.

    - For the Size property, set Width to 331 and Height to 287.

4. Now your ModifyDataTable form in the Design view should look like Figure 15-9.

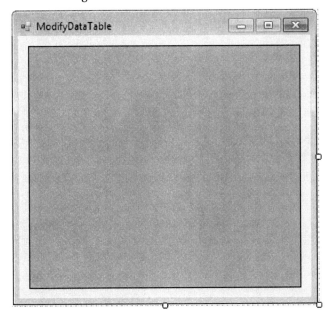

Figure 15-9. The Design view of the ModifyDataTable form

5. Double-click the empty surface of the ModifyDataTable.cs form, and it will
    open the code editor window, showing the ModifyDataTable _Load event.
    Modify the ModifyDataTable _Load event to look like Listing 15-4.

Listing 15-4. ModifyDataTable.cs

```
Using System.Data.SqlClient;
    private void ModifyDataTable_Load(object sender, EventArgs e)
    {
        // Connection string
        string connString = @"server=.\sql2012;database=AdventureWorks;Integrated
Security=true";

        // Query
        string sql = @"select  AddressLine2,City,StateProvinceID,PostalCode
                from Person.Address
                where City = 'Bothell'";

        // Create connection
        SqlConnection conn = new SqlConnection(connString);

        try
        {
            // Create Data Adapter
            SqlDataAdapter da = new SqlDataAdapter();
            da.SelectCommand = new SqlCommand(sql, conn);

            // Create and Fill Dataset
            DataSet ds = new DataSet();
            da.Fill(ds, "Person.Address");

            // Get data table reference
            DataTable dt = ds.Tables["Person.Address"];

            // FirstName column should be nullable
            dt.Columns["AddressLine2"].AllowDBNull = true;

            // Modify City in first row
            dt.Rows[0]["City"] = "Wilmington";

            // add a row
            DataRow newRow = dt.NewRow();

            newRow["PostalCode"] = "111111";
            newRow["StateProvinceID"] = "80";
            newRow["City"] = "Birmingham";
            dt.Rows.Add(newRow);

            // Display Rows
            gvAddress.DataSource = dt;
            gvAddress.Columns[0].Visible = false;
            gvAddress.Rows[0].DefaultCellStyle.BackColor  =  Color.Red;
```

```
        }
        catch (Exception ex)
        {
            MessageBox.Show(ex.Message + ex.StackTrace);
        }

        finally
        {
            // Connection close
            conn.Close();
        }
    }
}
```

6. To set the ModifyDataTable form as the start-up form, modify the `Program.cs` statement.

```
Application.Run(new DataView());
```

to appear as:

```
Application.Run(new ModifyDataTable());
```

Build the project, and run it by pressing Ctrl+F5. Your results should look like Figure 15-10.

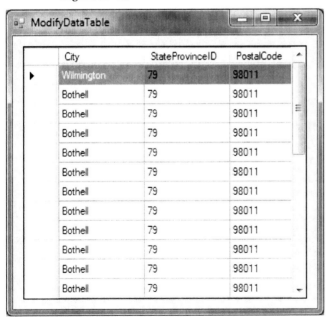

Figure 15-10. Modifying a data table

How It Works

As before, you use a single data table in a data set.

```
// Get data table reference
DataTable dt = ds.Tables["Person.Address"];
```

Next, you can see an example of how you can change the schema information. You select the FirstName column, whose AllowNull property is set to false in the database, and you change it—just for the purposes of demonstration—to true.

```
// AddressLine2 column should be nullable
dt.Columns["AddressLine2"].AllowDBNull = true;
```

Note that you can use an ordinal index (for example, dt.Columns[1]) if you know what the index for the column is, but using * to select all columns makes this less reliable since the position of a column may change if the database table schema changes.

You can modify a row using the same technique. You simply select the appropriate row and set its columns to whatever values you want, consistent with the column data types, of course. The following line shows the City column of the first row of the data set being changed to Wilmington:

```
// Modify City in first row
dt.Rows[o]["city"] = "Wilmington";
```

Next you add a new row to the data table.

```
// Add a row
DataRow newRow = dt.NewRow();

newRow["PostalCode"] = "111111";
newRow["StateProvinceID"] = "80";
newRow["City"] = "Birmingham";
dt.Rows.Add(newRow);
```

The NewRow method creates a data row (a System.Data.DataRow instance). You use the data row's indexer to assign values to its columns. Finally, you add the new row to the data table, calling the Add method on the data table's Rows property, which references the rows collection.

Updating data sources requires learning more about data adapter methods and properties. Let's take a look at these now.

Propagating Changes to a Data Source

You've seen how a data adapter populates a data set's data tables. What you haven't looked at yet is how a data adapter updates and synchronizes a data source with data from a data set. It has three properties that support this (analogous to its SelectCommand property, which supports queries).

- InsertCommand

- UpdateCommandDeleteCommand

We'll describe InsertCommand briefly and then put that to work.

InsertCommand Property

The data adapter uses the `InsertCommand` property for inserting rows into a table. Upon calling the `Update` method, all rows added to the data table will be searched for and propagated to the database.

Try It: Propagating New Data Set Rows to a Data Source

Let's propagate a new row to the database, in another variation on `ModifyDataTable.cs` in Listing 15-5.

1. Select the DataSetandDataAdapter project, right-click, and choose Add Windows Form. From the opened dialog, make sure the Windows form is selected, and rename `Form1.cs` to `PersistAdds.cs`. Click OK to add this form to the DataSetandDataAdapter project.

2. Select the PersistAdds form by clicking the form's title bar, and set the Size property's Width to 452 and Height to 163.

3. Drag a TextBox control to the form, and position it toward the center of the form. Select this TextBox control, navigate to the Properties window, and set the following properties:

    -   Set the Name property to txtDepartment.

    -   For the Location property, set X to 12 and Y to 12.

    -   For the Size property, set Width to 412 and Height to 95.

    -   Leave the Text property blank.

4. Now your PersistAdds form in the Design view should look like Figure 15-11.

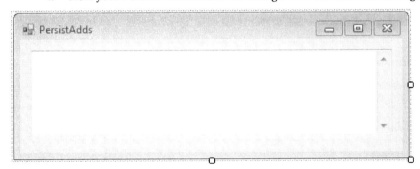

Figure 15-11. The Design view of the PersistAdds form

5. Double-click the empty surface of the `PersistAdds.cs` form, and it will open the code editor window, showing the `PersistAdds _Load` event. Modify the `PersistAdds _Load` event to look like Listing 15-5.

Listing 15-5. PersistAdds.cs

```
Using System.Data.SqlClient;
    private void PersistAdds_Load(object sender, EventArgs e)
    {
        // Connection string
        string connString = @" server=.\sql2012;database=AdventureWorks;Integrated
Security=true";

        // Query
        string qry = @" select *
                    from HumanResources.Department
                    where GroupName = 'Sales'";

        // SQL to insert employees
        string ins = @"insert into HumanResources.Department
                    (Name,GroupName, ModifiedDate)
                        values(@Name, @GroupName, @ModifiedDate)";

        // Create connection
        SqlConnection conn = new SqlConnection(connString);

        try
        {
            // Create data adapter
            SqlDataAdapter da = new SqlDataAdapter();
            da.SelectCommand = new SqlCommand(qry, conn);

            // Create and fill data set
            DataSet ds = new DataSet();
            da.Fill(ds, "HumanResources.Department");

            // Get data table reference
            DataTable dt = ds.Tables["HumanResources.Department"];

            // Add a row
            DataRow newRow = dt.NewRow();
            newRow["Name"] = "Microsoft Development";
            newRow["GroupName"] = "Global Development";
            newRow["ModifiedDate"] = "2012-04-28";
            dt.Rows.Add(newRow);

            // Display rows
            foreach (DataRow row in dt.Rows)
            {

                txtDepartment.AppendText(row["Name"].ToString());
                txtDepartment.AppendText("\t");
                txtDepartment.AppendText(row["GroupName"].ToString());
                txtDepartment.AppendText("\t");
                txtDepartment.AppendText(row["ModifiedDate"].ToString());
```

```
            txtDepartment.AppendText("\n");
        }

        // Create command
        SqlCommand cmd = new SqlCommand(ins, conn);
        //
        // Map parameters
        cmd.Parameters.Add("@Name", SqlDbType.NVarChar, 50,"Name");
        cmd.Parameters.Add("@GroupName",SqlDbType.NVarChar,50,"GroupName");
        cmd.Parameters.Add("@ModifiedDate",SqlDbType.DateTime,25,"ModifiedDate");

        // Insert department
        da.InsertCommand = cmd;
        da.Update(ds, "HumanResources.Department");
    }
    catch (Exception ex)
    {
        MessageBox.Show(ex.Message + ex.StackTrace);
    }

    finally
    {
        //Connection close
        conn.Close();
    }
}
```

6. To set the PersistAdds form as the start-up form, modify the Program.cs statement.

```
Application.Run(new ModifyDataTable());
```

to appear as:

```
Application.Run(new PersistAdds());
```

Build the project, and run it by pressing Ctrl+F5. You should see the results in Figure 15-12.

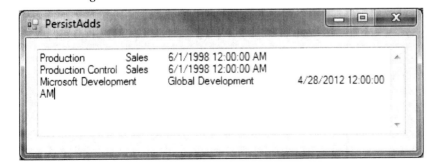

Figure 15-12. Adding a row

How It Works

You add an INSERT statement.

```
string ins = @"insert into HumanResources.Department
            (Name,GroupName, ModifiedDate)
            values(@Name, @GroupName, @ModifiedDate)";
```

Create a command for the INSERT query.

```
// create command
SqlCommand cmd = new SqlCommand(ins, conn);
```

Then you configure the command parameters. The three columns for which you'll provide values are each mapped to a named command parameter. You don't supply the primary key value since it's generated by SQL Server.

```
// Map parameters
 cmd.Parameters.Add("@Name", SqlDbType.NVarChar, 50,"Name");
 cmd.Parameters.Add("@GroupName",SqlDbType.NVarChar,50,"GroupName");
 cmd.Parameters.Add("@ModifiedDate",SqlDbType.DateTime,25,"ModifiedDate");
```

Finally, you set the data adapter's InsertCommand property with the command to insert into the Department table so it will be the SQL the data adapter executes when you call its Update method. You then call Update on the data adapter to propagate the change to the database. Here you add only one row, but since the SQL is parameterized, the data adapter will look for all new rows in the HumanResources.Department data table and submit inserts for all of them to the database.

```
// Insert department
da.InsertCommand = cmd;
da.Update(ds, "HumanResources.Department");
```

Figure 15-12 shows the new row, and if you check with Database Explorer or the SSMS with SQL Server 2012, you'll see the row has been propagated to the database. Microsoft Development is now in the Department table.

Command Builders

Although it's straightforward, it's a bit of a hassle to code SQL statements for the UpdateCommand, InsertCommand, and DeleteCommand properties, so each data provider has its own *command builder*. If a data table corresponds to a single database table, you can use a command builder to automatically generate the appropriate UpdateCommand, InsertCommand, and DeleteCommand properties for a data adapter. This is all done transparently when a call is made to the data adapter's Update method.

To be able to dynamically generate INSERT, DELETE, and UPDATE statements, the command builder uses the data adapter's SelectCommand property to extract metadata for the database table. If any changes are made to the SelectCommand property after invoking the Update method, you should call the RefreshSchema method on the command builder to refresh the metadata accordingly.

To create a command builder, you create an instance of the data provider's command builder class, passing a data adapter to its constructor. For example, the following code creates a SQL Server command builder:

```
SqlDataAdapter da = new SqlDataAdapter();
SqlCommandBuilder cb = new SqlCommandBuilder(da);
```

■ **Note** For a command builder to work, the SelectCommand data adapter property must contain a query that returns either a primary key or a unique key for the database table. If none is present, an InvalidOperation exception is generated, and the commands aren't generated.

Try It: Using SqlCommandBuilder

Here, you'll use SqlCommand Builder to insert a row into the database.

1. Select the DataSetandDataAdapter project, right-click, and choose Add ➤ Windows Form. From the opened dialog, make sure the Windows form is selected, and rename Form1.cs to PersistAddsBuilder.cs. Click OK to add this form to the DataSetandDataAdapter project.

2. Select the PersistAddsBuilder form by clicking the form's title bar, and set the Size property's Width to 483 and Height to 151.

3. Drag a TextBox control to the form, and position it toward the center of the form. Select this TextBox control, navigate to the Properties window, and set the following properties:

   • Set the Name property to txtDepartment.

   • For the Location property, set X to 12 and Y to 12.

   • For the Size property, set Width to 441 and Height to 89.

   • Leave the Text property blank.

4. Now your PersistAddsBuilder form in the Design view should look like Figure 15-13.

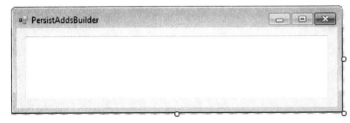

Figure 15-13. *The Design view of the PersistAddsBuilder form*

5. Double-click the empty surface of the PersistAddsBuilder.cs form, and it will open the code editor window, showing the PersistAddsBuilder _Load event. Modify the PersistAddsBuilder _Load event to look like Listing 15-6.

Listing 15-6. PersistAddsBuilder.cs

```csharp
Using System.Data.SqlClient;
    private void PersistAddsBuilder_Load(object sender, EventArgs e)
    {
        // Connection string
        string connString = @"server=.\sql2012;database=AdventureWorks;Integrated
Security=true";

        // Query
        string qry = @" select *
                    from HumanResources.Department
                    where GroupName = 'Research and Development' ";

        // Create connection
        SqlConnection conn = new SqlConnection(connString);

        try
        {
            // Create Data Adapter
            SqlDataAdapter da = new SqlDataAdapter();
            da.SelectCommand = new SqlCommand(qry, conn);

            // Create command builder
            SqlCommandBuilder cb = new SqlCommandBuilder(da);

            // Create and Fill Dataset
            DataSet ds = new DataSet();
            da.Fill(ds, "HumanResources.Department");

            // Get Data Table reference
            DataTable dt = ds.Tables["HumanResources.Department"];

            // Add a row
            DataRow newRow = dt.NewRow();
            newRow["Name"] = "Language Design";
            newRow["GroupName"] = "Research and Development";
            newRow["ModifiedDate"] = "2012-04-29";

            dt.Rows.Add(newRow);

            // Display rows
            foreach (DataRow row in dt.Rows)
            {
                txtDepartment.AppendText(row["Name"].ToString());
                txtDepartment.AppendText("\t\t");
                txtDepartment.AppendText(row["GroupName"].ToString());
                txtDepartment.AppendText("\t");
                txtDepartment.AppendText(row["ModifiedDate"].ToString());
                txtDepartment.AppendText("\n");
            }
```

```
        // Insert department
        da.Update(ds, "HumanResources.Department");
    }

    catch (Exception ex)
    {
        MessageBox.Show(ex.Message + ex.StackTrace);
    }

    finally
    {
        //Connection close
        conn.Close();
    }
}
```

6. To set the PersistAddsBuilder form as the start-up form, modify the `Program.cs` statement.

```
Application.Run(new PersistAdds());
```

to appear as:

```
Application.Run(new PersistAddsBuilder());
```

Build the project, and run it by pressing Ctrl+F5. You should see the results in Figure 15-14.

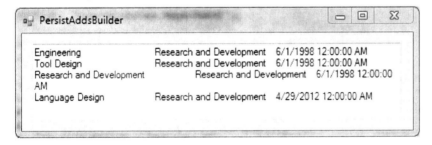

Figure 15-14. Adding a row using a command builder

How It Works

The most interesting thing to note isn't the line (yes, just one plus a comment) you add as much as what you replace.

```
// create command builder
SqlCommandBuilder cb = new SqlCommandBuilder(da);

// Add a row
DataRow newRow = dt.NewRow();
newRow["Name"] = "Language Design";
newRow["GroupName"] = "Research and Development";
```

```
newRow["ModifiedDate"] = "2012-04-29";

dt.Rows.Add(newRow);
```

Obviously, using command builders is preferable to manually coding SQL; however, remember that they work only on single tables and that the underlying database table must have a primary or unique key. Also, the data adapter `SelectCommand` property must have a query that includes the key columns.

■ **Note** Though all five of the data providers in the .NET Framework Class Library have command builder classes, no class or interface exists in the `System.Data` namespace that defines them. So, if you want to learn more about command builders, the best place to start is the description for the builder in which you're interested. The `System.Data.DataSet` class and the `System.Data.IDataAdapter` interface define the underlying components that command builders interact with, and their documentation provides the informal specification for the constraints on command builders.

Concurrency

You've seen that updating a database with data sets and data adapters is relatively straightforward. However, we've oversimplified things; you've been assuming that no other changes have been made to the database while you've been working with disconnected data sets.

Imagine two separate users trying to make conflicting changes to the same row in a data set and then trying to propagate these changes to the database. What happens? How does the database resolve the conflicts? Which row gets updated first, second, or at all? The answer is unclear. As with so many real-world database issues, it all depends on a variety of factors. However, ADO.NET provides a fundamental level of concurrency control that's designed to prevent update anomalies. The details are beyond the scope of this book, but the following is a good conceptual start.

Basically, a data set marks all added, modified, and deleted rows. If a row is propagated to the database but has been modified by someone else since the data set was filled, the data manipulation operation for the row is ignored. This technique is known as *optimistic concurrency* and is essentially the job of the data adapter. When the `Update` method is called, the data adapter attempts to reconcile all changes. This works well in an environment where users seldom contend for the same data.

This type of concurrency is different from what's known as *pessimistic concurrency,* which *locks* rows upon modification (or sometimes even on retrieval) to avoid conflicts. Most database managers use some form of locking to guarantee data integrity.

Disconnected processing with optimistic concurrency is essential to successful multitier systems. How to employ it most effectively given the pessimistic concurrency of DBMSs is a thorny problem. Don't worry about it now, but keep in mind that many issues exist, and the more complex your application, the more likely you'll have to become an expert in concurrency.

Using Data Sets and XML

XML is the fundamental medium for data transfer in .NET. In fact, XML is a major foundation for ADO.NET. Datasets organize data internally in XML format and have a variety of methods for reading and writing in XML. For example:

- You can import and export the structure of a data set as an XML schema using `System.Data.DataSet`'s `ReadXmlSchema` and `WriteXmlSchema` methods.

- You can read the data (and, optionally, the schema) of a data set from `ReadXml()` and write it to an xml file with `WriteXml()`. This can be useful when exchanging data with another application or making a local copy of a data set.

- You can bind a data set to an XML document (an instance of `System.Xml.XmlDataDocument`). The data set and data document are *synchronized*, so either ADO.NET or XML operations can be used to modify it.

Let's look at one of these in action: copying a data set to an XML file.

■ **Note** If you're unfamiliar with XML, don't worry. ADO.NET doesn't require any detailed knowledge of it. Of course, the more you know, the better you can understand what's happening transparently.

Try It: Extracting a Data Set to an XML File

You can preserve the contents and schema of a data set in one XML file using the data set's `WriteXml` method or in separate files using `WriteXml()` and `WriteXmlSchema()`. `WriteXml()` is overloaded, and in this example we'll show a version that extracts both data and schema.

1. Select the DataSetandDataAdapter project, right-click, and choose Add ➤ Windows Form. From the opened dialog, make sure the Windows form is selected, and rename Form1.cs to WriteXML.cs. Click OK to add this form to the DataSetandDataAdapter project.

2. Select the WriteXML form by clicking the form's title bar, and set the Size property's Width to 289 and Height to 124.

3. Drag a Button control to the form, and position it toward the center of the form. Select this Button control, navigate to the Properties window, and set the following properties:

    - Set the Name property to btnXML.

    - For the Location property, set X to 74 and Y to 30.

    - For the Size property, set Width to 128 and Height to 23.

    - Set the Text property to Generate XML.

4. Now your WriteXML form in the Design view should look like Figure 15-15.

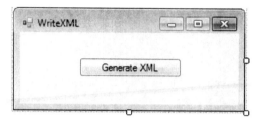

Figure 15-15. The Design view of the WriteXML form

5. Double-click the empty surface of the WriteXML.cs form, and it will open the code editor window, showing the WriteXML _Load event. Modify the WriteXML _Load event to look like Listing 15-7.

Listing 15-7. WriteXML.cs

```
Using System.Data.SqlClient;
    private void btnXML_Click(object sender, EventArgs e)
    {
        // Connection string
        string connString = @" server=.\sql2012; database=AdventureWorks;
                        Integrated Security=true";

        // Query
        string qry = @"select Name ,ProductNumber
                    from Production.Product";

        // Create connection
        SqlConnection conn = new SqlConnection(connString);

        try
        {
            // Create Data Adapter
            SqlDataAdapter da = new SqlDataAdapter();
            da.SelectCommand = new SqlCommand(qry, conn);

            // Open connection
            conn.Open();

            // Create and Fill Dataset
            DataSet ds = new DataSet();
            da.Fill(ds, "Production.Product");

            // Extract data set to XML file
            ds.WriteXml(@"c:\productstable.xml");
            MessageBox.Show("The XML file is Created");
        }

        catch (Exception ex)
        {
```

```
        MessageBox.Show(ex.Message + ex.StackTrace);
    }

    finally
    {
        // Connection close
        conn.Close();
    }
}
```

6. To set the WriteXML form as the start-up form, modify the `Program.cs` statement.

```
Application.Run(new PersistAddsBuilder());
```

to appear as

```
Application.Run(new WriteXML());
```

Build the project, and run it by pressing Ctrl+F5. Your results should look like Figure 15-16.

Figure 15-16. Extracting a data table as XML

7. Not much seems to have happened, but that's because you wrote to a file rather than to the screen. Open `productstable.xml` (the path we saved this table to was c:\; if you have changed the path, please refer to that) to see the

XML. (One way in Visual Studio is to use File Open File.) Figure 15-17 shows
the XML extracted for the first five product rows.

```
productstable.xml ⊕ ✕
    <?xml version="1.0" standalone="yes"?>
    <NewDataSet>
        <Production.Product>
            <Name>Adjustable Race</Name>
            <ProductNumber>AR-5381</ProductNumber>
        </Production.Product>
        <Production.Product>
            <Name>Bearing Ball</Name>
            <ProductNumber>BA-8327</ProductNumber>
        </Production.Product>
        <Production.Product>
            <Name>BB Ball Bearing</Name>
            <ProductNumber>BE-2349</ProductNumber>
        </Production.Product>
        <Production.Product>
            <Name>Headset Ball Bearings</Name>
            <ProductNumber>BE-2908</ProductNumber>
        </Production.Product>
        <Production.Product>
            <Name>Blade</Name>
            <ProductNumber>BL-2036</ProductNumber>
        </Production.Product>
```

Figure 15-17. Data table extracted as XML

■ **Tip** By default, extracted XML documents are plain-text files. You can open the productstable.xml file in any
editor or even use the type or more commands to view it from the command line.

How It Works

First we need to create a Select query to pull data from database.

```
// Query
 string qry = @"select Name ,ProductNumber
            from Production.Product";
```

Next we need to Create Data Set and Data Adapter

```
// Create Data Adapter
SqlDataAdapter da = new SqlDataAdapter();
da.SelectCommand = new SqlCommand(qry, conn);
```

After creation of data set and data adapter, Store data set into the xml file.

```
// Create and Fill Dataset
 DataSet ds = new DataSet();
 da.Fill(ds, "Production.Product");

// Extract dataset to XML file
ds.WriteXml(@"c:\productstable.xml");
```

Note that the XML has simply mapped the data set as a hierarchy. The first XML element, `<NewDataSet>`, is the data set name (defaulting to `NewDataSet` since you don't specify one). The next element, `<Production.Product>`, uses the data table name (you have only one data table since you use only one query to populate the data set), and it's nested inside the data set element. The data column elements, `<Name>` and `<ProductNumber>`, are nested inside this element.

The data for each column appears (as plain text) between the *start tag* (for example, `<Name>`) and the *end tag* (for example, `</Name>`) for each column element. Note that the `<Production.Product>` elements represent individual rows, not the whole table. So, the column elements are contained within the start tag `<Production.Product>` and end tag `</Production.Product>` for each row.

If you scroll to the bottom of the XML file, you'll find the end tag `</NewDataSet>` for the data set.

Understanding Typed and Untyped Data Sets

Data sets can be *typed* or *untyped*. The data sets you've used so far have all been untyped. They were instances of `System.Data.DataSet`. An untyped data set has no built-in schema. The schema is only implicit. It grows as you add tables and columns to the data set, but these objects are exposed as collections rather than as XML schema elements. However, as we mentioned in passing in the previous section, you can explicitly export a schema for an untyped data set with `WriteXmlSchema` (or `WriteXml`).

A typed data set is one that's derived from `System.Data.DataSet` and uses an XML schema (typically in an `.xsd` file) in declaring the data set class. Information from the schema (tables, columns, and so on) is extracted, generated as C# code, and compiled, so the new data set class is an actual .NET type with appropriate objects and properties.

Either typed or untyped data sets are equally valid, but typed data sets are more efficient and can make code somewhat simpler. For example, using an untyped data set, you'd need to write this:

```
ds.Tables[o].Rows[o]["CompanyName"];
```

to get the value for the CompanyName column of the Customers table, assuming that the data table was the first in the data set. With a typed data set, you can access its data tables and data columns as class members. You could replace the previous code with this:

```
 ds.Customers[o].CompanyName;
```

making the code more intuitive. In addition, the Visual Studio code editor has IntelliSense support for typed data sets.

Typed data sets are more efficient than untyped data sets because typed data sets have a defined schema, and when they're populated with data, runtime type identification and conversion aren't necessary, since this has been taken care of at compile time. Untyped data sets have a lot more work to do every time a result set is loaded.

However, typed data sets aren't always the best choice. If you're dealing with data that isn't well defined, whose definition dynamically changes, or is only of temporary interest, the flexibility of untyped data sets can outweigh the benefits of typed ones.

This chapter is already long enough. Since we're not concerned with efficiency in our small sample programs, we won't use typed data sets, and we don't need to cover creating them here.

Our emphasis in this book is explaining how C# works with ADO.NET by showing you how to code fundamental operations. If you can code them yourself, you'll have insight into what C# does when it generates things for you, as in the next chapter on using Windows Forms. This is invaluable for understanding how to configure generated components and debugging applications that use them.

Although you can code an `.xsd` file yourself (or export an XSL schema for an untyped data set with `System.Data.DataSet.WriteXmlSchema()` and modify it) and then use the `xsd.exe` utility to create a class for a typed data set, it's a lot of work, is subject to error, and is something you'll rarely (if ever) want or need to do.

Summary

In this chapter, we covered the basics of data sets and data adapters. A data set is a relational representation of data that has a collection of data tables, and each data table has collections of data rows and data columns. A data adapter is an object that controls how data is loaded into a data set (or data table) and how changes to the data set data are propagated back to the data source.

We presented basic techniques for filling and accessing data sets, demonstrated how to filter and sort data tables, and noted that though data sets are database-independent objects, disconnected operation isn't the default mode.

We discussed how to propagate data modifications back to databases with parameterized SQL and the data adapter's `UpdateCommand`, `InsertCommand`, and `DeleteCommand` properties, and how command builders simplify this for single-table updates.

We briefly mentioned the important issue of concurrency and then introduced XML, the fundamental technology behind ADO.NET.

Finally, we discussed typed and untyped data sets.

Now that you've seen, understood, and practiced ADO.NET with Windows applications, in the next chapter we'll explore using data control with ASP.NET applications.

Using Data Controls with ASP.NET Applications

This chapter focuses on the concepts behind web application development and the key components of a web environment, and it shows you how to work with an ASP.NET web site project while developing a web application. (Covering the ASP.NET framework in detail is out of the scope of this book.)

Normally, a fully functional web project requires Internet Information Services (IIS) to be installed and configured on the machine. But in this chapter, to keep things simple and to help you understand the fundamentals of an ASP.NET web site project that uses a data control, IIS is not required. However, if you have it, you do not need to uninstall it.

In this chapter, I'll cover the following:

- Understanding web functionality

- Understanding ASP.NET and web pages

- Understanding the Visual Studio 2012 web site types

- Understanding the layout of an ASP.NET web site

- Understanding the web UI of ASP.NET web apps

- Using the Repeater control

Understanding Web Functionality

When you work within the .NET Framework, you use ASP.NET Web Forms to build web applications. The Web Forms technology works in the ASP.NET environment and accepts code functionality from any .NET-compliant language, such as C#.

Before you dive into Web Forms and learn how to develop a web application, you need to understand what components drive this technology and how these components serve various applications running over the Web.

Basically, there are three key players that make all web applications functional: the web server, the web browser, and Hypertext Transfer Protocol (HTTP). Let's take a look at their communication process:

1. The web browser initiates a request to the web server for a resource.

2. HTTP sends a GET request to the web server, and the web server processes that request. The web server initiates a response; HTTP sends the response to the web browser.

3. The web browser processes the response and displays the result on the web page.

4. The user inputs data or performs some action that forces data to be sent again to the web server.

5. HTTP will POST the data back to the web server, and the web server processes that data.

6. HTTP sends the response to the web browser.

7. The web browser processes the response and displays the result on the web page.

Now that you have a general understanding of the communication process, let's take a closer look at each of the key components.

The Web Server

The web server is responsible for receiving and handling all requests coming from browsers through HTTP. After receiving a request, the web server will process that request and return the response to the browser. Right after this, usually the web server will close its connection with the database and release all resources, opened files, network connections, and so forth, which become part of the request to be processed on the web server.

The web server does all this cleaning of data, resources, and so on, in order to be stateless. The term *state* refers to the data that gets stored between the request sent to the server and the response delivered to the browser.

Most of today's web sites run as applications and consist of many web pages, and data on one web page is often responsible for the output that will be displayed on the next web page. In this situation, being stateless defeats the whole purpose of such web sites; therefore, maintaining state becomes important.

To be stateful, the web server will keep connections and resources alive for a period of time by anticipating that there will be an additional request from the web browser. ASP.NET offers various techniques as counter approaches for stateless behavior, such as cookie, view state, query strings, session and application state, and so on.

The Web Browser and HTTP

The web browser is the client-side application that displays web pages. The web browser works with HTTP to send a request to the web server, and then the web server responds to the web browser or web client's request with the data the user wants to see or work with.

HTTP is a communication protocol that is used to request web pages from the web server and then to send the response to the web browser.

Understanding ASP.NET and Web Pages

ASP.NET is available to all .NET developers, because it comes with the Microsoft .NET Framework. ASP.NET provides a web development model to build web applications by using any .NET-compliant language, such as C#. ASP.NET code is compiled rather than interpreted, and it supports the basic features of the .NET Framework such as strong typing, performance optimizations, and so on. After the code has been compiled, the .NET CLR will further compile the ASP.NET code to native code, which provides improved performance.

Web pages serve the purpose of a user interface for your web application. ASP.NET adds programmability to the web page. ASP.NET implements application logic using code, which will be sent for execution on the server side. ASP.NET web pages have the following traits:

- They are based on Microsoft ASP.NET technology, in which code that runs on the server dynamically generates web page output to the browser or client device.

- They are compatible with any language supported by the .NET common language runtime, including Microsoft Visual Basic and Microsoft Visual C#.

- They are built on the Microsoft .NET Framework. This provides all the benefits of the framework, including a managed environment, type safety, and inheritance.

The web page consists of application code that serves requests by users; to do so, ASP.NET compiles the code into the assemblies. *Assemblies* are files that contain metadata about the application and have the file extension `.dll`. After the code is compiled, it is translated into a language-independent and CPU-independent format called *Microsoft Intermediate Language* (MSIL), also known as *Intermediate Language* (IL). While running the web site, MSIL runs in the context of the .NET Framework and gets translated into CPU-specific instructions for the processor on the PC running the web application.

Understanding the Visual Studio 2012 Web Site Types

Visual Studio 2012 offers various ways of creating a web project or web site. Though web sites are meant only for the Internet or intranets, Visual Studio 2012 has three types, based on location that can serve as a foundation for any web site that web developers are working on. The purpose of having these options is that they really simplify the system requirements on the developer's machine.

If you have ever worked with classic ASP applications (not ASP.NET), recall the days of Visual Studio 6.0, when developers were required to use Internet Information Services (IIS) to work with and test an ASP web application. This issue has been resolved with the evolution of Visual Studio; now you can develop a web site without having IIS installed on your machine.

■ **Note** IIS is a flexible, secure, and easy-to-manage web server for Windows to host anything on the Web. IIS provides a complete web administration facility to the web applications hosted inside it.

A new web site project can be built in the Visual Studio 2012 IDE by accessing File ➤ New ➤ Web Site.

Let's take a look at the types of web sites offered by Visual Studio 2012.

■ **Note** In the following section, I have selected ASP.NET Empty Web Site in the available project template list. The following sections (about file system, HTTP, and FTP web sites) apply to all the web site templates available in the list, as shown in Figure 16-1.

File System Web Site

A file system–based web site is stored on the computer like any other folder structure. The main feature of this type of web site is that it uses a very lightweight ASP.NET development server that is part of Visual Studio 2012, so it does not require IIS to be available on the developer's local machine.

To view or test a file system web site, ASP.NET Development Server plays the role of the web server. The ASP.NET Development Server is a server that runs locally on your Windows computer and serves ASP.NET web pages, which makes it suitable for testing your file system–based web application.

Figure 16-1 shows the New Web Site dialog box with the web site location set to File System; notice also the path of the folder where this web site will be stored: the local path on your disk.

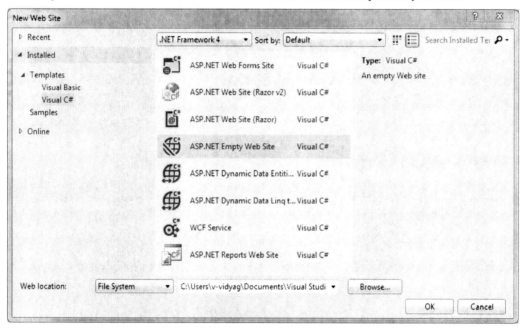

Figure 16-1. Specifying a file system web site

FTP Web Site

A web site based on the File Transfer Protocol (FTP) helps you manage and transfer files between a local machine and a remote web site. The FTP web site offers a Windows Explorer–like interface and exposes the folder structure where files, documents, and so on, are kept for sharing purposes.

You can access the FTP site to share, transfer, or download files from a remote FTP site to your local computer, or you can upload files to the remote FTP site.

To view or test the FTP web site, the server computer must have a location to browse, that is, an HTTP URL that points to the same files as the FTP site.

Figure 16-2 shows the New Web Site dialog box with the web site location set to FTP.

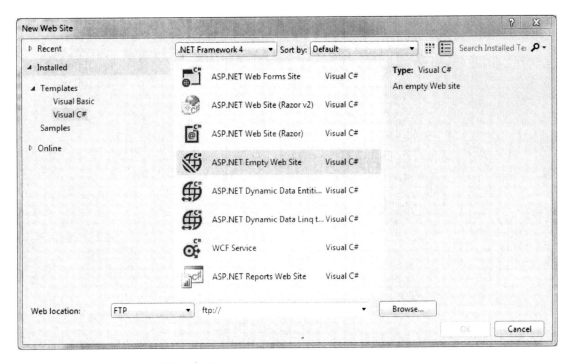

Figure 16-2. Specifying an FTP web site

Note Building FTP sites requires a user's credentials to be passed. Usually there is no anonymous FTP site; you should specify the FTP address using the `ftp://user:pwd@ftpaddress:port` syntax.

HTTP Web Site

A web site based on the Hypertext Transfer Protocol (HTTP) is preferable for building commercial and enterprise web-based products. The HTTP web site requires IIS on the local machine of the developer, because it is configured as an application in the virtual directory of IIS.

Note IIS Express is a light version of IIS that is included with Visual Studio 2012. The IIS Express server brings a lot of administrative power to web applications sitting inside IIS Express.

Figure 16-3 shows the New Web Site dialog box with the web site location set to HTTP.

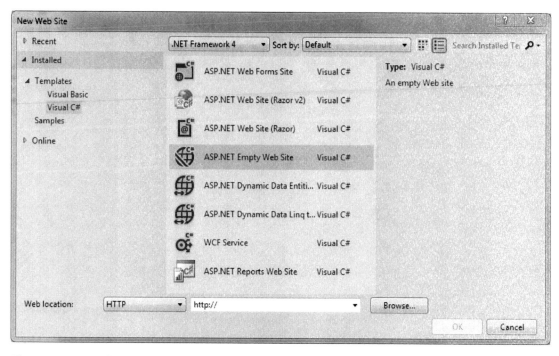

Figure 16-3. Specifying an HTTP web site

Understanding the Layout of an ASP.NET Web Site

When you pick Visual Studio–provided templates other than ASP.NET Empty Web Site, Visual Studio 2012 offers many forms and components needed for most of the large web applications. To keep things simple and help you stay focused, let's work with an empty web site, add a web form to it, and explore its layout.

Open the Visual Studio 2012 IDE, and select File ➤ New ➤ Web Site. In the New Web Site dialog box, select ASP.NET Empty Web Site as the project template, and then choose File System as the location and Visual C# as the language, as shown in Figure 16-1. In the text box adjacent to the "Web location" drop-down box, modify the path to the directory path, which indicates you are going to create a web site on the file system with the name Chapter16. Click OK. After you create the project, it will open, as shown in Figure 16-4.

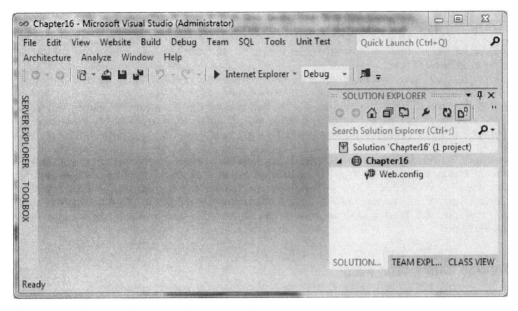

Figure 16-4. Layout of an empty file system web site

This empty web application loads with only one component in it, and that is the web.config file, explained next.

The web.config File

The web.config file is a very important file of a web project. This file helps the developer by providing a central location where all the settings required for various actions such as database connections, debugging mode, and so on, can be set, and these settings will be applied and accessible throughout the project.

■ **Note** The web.config file is not automatically added to the ASP.NET web site project if you select File System as the storage location.

Another feature of the web.config file is that it is simple to read and write to, just like a Notepad file, because it comes in XML format.

The web.config file has a lot of predefined tags that help you organize the configuration settings for your web application. The most important thing to remember is that all tags need to be embedded inside the parent tags <Configuration> </Configuration>.

Understanding the Web UI of ASP.NET Web Apps

The UI of an ASP.NET application or web site is a web form or web page with an extension of `.aspx`, which means Active Server Pages.

Each web form or web page will contain the UI design or presentation in HTML format and the code functionality in an associated code-behind file with an extension of `.cs`. Hence, if your form is `Default.aspx`, this represents the presentation, and the `Default.aspx.cs` file represents the code. You will work with these files later in this chapter. Unlike the old version of ASP known as classical ASP, this approach helps keep the presentation separate from the logic and makes it easy to work with for a developer.

Also, as shown in previous chapters, ASP.NET-based applications are capable of containing multiple pages. You make one form the default page to load an application with, and then you move between the pages. Unlike Windows Forms, ASP.NET uses a different mechanism to switch to another form after an acknowledgment of an event. The mechanism is known as *redirect*, and this is available under the `Response` object of ASP.NET. Later in this chapter, you will see how these most widely used functions and objects work together.

Try It: Working with a Web Form

In this exercise, you will add a web form with basic controls to your project, and then you will add the required functionality to the controls.

1. Navigate to Solution Explorer, select the Chapter16 project, right-click it, and select Add New Item.

2. In the Add New Item dialog box, modify the form name to appear as Login, and ensure that the Language drop-down list shows Visual C#. Click OK to add the Login form to your project.

3. Right-click the `Login.aspx` web form, and select the View Designer option; this will open the `Login.aspx` page in the Design view, where you can drag and drop controls onto the web page, as shown in Figure 16-5.

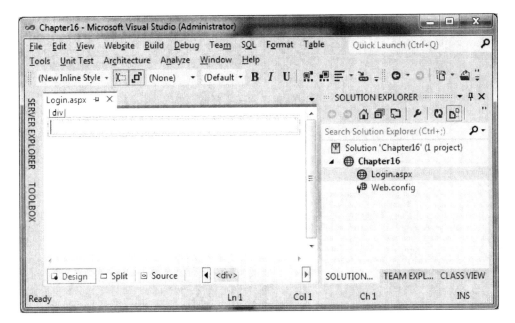

Figure 16-5. The Design view of a newly added web page

4. In the Toolbox, from the Standard bar, drag a Label control (named Label1) onto the form inside the area titled div, as shown in Figure 16-5. Select the Label control, and if the Properties window is not shown already, press F4. Go to the properties of the Label control, and set its Id property to lblUserName and its Text property to Enter User Name.

Note Just like Name property of Windows Forms and Windows controls, ASP.NET has an Id property for the names of the controls.

---

5. Drag a TextBox control (with an Id of TextBox1) onto the form and place it next to the Label control. Select the TextBox, and change its Id property to txtUserName.

6. Drag a Button control (named Button1) onto the form, and place it next to the TextBox control. Select the Button control, and set its Id property to btnLogin and its Text property to Login. All three controls should appear in one line, as shown in Figure 16-6.

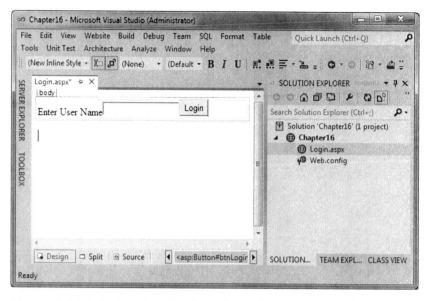

Figure 16-6. The Design view of the login form after adding controls

7. Now let's add one more web form to the application like done in step 2 and name the form WebDataForm.

8. Your web project will now have two forms, Login and WebDataForm, as shown in Figure 16-7.

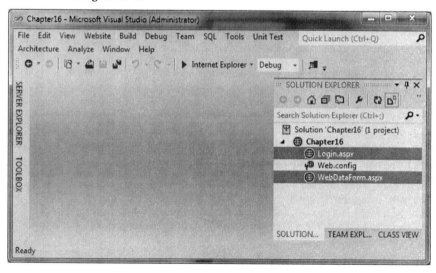

Figure 16-7. Project showing two web forms

9.   Now let's add the functionality. Open `Login.aspx` in the Design view by selecting it, right-clicking, and choosing View Designer. It will open as shown in Figure 16-6. Double-click the Login button, which will open the blank template for the btnLogin_click event. Modify the btnLogin_click event to look like Listing 16-1.

Listing 16-1. *Login.aspx.cs*

```
protected void btnLogin_Click(object sender, EventArgs e)
{
    if (txtUserName.Text == "agarwal")
    {
        Response.Redirect("WebDataForm.aspx");
    }
    else
    {
        Response.Write("Invalid User Name, please try again!");
    }
}
```

10.   Build the project and run the application by pressing Ctrl+F5. The `Login.aspx` form will appear in the browser. Enter a name in the provided text box, and click the Login button. If you will enter any other string than Agarwal, you should receive an "Invalid User Name, please try again!"error similar to that shown in Figure 16-8.

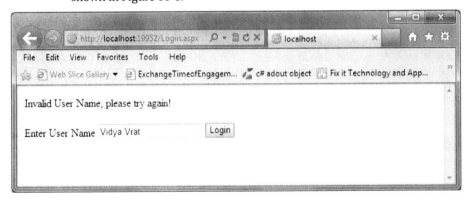

Figure 16-8. *Running and testing the Login form*

11.   In an ideal case, when you enter Agarwal, you will be taken to `WebDataForm.aspx`. But before we try that, let's add the functionality to the WebDataForm form first.

How It Works

First, you verify whether you have a successful log.

```
if (txtUserName.Text == "agarwal")
```

Once this condition is true, you want the user to be able to automatically navigate to WebDataForm. For this purpose, you used ASP.NET's Response object and its Redirect function, which takes the page name you would like to redirect to.

```
Response.Redirect("WebDataForm.aspx");
```

In the event of incorrect login, we are also showing an error message to the user. To show this error, we used Response object's Write method, which takes the string that you want to display on the page.

```
Response.Write("Invalid User Name, please try again!");
```

Using the Repeater Control

The Repeater control is an ASP.NET-specific control; in other words, it doesn't exist in Windows Forms. The Repeater control serves the purpose of a container control, which allows you to create custom lists to present data on the web page. Another feature of the Repeater control is that it does not have a built-in rendering of its own, which means that a web developer must provide the layout for the Repeater control with the help of templates. The Repeater control is capable of using various type of templates, such as ItemTemplate, HeaderTemplate, SeperatorTemplate, and FooterTemplate.

When the web page loads with a Repeater control, the Repeater control iterates through the data rows in the data source and renders data for each record found.

Unlike ListBox, GridView, TextBox, and so on, which you have used with database in earlier chapters, the Repeater control has no default look; hence, it makes it very flexible and powerful to be used with any type of lists, including a table layout, a comma-delimited list, or an XML-formatted list.

Now you have half the application ready and working, as shown in Figure 16-8. The next task will be to add functionality to WebDataForm; for this purpose, you will use one of the ASP.NET-specific data controls called the Repeater control, as discussed earlier.

Try It: Working with Repeater Control

In this exercise, you will add a Repeater control to a web form, and then you will write the required functionality to populate it with the data from a database.

1. Navigate to Solution Explorer. Right-click the WebDataForm.aspx web form, and select the View Designer option; this will open the WebDataForm.aspx page in the Design view, where you can drag and drop controls onto the web page.

2. Navigate to the Toolbox, expand the Data tab, and then drag a Repeater control to WebDataForm.aspx, positioning it toward the top left of the form.

3. Now press F4 to open the Properties window. Select the Repeater control, navigate to the Properties window, and set the Id property to RepData. Your WebDataForm will now look like Figure 16-9.

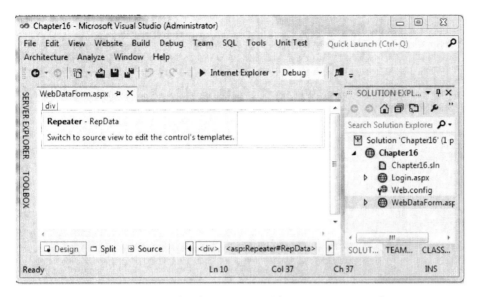

Figure 16-9. The Design view of WebDataForm with a Repeater control

4. Now you need to bind the data access code to WebDataForm. Double-click the empty surface of the WebDataForm as you have done already in Windows Forms applications. This will open the Page_Load event.

5. Modify the Page_Load event of WebDataForm.aspx.cs to look like Listing 16-2.

Listing 16-2. WebDataForm.aspx.cs

```csharp
using System.Data;
using System.Data.SqlClient

protected void Page_Load(object sender, EventArgs e)
{
    // Connection string
    string connString = @"server=.\sql2012;database=AdventureWorks;
                Integrated Security=true";

    //Query
    string query = @" SELECT  Title, BirthDate
                FROM    HumanResources.Employee";

    DataTable dt = new DataTable();

    try
    {
        SqlDataAdapter da = new SqlDataAdapter(query, connString);
        da.Fill(dt);
    }
```

```
        catch (Exception ex)
        {
            Response.Write(ex.Message.ToString());
        }

        //Populate Repeater control with data
        RepData.DataSource = dt;
        RepData.DataBind();
    }
```

6. Save the project and build the code by pressing Ctrl+Shift+B. It should build
    successfully.

7. Because you added the data access code, you need to enable the Repeater
    control to access this data. To do so, you need to tweak the HTML of
    WebDataForm.

8. Close WebDataForm.aspx.cs if open. Go to Solution Explorer, right-click
    WebDataForm, and select View Markup; you should see the HTML of
    WebDataForm.aspx, as shown in Figure 16-10.

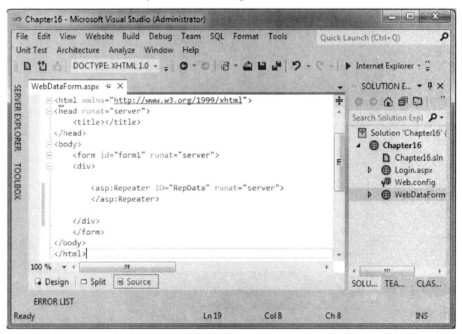

Figure 16-10. Markup view of WebDataForm

9. Modify the <body> HTML code segment to look like Listing 16-3.

Listing 16-3. HTML Code for WebDataForm.aspx

```
<body>
    <form id="form1" runat="server">
    <h3>HumanResources - Employee data</h3>
      <p>
      <asp:Repeater id=RepData runat="server">

        <HeaderTemplate>
            <table border=1>
                <tr>
                    <td><b>Title</b></td>
                    <td><b>BirthDate</b></td>
                </tr>
        </HeaderTemplate>

        <ItemTemplate>
            <tr>
                <td>
                    <%# DataBinder.Eval(Container.DataItem, "Title") %>
                </td>
                <td>
                    <%# DataBinder.Eval(Container.DataItem, "BirthDate") %>
                </td>
            </tr>
        </ItemTemplate>

        <FooterTemplate>
            </table>
        </FooterTemplate>
      </asp:Repeater>
      <p>
    </form>
</body>
```

10. Save the project, and build the project by pressing Ctrl+Shift+B. After successfully building, run the web application by pressing Ctrl+F5.

The project will load with Login.aspx, as shown in Figure 16-8, but this time you will enter correct user name **agarwal**, which is hard-coded in the if condition of the Login button. After entering the user name, and click the Login button; you will be redirected to WebDataForm.aspx, as shown in Figure 16-11.

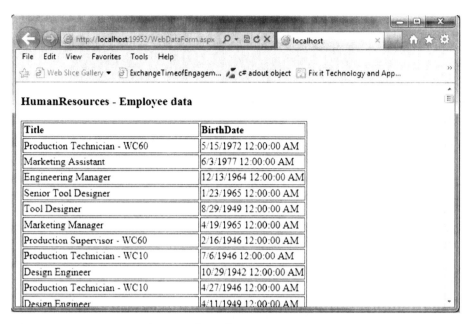

Figure 16-11. Running and testing the WebDataForm

How It Works

First you have to add the data access code to WebDataForm.aspx.cs, which builds the query and then loads the data table.

```
//Query
        string query = @" SELECT  Title, BirthDate
                    FROM    HumanResources.Employee";

        DataTable dt = new DataTable();
```

After building the data table, you fill the DataAdapter object using this DataTable object.

```
        try
        {
            SqlDataAdapter da = new SqlDataAdapter(query, connString);
            da.Fill(dt);
        }
```

Next you populate the Repeater control with the data.

```
    //Populate Repeater control with data
    RepData.DataSource = dt;
    RepData.DataBind();
```

Summary

In this chapter, you learned a few basics about the web technology called ASP.NET. You also learned about the various types of web sites you can create in Visual Studio 2012. You saw how to work with web pages and then use data access code and the Repeater control. In the next chapter, you will learn how work with text and binary data.

CHAPTER 17

Working with Text and Binary Data

Some kinds of data have special formats, are very large, or vary greatly in size. Here, I'll show you techniques for working with text and binary data. In this chapter, I'll cover the following:

- Understanding SQL Server text and binary data types

- Storing images in a database

- Retrieving images from a database

- Working with text data

I'll also present the T-SQL for creating tables in the tempdb database, which is intended to hold any temporary table. I'll start by covering what data types support these kinds of data.

Understanding SQL Server Text and Binary Data Types

SQL Server provides the types CHAR, NCHAR, VARCHAR, NVARCHAR, BINARY, and VARBINARY for working with reasonably small text and binary data. You can use these with text (character) data up to a maximum of 8,000 bytes (4,000 bytes for Unicode data, NCHAR, and NVARCHAR, which use 2 bytes per character).

For larger data, which SQL Server 2012 calls *large-value data types*, you should use the VARCHAR(MAX), NVARCHAR(MAX), and VARBINARY(MAX) data types. VARCHAR(MAX) is for non-Unicode text, NVARCHAR(MAX) is for Unicode text, and VARBINARY(MAX) is for images and other binary data.

■ **Warning** In SQL Server 2000, large data was stored using NTEXT, TEXT, and IMAGE data types. These data types were deprecated and was removed with the release of newer versions of SQL Server. If you work with legacy applications, you should consider converting NTEXT, TEXT, and IMAGE to NVARCHAR(MAX), VARCHAR(MAX), and VARBINARY(MAX), respectively. However, the System.Data.SqlDbType enumeration does not yet include members for these data types, so we use VARCHAR(MAX) and VARBINARY(MAX) for column data types, but Text and Image when specifying data types for command parameters.

An alternative to using these data types is to not store the data itself in the database but instead define a column containing a path that points to where the data is actually stored. This can be more efficient for accessing large amounts of data, and it can save resources on the database server by transferring the demand to a file server. It does require more complicated coordination and has the potential for database and data files to get out of sync. I won't use this technique in this chapter.

■ **Tip** If you are using a SQL Server Express database that cannot exceed 4GB or if you don't want your database to store a lot of information and grow beyond a certain size limit, using SQL Server–provided text and binary data types may be your only alternative for very large text and image data.

Within a C# program, binary data types map to an array of bytes (byte[ ]), and character data types map to strings or character arrays (char[ ]).

■ **Note** DB2, MySQL, Oracle, and the SQL standard call such data types *large objects* (LOBs); specifically, they're binary large objects (BLOBs) and character large objects (CLOBs). But, as with many database terms, whether BLOB was originally an acronym for anything is debatable. Needless to say, it has always implied a data type that can handle large amounts of (amorphous) data, and SQL Server documentation uses BLOB as a generic term for large data and data types.

Storing Images in a Database

Let's start by creating a database table for storing images and then loading some images into it. We'll use small images but use VARBINARY(MAX) to store them. In the examples, I'll demonstrate using images from the code directory path C:\VidyaVrat\C#2012 and SQL 2012\Chapter17\Code; you can use the path of the location where you have some images on your computer.

Try It: Loading Image Binary Data from Files

In this example, you'll write a program that creates a database table and then load and stores images in it.

1. Create a new Windows Forms Application project named Chapter17. When Solution Explorer opens, save the solution.

2. Rename the Chapter17 project to Text and Binary Data. Rename the Form1.cs file to LoadImages.cs . Select the LoadImages form by clicking the form's title bar, and set the Size property's Width to 439 and Height to 178.

3. Drag a TextBox control to the form, and position it toward the center of the form. Select this TextBox control, navigate to the Properties window, and set the following properties:

    •   Set the Name property to txtLoadImages.

- For the Location property, set X to 12 and Y to 12.

- Set the Multiline property to True.

- For the Size property, set Width to 401 and Height to 117.

- Leave the Text property blank.

4. Now your LoadImages form in the Design view should look like Figure 17-1.

Figure 17-1. The Design view of the LoadImages form

5. Navigate to Solution Explorer, select the LoadImages.cs form, right-click, and select View Code; this will take you to the code editor window. Add the code to LoadImages.cs shown in Listing 17-1.

Listing 17-1. LoadImages.cs

```
using System.Data;
using System.Data.SqlClient;
using System.IO;
 // change this path to the location of image in your computer
 string imageFileLocation = @"C:\VidyaVrat\C#2012 and SQL 2012\Chapter17\Code\";

 string imageFilePrefix = "SpaceNeedle";
 string imageFileType = ".jpg";

 int numberImageFiles = 1;
 int maxImageSize = 10000;

 SqlConnection conn = null;
 SqlCommand cmd = null;

 private void LoadImages_Load(object sender, EventArgs e)
 {
    try
     {
        // Create connection
        conn = new SqlConnection(@"server = .\sql2012;integrated security = true;
                           database = SQL2012Db");
```

```
        // Open connection
        conn.Open();

        //Create command
        cmd = new SqlCommand();
        cmd.Connection = conn;

         // Create table
        CreateImageTable();

        // Prepare insert
        PrepareInsertImages();

        // Loop for Inserting images
        for (int i = 1; i <= numberImageFiles; i++)
        {
            ExecuteInsertImages(i);
        }
    }

    catch (SqlException ex)
    {
        MessageBox.Show(ex.Message + ex.StackTrace);
    }

    finally
    {
        // Close connection
        conn.Close();
        txtLoadImages.AppendText(Environment.NewLine);
        txtLoadImages.AppendText("Connection Closed.");
    }
}

private void ExecuteCommand(string cmdText)
{
    int cmdResult;
    cmd.CommandText = cmdText;
    //txtLoad.AppendText("Executing command:\n");
  // txtLoad.AppendText(cmd.CommandText);
    //txtLoad.AppendText(Environment.NewLine);
    cmdResult = cmd.ExecuteNonQuery();
}

private void CreateImageTable()
{
    ExecuteCommand(@"if exists
                        (select * from
                          INFORMATION_SCHEMA.TABLES
                          where TABLE_NAME = 'ImageTable')
```

```
                        drop table ImageTable

                        create table ImageTable
                        (
                            ImageFile nvarchar(20),
                            ImageData varbinary(max)
                        )");
}

private void PrepareInsertImages()
{
    cmd.CommandText = @"insert into ImageTable
                        values (@ImageFile, @ImageData)";

    cmd.Parameters.Add("@imagefile", SqlDbType.NVarChar, 20);
    cmd.Parameters.Add("@imagedata", SqlDbType.Image, 1000000);

    cmd.Prepare();
}

private void ExecuteInsertImages(int imageFileNumber)
{
    string imageFileName = null;
    byte[] imageImageData = null;

    imageFileName = imageFilePrefix + imageFileNumber.ToString() + imageFileType;
    imageImageData = LoadImageFile(imageFileName, imageFileLocation, maxImageSize);

    cmd.Parameters["@ImageFile"].Value = imageFileName;
    cmd.Parameters["@ImageData"].Value = imageImageData;

    ExecuteCommand(cmd.CommandText);
}

private byte[] LoadImageFile(string fileName,string fileLocation,int maxImageSize)
{
    byte[] imagebytes = null;
    string fullpath = fileLocation + fileName;
    txtLoadImages.AppendText("Loading File:");
    txtLoadImages.AppendText(Environment.NewLine);
    txtLoadImages.AppendText(fullpath);
    FileStream fs = new FileStream(fullpath, FileMode.Open, FileAccess.Read);
    BinaryReader br = new BinaryReader(fs);
    imagebytes = br.ReadBytes(maxImageSize);
    txtLoadImages.AppendText(Environment.NewLine);

    txtLoadImages.AppendText("Imagebytes has length " +
            imagebytes.GetLength(0).ToString() + "bytes.");

    return imagebytes;
}
```

337

6. Build the project, and run the program by pressing Ctrl+F5. You should see output similar to that in Figure 17-2. It shows the information for loading an image into the database that you have on your computer at the specified location, and it shows the size of each image.

Figure 17-2. Loading image data

7. To see the image you have inserted into the database, open SQL Server Management Studio and run a SELECT query on the image table you have created in the SQL2012Db database, which was created in Chapter 3 (see Figure 17-3).

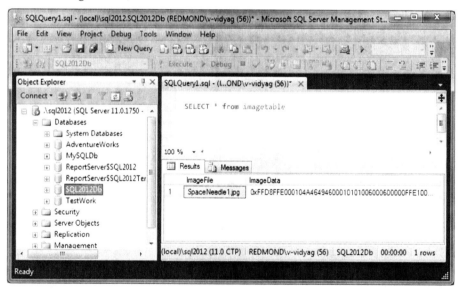

Figure 17-3. Viewing image data

How It Works

In LoadImages.cs, you do three major things other than creating and opening a connection. You connect to SQL2012Db, the database that you created in Chapter 3.

```
// Create connection
conn = new SqlConnection(@"server = .\sql2012;integrated security = true;
                          database = SQL2012Db");

// Open connection
conn.Open();
```

You call a private class-level method to create a table to hold images.

```
// Create table
CreateImageTable();
```

You call a private class-level method to prepare a command (yes, you finally prepare a command, since you expect to run it multiple times) to insert images.

```
// Prepare insert
PrepareInsertImages();
```

You then loop through the image files and insert them into the table.

```
// Loop for Inserting images
for (int i = 1; i <= loader.numberImageFiles; i++)
{
    ExecuteInsertImages(i);
}
```

Because there could already be a table, you have to take care of dropping the table if it exists and then creating it. This step is repeated on each run of the application.

When you create the table, a simple one containing the image file name and the image, you use the VARBINARY(MAX) data type for the imagedata column.

```
private void CreateImageTable()
{
    ExecuteCommand(@"if exists
                        (select * from
                          INFORMATION_SCHEMA.TABLES
                          where TABLE_NAME = 'ImageTable')

                     drop table ImageTable

                     create table ImageTable
                     (
                         ImageFile nvarchar(20),
                         ImageData varbinary(max)
                     )");
}
```

But when you configure the INSERT command, you use the Image member of the SqlDbType enumeration, since there is no member for the VARBINARY(MAX) data type. You specify lengths for both variable-length data types, since you can't prepare a command unless you do.

```
private void PrepareInsertImages()
{
    cmd.CommandText = @"insert into ImageTable
                        values (@ImageFile, @ImageData)";
```

```
cmd.Parameters.Add("@imagefile", SqlDbType.NVarChar, 20);
cmd.Parameters.Add("@imagedata", SqlDbType.Image, 1000000);

    cmd.Prepare();
}
```

The ExecuteInsertImages method accepts an integer to use as a suffix for the image file name, calls LoadImageFile to get a byte array containing the image, assigns the file name and image to their corresponding command parameters, and then executes the command to insert the image.

```
private void ExecuteInsertImages(int imageFileNumber)
{
    string imageFileName = null;
    byte[] imageImageData = null;

    imageFileName = imageFilePrefix + imageFileNumber.ToString() + imageFileType;
    imageImageData = LoadImageFile(imageFileName, imageFileLocation, maxImageSize);

    cmd.Parameters["@ImageFile"].Value = imageFileName;
    cmd.Parameters["@ImageData"].Value = imageImageData;

    ExecuteCommand(cmd.CommandText);
}
```

The LoadImageFile method reads the image file, displays the file name and number of bytes in the file, and returns the image as a byte array.

```
private byte[] LoadImageFile(string fileName,string fileLocation,int maxImageSize)
{
    byte[] imagebytes = null;
    string fullpath = fileLocation + fileName;
    txtLoadImages.AppendText("Loading File:");
    txtLoadImages.AppendText(Environment.NewLine);
    txtLoadImages.AppendText(fullpath);
    FileStream fs = new FileStream(fullpath, FileMode.Open, FileAccess.Read);
    BinaryReader br = new BinaryReader(fs);
    imagebytes = br.ReadBytes(maxImageSize);
    txtLoadImages.AppendText(Environment.NewLine);

    txtLoadImages.AppendText("Imagebytes has length " +
            imagebytes.GetLength(0).ToString() + " bytes.");

    return imagebytes;
}
```

Retrieving Images from a Database

Now that you've stored some image(s), you'll see how to retrieve and display them with a Windows Forms application.

Try It: Displaying Stored Images

To display your stored images, follow these steps:

1. Select the Text and Binary Data project, right-click, and choose Add ➤ Windows Form. From the opened dialog, make sure Windows Form is selected, and rename Form1.cs to DisplayImages.cs; click OK to add this form to the Text and Binary Data project.

2. Select the DisplayImages form, and set the Size property's Width to 330 and Height to 332.

3. Drag a Label control to the form, and position it toward the top-left corner of the form. Select this Label control, navigate to the Properties window, and set the following properties:

   - Set the Name property to lblImageName.

   - For the Location property, set X to 12 and Y to 22.

   - For the Text property, set to Image Name.

4. Drag a TextBox control to the form, and position it next to the Label control. Select this TextBox control, navigate to the Properties window, and set the following properties:

   - Set the Name property to txtImageName.

   - For the Location property, set X to 85 and Y to 22.

   - Leave the Text property blank.

5. Drag a Button control to the form, and position it next to the TextBox control. Select this Button control, navigate to the Properties window, and set the following properties:

   - Set the Name property to btnShowImage.

   - For the Location property, set X to 277 and Y to 22.

   - Set the Text property to Show Image.

6. Drag a PictureBox control to the form, and position it toward the center of the form. Select this PictureBox control, navigate to the Properties window, and set the following properties:

   - Set the Name property to ptbImage.

   - For the Location property, set X to 44 and Y to 61.

   - For the Size property, set Height to 220 and Width to 221.

7. Now your DisplayImages form in the Design view should look like Figure 17-4.

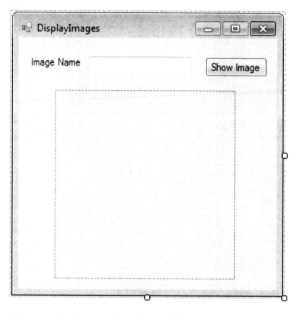

Figure 17-4. The Design view of the DisplayImages form

8. Add a new class named Images to this Windows Form project. To add this, select the Text and Binary Data project, right-click, select Class… in the Add New Item dialog, name the class Images.cs, and click Add to have it listed under your project. Once it's added, replace the code in Images.cs with the code in Listing 17-2.

Listing 17-2. Images.cs

```
using System.Data.SqlClient;
using System.IO;
using System.Drawing;

namespace Text_and_Binary_Data
{
    public class Images
    {
        string imageFilename = null;
        byte[] imageBytes = null;

        SqlConnection imageConnection = null;
        SqlCommand imageCommand = null;
        SqlDataReader imageReader = null;

        // Constructor
        public Images()
        {
```

```csharp
        imageConnection = new SqlConnection(@"data source = .\sql2012;
                integrated security = true; initial catalog = SQL2012db;");

        imageCommand = new SqlCommand(@" select imagefile,imagedata
                                    from ImageTable", imageConnection);

        // Open connection and create data reader
        imageConnection.Open();
        imageReader = imageCommand.ExecuteReader();
    }

    public Bitmap GetImage()
    {
        MemoryStream ms = new MemoryStream(imageBytes);
        Bitmap bmap = new Bitmap(ms);

        return bmap;
    }

    public string GetFilename()
    {
        return imageFilename;
    }

    public bool GetRow()
    {
        if (imageReader.Read())
        {
            imageFilename = (string)imageReader.GetValue(0);
            imageBytes = (byte[])imageReader.GetValue(1);

            return true;
        }
        else
        {
            return false;
        }
    }

    public void EndImages()
    {
        // Close the reader and the connection.
        imageReader.Close();
        imageConnection.Close();
    }
  }
}
```

9. Next, insert the code in Listing 18-3 into DisplayImages.cs in the constructor. You can access DisplayImages.cs by right-clicking DisplayImages.cs and selecting View Code, which will take you to the Code view.

Listing 17-3. Initializing Image Display in the DisplayImages Constructor

```
public DisplayImages()
{
    InitializeComponent();

    if (images.GetRow())
    {
        this.txtImageName.Text = images.GetFilename();
        this.ptbImage.Image = (Image)images.GetImage();
    }
    else
    {
        this.txtImageName.Text = "DONE";
        this.ptbImage.Image = null;
    }
}
```

10. Insert the code in Listing 18-3 into the btnShowImage button's Click event handler. You can access the btnShowImage_Click event handler by navigating to the Design view of the DisplayImages form and double-clicking the btnShowImage Button control.

Listing17-4. btnShowImage_Click Event in DisplayImages.cs

```
private void btnShowImage_Click(object sender, EventArgs e)
{
    if (images.GetRow())
    {
        this.txtImageName.Text = images.GetFilename();
        this.ptbImage.Image = (Image)images.GetImage();
    }
    else
    {
        this.txtImageName.Text = "DONE";
        this.ptbImage.Image = null;
    }
}
```

11. To set the TypedAccessor form as the start-up form, modify the Program.cs statement.

```
Application.Run(new LoadImages());
```

to appear as

```
Application.Run(new DisplayImages());
```

Build the project, and run it by pressing Ctrl+F5. You should see the results in Figure 17-5.

Figure 17-5. *Displaying images*

How It Works

You declare a type, Images, to access the database and provide methods for the form components to easily get and display images. In its constructor, you connect to the database and create a data reader to handle the result set of a query that retrieves all the images you stored earlier.

```
// Constructor
public Images()
{
    imageConnection = new SqlConnection(@"data source = .\sql2012;
            integrated security = true; initial catalog = SQL2012db;");

    imageCommand = new SqlCommand(@" select imagefile,imagedata
                                from ImageTable", imageConnection);

    // Open connection and create data reader
    imageConnection.Open();
    imageReader = imageCommand.ExecuteReader();
}
```

When the form is initialized, the new code creates an instance of Images, looks for an image with GetRow(), and, if it finds one, assigns the file name and image to the text box and picture box with the GetFilename and GetImage methods, respectively.

```
images = new Images();
if (images.GetRow())
{
    this.textBoxl.Text = images.GetFilename();
    this.pictureBoxl.Image = (Image)images.GetImage();
}
else
{
    this.textBoxl.Text = "DONE";
    this.pictureBoxl.Image = null;
}
```

You use the same if statement in the Next button's click event handler to look for the next image. If none is found, you displayed the word *DONE* in the text box.

The image is returned from the database as an array of bytes. The PictureBox control's Image property can be a Bitmap, Icon, or Metafile (all derived classes of Image). Bitmap supports a variety of formats including BMP, GIF, and JPEG. The getImage method, shown here, returns a Bitmap object:

```
public Bitmap GetImage()
{
    MemoryStream ms = new MemoryStream(imageBytes);
    Bitmap bmap = new Bitmap(ms);

    return bmap;
}
```

Bitmap's constructor doesn't accept a byte array, but it will accept a MemoryStream (which is effectively an in-memory representation of a file), and MemoryStream has a constructor that accepts a byte array. So, you create a memory stream from the byte array and then create a bitmap from the memory stream.

Working with Text Data

Handling text is similar to handling images except for the data type used for the database column.

Try It: Loading Text Data from a File

To load text data from a file, follow these steps:

1. Select the Text and Binary Data project, right-click, and choose Add ➤ Windows Form. From the opened dialog, make sure Windows Form is selected, and rename Form1.cs to LoadText.cs; click OK to add this form to the Text and Binary Data project.

2. Select the LoadText form, and set the Size property's Width to 496 and Height to 196.

3. Drag a TextBox control to the form, and position it toward the center of the form. Select this TextBox control, navigate to the Properties window, and set the following properties:

   • Set the Name property to txtLoadText.

- For the Location property, set X to 12 and Y to 12.

- For the Size property, set Width to 456 and Height to 135.

- Leave the Text property blank.

4. Now your LoadText form in the Design view should look like Figure 17-6.

Figure 17-6. The Design view of the LoadText form

5. Next, insert the code in Listing 17-5 into LoadText.cs. You can access
LoadText.cs by right-clicking LoadText.cs and selecting View Code, which will
take you to the Code view.

Listing 17-5. LoadText.cs

```
using System.Data;
using System.Data.SqlClient;
using System.IO

static string fileName =
        @"C:\VidyaVrat\C#2012 and SQL 2012\Chapter17\Code\Text and Binary Data\LoadText.cs";

        SqlConnection conn = null;
        SqlCommand cmd = null;

        public LoadText()
        {
            InitializeComponent();
        }

        private void LoadText_Load(object sender, EventArgs e)
        {
            try
            {
                // Create connection
                conn = new SqlConnection(@"data source = .\sql2012;
                    integrated security = true;initial catalog = SQL2012Db;");

                //Create command
```

```
            cmd = new SqlCommand();
            cmd.Connection = conn;

            // Open connection
            conn.Open();

            // Create table
            CreateTextTable();

            // Prepare insert command
            PrepareInsertTextFile();

            // Load text file
            ExecuteInsertTextFile(fileName);

            txtLoadText.AppendText("Loaded "+fileName+" into TextTable.\n");

        }
        catch (SqlException ex)
        {
            MessageBox.Show(ex.ToString());
        }
        finally
        {
            // Close connection
            conn.Close();
        }
    }

    private void CreateTextTable()
    {
        ExecuteCommand(@"if exists(select *
                            from INFORMATION_SCHEMA.TABLES
                            where TABLE_NAME = 'TextTable')

                    drop table TextTable ");

        ExecuteCommand(@"create table TextTable
                    (
                            TextFile varchar(255),
                            TextData varchar(max)
                    )");
    }

    private void ExecuteCommand(string commandText)
    {
        cmd.CommandText = commandText;
        cmd.ExecuteNonQuery();
        txtLoadText.AppendText("\n");
    }

    private void PrepareInsertTextFile()
```

```csharp
{
    cmd.CommandText = @"insert into TextTable
                        values (@textfile, @textdata)";

    cmd.Parameters.Add("@textfile", SqlDbType.NVarChar, 30);
    cmd.Parameters.Add("@textdata", SqlDbType.Text, 1000000);
}

private void ExecuteInsertTextFile(string textFile)
{
    string textData = GetTextFile(textFile);
    cmd.Parameters["@textfile"].Value = textFile;
    cmd.Parameters["@textdata"].Value = textData;
    ExecuteCommand(cmd.CommandText);
}

private string GetTextFile(string textFile)
{
    string textBytes = null;
    txtLoadText.AppendText("Loading File: " + textFile);

    FileStream fs = new FileStream(textFile, FileMode.Open, FileAccess.Read);
    StreamReader sr = new StreamReader(fs);
    textBytes = sr.ReadToEnd();

    txtLoadText.AppendText("TextBytes has length" + textBytes.Length + " bytes.\n");

    return textBytes;
}
```

6. To set the LoadText form as the start-up form, modify the `Program.cs` statement.

   ```csharp
   Application.Run(new DisplayImages());
   ```

   to appear as

   ```csharp
   Application.Run(new LoadText());
   ```

   Build the project, and run it by pressing Ctrl+F5. You should see the results in Figure 17-7.

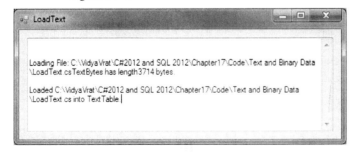

Figure 17-7. Loading a text file into a table

How It Works

You simply load the source code for the LoadText program.

```
// change this path to the location of text in your computer
        static string fileName =
            @"C:\VidyaVrat\C#2012 and SQL 2012\Chapter17\Code\Text and Binary Data\LoadText.cs";
```

Set CommandText with the insert staterment and add parameters:

```
cmd.CommandText = @"insert into TextTable
                    values (@textfile, @textdata)";
```

```
cmd.Parameters.Add("@textfile", SqlDbType.NVarChar, 30);
cmd.Parameters.Add("@textdata", SqlDbType.Text, 1000000);
```

Execute command to drop the existing table and create a fresh one:

```
ExecuteCommand(@"if exists(select *
                    from INFORMATION_SCHEMA.TABLES
                    where TABLE_NAME = 'TextTable')
                    drop table TextTable ");

        ExecuteCommand(@"create table TextTable
                    (
                        TextFile varchar(255),
                        TextData varchar(max))"
                    );
```

Note that you first check to see whether the table exists. If it does, you drop it so you can re-create it.

Note The `information_schema.tables` *view* (a named query) is compatible with the SQL standard `INFORMATION_SCHEMA` view of the same name. It limits the tables you can see to the ones you can access. Microsoft recommends you use the new *catalog views* to get database metadata in SQL Server 2012, and SQL Server itself uses them internally. The catalog view for this query would be `sys.tables`, and the column name would be name. We've used the `INFORMATION SCHEMA` view here because you may still see it often.

Instead of the BinaryReader you use for images, GetTextFile uses a StreamReader (derived from System.IO.TextReader) to read the contents of the file into a string.

```
        private string GetTextFile(string textFile)
        {
            string textBytes = null;
            txtLoadText.AppendText("Loading File: " + textFile);

            FileStream fs = new FileStream(textFile, FileMode.Open, FileAccess.Read);
            StreamReader sr = new StreamReader(fs);
            textBytes = sr.ReadToEnd();
```

```
        txtLoadText.AppendText("TextBytes has length" + textBytes.Length + " bytes.\n");

        return textBytes;
    }
```

Otherwise, the processing logic is basically the same as you've seen many times throughout the book: open a connection, access a database, and then close the connection.

Now let's retrieve the text you just stored.

Retrieving Data from Text Columns

Retrieving data from text columns is just like retrieving it from the smaller character data types. You'll now write a simple console program to see how this works.

Try It: Retrieving Text Data

To retrieve data from text columns, follow these steps:

1. Select the Text and Binary Data project, right-click, and choose Add ➤ Windows Form. From the opened dialog, make sure Windows Form is selected and rename `Form1.cs` to `RetrieveText.cs`; click OK to add this form to the Text and Binary Data project.

2. Select the RetrieveText form, and set the Size property's Width to 438 and Height to 334.

3. Drag a TextBox control to the form, and position it toward the center of the form. Select this TextBox control, navigate to the Properties window, and set the following properties:

   - Set the Name property to txtRetrieveText.

   - For the Location property, set X to 12 and Y to 12.

   - For the Size property, set Width to 401 and Height to 269.

   - Leave the Text property blank.

4. Now your LoadText form in the Design view should look like Figure 17-8.

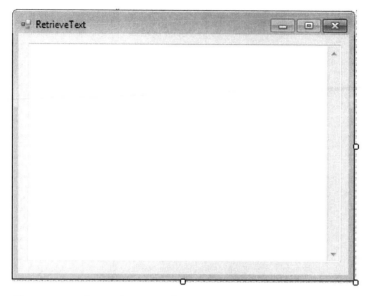

Figure 17-8. *The Design view of the RetrieveText form*

5. Next, insert the code in Listing 17-6 into RetrieveText.cs. You can access
    RetrieveText.cs by right-clicking RetrieveText.cs and selecting View Code,
    which will take you to the Code view.

Listing 17-6. *RetrieveText.cs*

```
using System.Data;
using System.Data.SqlClient;

    string textFile = null;
    char[] textChars = null;
    SqlConnection conn = null;
    SqlCommand cmd = null;
    SqlDataReader dr = null;

    public RetrieveText()
    {
        InitializeComponent();

        // Create connection
        conn = new SqlConnection(@"data source = .\sql2012;integrated security = true;
                                    initial catalog = SQL2012Db;");

        // Create command
        cmd = new SqlCommand(@"select textfile, textdata
                            from TextTable", conn);
```

```csharp
        // Open connection
        conn.Open();

        // Create data reader
        dr = cmd.ExecuteReader();
    }

    public void RetrieveText_Load(object sender, EventArgs e)
    {
        try
        {
            while (GetRow() == true)
            {
                txtRetrieveText.AppendText ("----- end of file\n");
                txtRetrieveText.AppendText(textFile);
                txtRetrieveText.AppendText("\n=============================\n");
            }
        }
        catch (SqlException ex)
        {
            Console.WriteLine(ex.ToString());
        }

        finally
        {
            // Close the reader and the connection.
            dr.Close();
            conn.Close();
        }
    }

    public bool GetRow()
    {
        long textSize;
        int bufferSize = 100;
        long charsRead;
        textChars = new Char[bufferSize];

        if (dr.Read())
        {
            // Get file name
            textFile = dr.GetString(0);
            txtRetrieveText.AppendText("------ start of file\n");
            txtRetrieveText.AppendText(textFile);
            txtRetrieveText.AppendText("\n");
            textSize = dr.GetChars(1, 0, null, 0, 0);
            txtRetrieveText.AppendText("--- size of text: " + textSize + " characters ---
");

            txtRetrieveText.AppendText("\n--- first 100 characters in text -----\n");
            charsRead = dr.GetChars(1, 0, textChars, 0, 100);
            txtRetrieveText.AppendText(new String(textChars));
```

```
        txtRetrieveText.AppendText("\n");
        txtRetrieveText.AppendText("\n--- last 100 characters in text -----\n");
        charsRead = dr.GetChars(1, textSize - 100, textChars, 0, 100);
        txtRetrieveText.AppendText(new String(textChars));

        return true;
    }
    else
    {
        return false;
    }
}
```

6. To set the LoadText form as the start-up form, modify the `Program.cs` statement.

    ```
    Application.Run(new LoadText());
    ```

    to appear as

    ```
    Application.Run(new RetrieveText());
    ```

    Build the project, and run it by pressing Ctrl+F5. You should see the results in Figure 17-9.

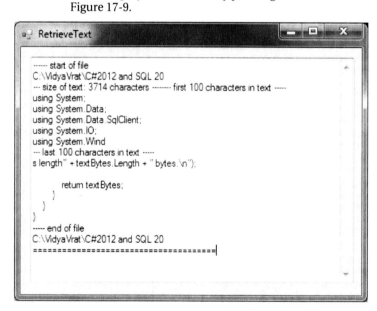

Figure 17-9. Retrieving text from a table

How It Works

After querying the database, like so:

```
// Create connection
    conn = new SqlConnection(@"data source = .\sql2012;integrated security = true;
                                initial catalog = SQL2012Db;");

    // Create command
    cmd = new SqlCommand(@"select textfile, textdata
                          from TextTable", conn);

    // Open connection
    conn.Open();

    // Create data reader
    dr = cmd.ExecuteReader();
```

you loop through the result set (but here there is only one row), get the file name from the table with GetString(), and print it to show which file is displayed. You then call GetCharsQ with a null character array to get the size of the VARCHAR(MAX) column.

```
        if (dr.Read())
        {
            // Get file name
            textFile = dr.GetString(0);
            txtRetrieveText.AppendText("------ start of file\n");
            txtRetrieveText.AppendText(textFile);
            txtRetrieveText.AppendText("\n");
            textSize = dr.GetChars(1, 0, null, 0, 0);
            txtRetrieveText.AppendText("--- size of text: " + textSize + " characters ---
");

            txtRetrieveText.AppendText("\n--- first 100 characters in text -----\n");
            charsRead = dr.GetChars(1, 0, textChars, 0, 100);
            txtRetrieveText.AppendText(new String(textChars));
            txtRetrieveText.AppendText("\n");
            txtRetrieveText.AppendText("\n--- last 100 characters in text -----\n");
            charsRead = dr.GetChars(1, textSize - 100, textChars, 0, 100);
            txtRetrieveText.AppendText(new String(textChars));

            return true;
        }
        else
        {
            return false;
        }
```

Rather than print the whole file, you display the first 100 bytes, using GetChars() to extract a substring. You do the same thing with the last 100 characters.

Otherwise, this program is like any other that retrieves and displays database character data.

Summary

In this chapter, you explored SQL Server's text and binary data types. You also practiced storing and retrieving binary and text data using data types for SQL Server large objects and ADO.NET.

In the next chapter, you will learn about another database query technique known as Language Integrated Query (LINQ).

CHAPTER 18

Using LINQ

Writing software means you need to have a database sitting on the back end, and most of your time goes into writing queries to retrieve and manipulate data. Whenever someone talks about data, we tend to think of the information that is contained in a relational database or in an XML document.

The kind of data access that we had prior to the release of .NET 3.5 was meant only for data that resides in traditional data sources like the two just mentioned. But with the release of .NET 3.5 and newer versions like .NET 4.0 and .NET 4.5, which have Language Integrated Query (LINQ) incorporated into them, it is now possible to deal with data residing beyond traditional information storage. For instance, you can query a generic List type containing a few hundred integer values and write a LINQ expression to retrieve a subset that meets your criterion, such as either even or odd numbers.

LINQ, as you may have gathered, is one of the major differences between .NET 3.0 and .NET 3.5. It is a set of features in Visual Studio 2012 that extends powerful query capabilities into the language syntax of C# and VB .NET.

LINQ introduces a standard, unified, easy-to-learn approach for querying and modifying data and can be extended to support potentially any type of data store. Visual Studio 2012 includes LINQ provider assemblies that enable the use of LINQ queries with various types of data sources including relational data, XML, and in-memory data structures.

In this chapter, we'll cover the following:

- Introduction to LINQ
- Architecture of LINQ
- LINQ project structure
- Using LINQ to Objects
- Using LINQ to SQL
- Using LINQ to XML

Introduction to LINQ

LINQ is an innovation that Microsoft made with the release of Visual Studio 2008 and .NET Framework version 3.5 that promises to revolutionize the way developers work with data. Microsoft has continued to improve LINQ with the recent releases of .NET 4.0/4.5 and Visual Studio 2012. As mentioned, LINQ allows you to query various types of data sources including relational databases, XML documents, and even in-memory data structures. LINQ supports all these types of data stores with the help of LINQ query expressions of first-class language constructs in C# 2012. LINQ offers the following advantages:

- LINQ offers common syntax for querying any type of data source; for example, you can query an XML document in the same way you query a SQL database, an ADO.NET dataset, an in-memory collection, or any other remote or local data source that you have chosen to connect to and access by using LINQ.

- LINQ bridges the gap and strengthens the connection between relational data and the object-oriented world.

- LINQ speeds development time by catching many errors at compile time and including IntelliSense and debugging support.

- LINQ query expressions (unlike traditional SQL statements) are strongly typed.

Note Strongly typed expressions ensure access to values as the correct type at compile time and so prevent type mismatch errors from being caught when the code is compiled rather than at runtime.

The LINQ assemblies provide all the functionality of accessing various types of data stores under one umbrella. Table 18-1 lists the core LINQ assemblies.

Table 18-1. Core LINQ Assemblies

Assembly Name	Description
System.LINQ	Provides classes and interfaces that support LINQ queries
System.Collections.Generic	Allows users to create strongly typed collections that provide better type safety and performance than nongeneric strongly typed collections (LINQ to Objects)
System.Data.LINQ	Provides the functionality to use LINQ to access relational databases (LINQ to SQL)
System.XML.LINQ	Provides functionality for accessing XML documents using LINQ (LINQ to XML)
System.Data.Linq.Mapping	Designates a class as an entity class associated with a database

Note Though it's called Language Integrated *Query*, LINQ can be used to update database data. We'll cover only simple queries here to give you your first taste of LINQ, but LINQ is a general-purpose facility for accessing data.

Architecture of LINQ

LINQ consists of three major components:

- LINQ to Objects
- LINQ to ADO.NET, which includes
  - LINQ to SQL (formerly called DLinq)
  - LINQ to DataSets (formerly called LINQ over DataSets)
  - LINQ to Entities
- LINQ to XML (formerly called XLinq)

Figure 18-1 depicts the LINQ architecture, which clearly shows the various components of LINQ and their related data stores.

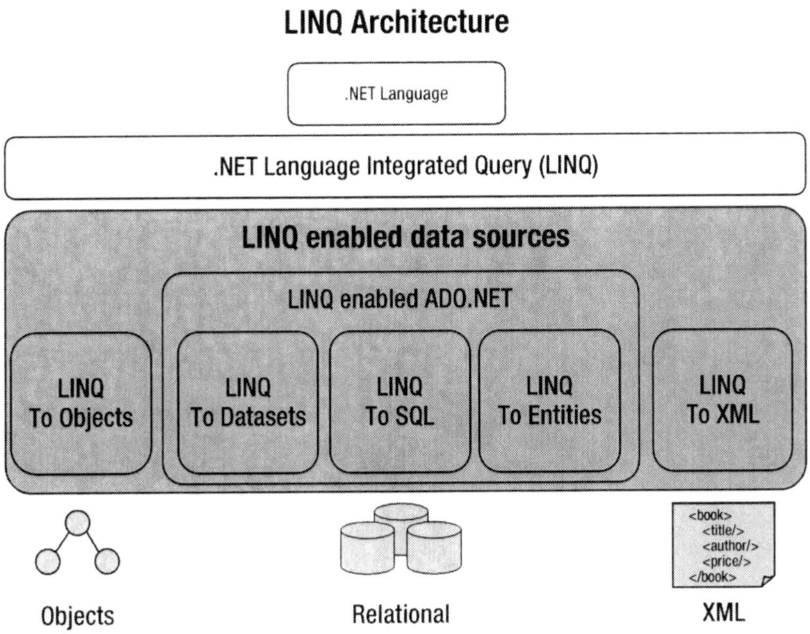

Figure 18-1. *LINQ architecture*

LINQ to Objects deals with in-memory data. Any class that implements the `IEnumerable<T>` interface (in the `System.Collections.Generic` namespace) can be queried with Standard Query Operators (SQOs).

> **Note** SQOs are a collection of methods that form the LINQ pattern. SQO methods operate on sequences, where a *sequence* represents an object whose type implements the interface IEnumerable<T> or the interface IOueryable<T>. The SQO provides query capabilities including filtering, projection, aggregation, sorting, and so forth.

LINQ to ADO.NET (also known as LINQ-enabled ADO .NET) deals with data from external sources, basically anything ADO.NET can connect to. Any class that implements IEnumerable<T> or IOueryable<T> (in the System.Linq namespace) can be queried with SQOs. The LINQ to ADO.NET functionality can be achieved by using the System.Data.Linq namespace.

LINQ to XML is a comprehensive API for in-memory XML programming. Like the rest of LINQ, it includes SQOs, and it can also be used in concert with LINQ to ADO.NET, but its primary purpose is to unify and simplify the kinds of things that disparate XML tools, such as XQuery, XPath, and XSLT, are typically used to do. The LINQ to XML functionality can be achieved by using the System.Xml.Linq namespace.

> **Note** LINQ on the .NET Compact Framework includes a subset of the desktop LINQ features. One of the differences between LINQ on the .NET Framework and LINQ on the .NET Compact Framework is that on the .NET Compact Framework, only SQOs are supported. LINQ to DataSets and LINQ to DataTables are supported, and LINQ to XML is also supported except for XPath extensions.

In this chapter, we'll work with the techniques LINQ to Objects, LINQ to SQL, and LINQ to DataSets, since they're most closely related to the C# 2012 database programming we've covered in this book.

LINQ Project Structure

Visual Studio 2012 allows you to use LINQ queries. To create a LINQ project, follow these steps:

1. Open Visual Studio 2012 and select File ➤ New ➤ Project.

2. In the New Project dialog box that appears, by default .NET Framework 4.5 is chosen in the list of available .NET Framework versions supported by Visual Studio 2012. Select the type of project you want the LINQ feature to be part of. For this example, we will be using a Windows Forms Application project.

3. Specify the name Chapter18 for the chosen project, and click OK. A new Windows Forms application named Chapter18 will be created. Select the project named Chapter18 underneath the solution and rename it to Linq. Save all the changes.

4. Open the References folder in Solution Explorer. You should see Linq-related assembly references added by default, as shown in Figure 18-2.

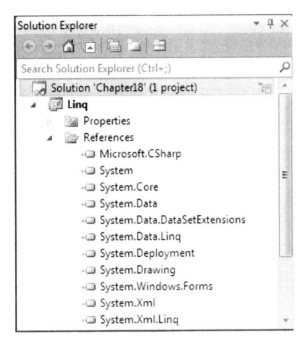

Figure 18-2. *LINQ references*

Now you are ready to work with a LINQ project, and all you need to do is add the code functionality and required namespaces to the project and test the application. Let's begin using LINQ.

Using LINQ to Objects

The term LINQ to Objects refers to the use of LINQ queries to access in-memory data structures. You can query any type that supports IEnumerable<T>. This means you can use LINQ queries not only with user-defined lists, arrays, dictionaries, and so on, but also in conjunction with .NET Framework APIs that return collections. For example, you can use the System.Reflection classes to return information about types stored in a specified assembly and then filter those results by using LINQ. Or you can import text files into enumerable data structures and compare the contents to other files, extract lines or parts of lines, group matching lines from several files into a new collection, and so on. LINQ queries offer three main advantages over traditional foreach loops:

- They are more concise and readable, especially when filtering multiple conditions.

- They provide powerful filtering, ordering, and grouping capabilities with a minimum of application code.

- They can be ported to other data sources with little or no modification.

In general, the more complex the operation you want to perform on the data, the greater the benefit you will realize by using LINQ as opposed to traditional iteration techniques.

Try It: Coding a Simple LINQ to Objects Query

In this exercise, you'll create a Windows Forms application that has one TextBox. The application will retrieve and display some names from an array of strings in a TextBox control by using Linq to Objects.

1. Right-click Form1.cs in the Chapter18 solution, select the Rename option, and rename the form to LinqToObjects.

2. Select the LinqToObjects form by clicking the form's title bar, and set the Size property's Width to 308 and Height to 311.

3. Drag a TextBox control onto the form, and position it toward the center of the form. Select this TextBox, navigate to the Properties window, and set the following properties:

   - Set the Name property to txtDisplay.

   - For the Size property, set Width to 244 and Height to 216.

   - Set the Multiline property to True.

4. Now your LinqToObjects form in the Design view should look like Figure 18-3.

Figure 18-3. The Design view of the LinqToObjects form

5. Double-click the empty surface of the LinqToObjects.cs form, and it will open the code editior window, showing the LinqToObject_Load event. Place the code in Listing 18-1 in the LinqToObjects_Load event.

Listing 18-1. `LinqToObjects.cs`

```
//Define string array
string[] names = { "Life is Beautiful",
                   "Arshika Agarwal",
                   "Seven Pounds",
                   "Rupali Agarwal",
                   "Pearl Solutions",
                   "Vamika Agarwal",
                   "Vidya Vrat Agarwal",
                   "Lionbridge Technologies"
                 };

//Linq query
IEnumerable<string> namesOfPeople = from name in names
                                    where name.Length <= 16
                                    select name;

foreach (var name in namesOfPeople)
{
    txtDisplay.AppendText(name+"\n");
}
```

6. Run the program by pressing Ctrl+F5, and you should see the results shown in Figure 18-4.

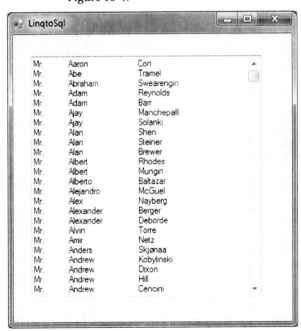

Figure 18-4. Retrieving names from a string array using LINQ to Objects

How It Works

You declare a string array called names.

```
string[] names = {"Life is Beautiful",
                  "Arshika Agarwal",
                  "Seven Pounds",
                  "Rupali Agarwal",
                  "Pearl Solutions",
                  "Vamika Agarwal",
                  "Vidya Vrat Agarwal",
                  "Lionbridge Technologies" };
```

To retrieve names from the string array, you query the string array using IEnumerable<string> and also loop through the names array with the help of foreach using the LINQ to Objects query syntax.

```
IEnumerable<string> namesOfPeople = from name in names
                        where name.Length <= 16
                        select name; foreach (var name in namesOfPeople)
```

Using LINQ to SQL

LINQ to SQL is a facility for managing and accessing relational data as objects. It's logically similar to ADO.NET in some ways, but it views data from a more abstract perspective that simplifies many operations. It connects to a database, converts LINQ constructs into SQL, submits the SQL, transforms results into objects, and even tracks changes and automatically requests database updates.

A simple LINQ query requires three things:

- Entity classes

- A data context

- A LINQ query

Try It: Coding a Simple LINQ to SQL Query

In this exercise, you'll use LINQ to SQL to retrieve all contact details from the AdventureWorks Person.Contact table.

1. Navigate to Solution Explorer, right-click the Linq project, and select Add ➤ Windows Form. In the opened Add New Item dialog, make sure Windows Form is selected and then rename Form1.cs to LinqToSql. Click Add.

2. Select the LinqToSql form by clicking the form's title bar, and set the Size property's Width to 355 and Height to 386.

3. Drag a TextBox control onto the form, and position it toward the center of the form. Select this TextBox, navigate to the Properties window, and set the following properties:

   - Set the Name property to txtLinqToSql.

   - Set the Multiline property to True.

- Set the ScrollBars property to Vertical.

4. For the Size property, set Width to 315 and Height to 320. Now your LinqToSql form in the Design view should look like Figure 18-5.

Figure 18-5. *The Design view of the LinqToSql form*

5. Before you begin coding the functionality, you must add the required assembly references. LinqToSql will require an assembly reference of `System.Data.Linq` to be added to the Linq project. To do so, select References, right-click, and choose Add Reference. From the opened Reference Manager dialog, scroll down to the assembly list, and select System.Data.Linq, as shown in Figure 18-6. Click OK.

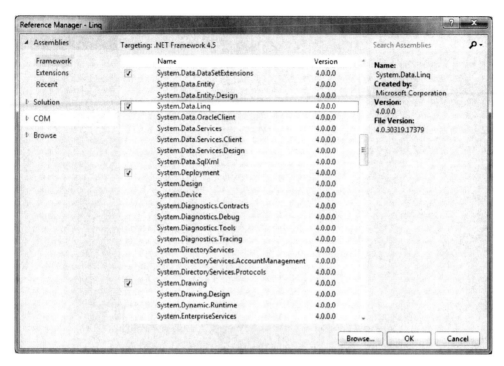

Figure 18-6. Adding References to Linq assemblies.

6.   Open the newly added form LinqToSql.cs in the Code view. Add the code shown in Listing 18-2 in LinqToSql.cs.

Listing 18-2. LinqToSql.cs

```
// Must add these two namespaces for LinqToSql
using System.Data.Linq;
using System.Data.Linq.Mapping;

[Table(Name = "Person.Person")]
      public class Contact
      {
          [Column]
          public string Title;
          [Column]
          public string FirstName;
          [Column]
          public string LastName;
      }

       private void LinqToSql_Load(object sender, EventArgs e)
       {
           // connection string
```

```
        string connString = @"server = .\sql2012;integrated security = true;
                    database = AdventureWorks";

        try
        {
            // Create data context
            DataContext db = new DataContext(connString);

            // Create typed table
            Table<Contact> contacts = db.GetTable<Contact>();

            // Query database
            var contactDetails =
                from c in contacts
                where c.Title == "Mr."
                orderby c.FirstName
                select c;

            // Display contact details
            foreach (var c in contactDetails)
            {
                txtLinqtoSql.AppendText(c.Title);
                txtLinqtoSql.AppendText("\t");
                txtLinqtoSql.AppendText(c.FirstName);
                txtLinqtoSql.AppendText("\t");
                txtLinqtoSql.AppendText(c.LastName);
                txtLinqtoSql.AppendText("\n");
            }
        }

        catch (Exception ex)
        {
            MessageBox.Show(ex.Message);
        }
    }
```

7. Now, to set the LinqToSql form as the start-up form, open `Program.cs` in the code editor, and modify `Application.Run(new LinqToObjects());` to be `Application.Run(new LinqToSql());`.

8. Build the solution, and then run the program by pressing Ctrl+F5; you should see the results shown in Figure 18-7.

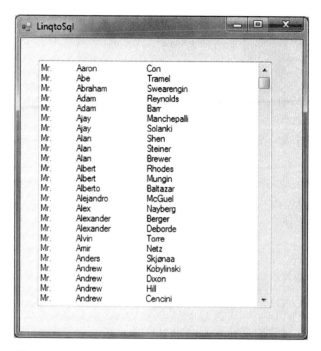

Figure 18-7. Retrieving contact details with LINQ to SQL

How It Works

You define an *entity class*, Contact.

```
[Table(Name = "Person.Person")]
    public class Contact
    {
        [Column]
        public string Title;
        [Column]
        public string FirstName;
        [Column]
        public string LastName;
    }
```

Entity classes provide objects in which LINQ stores data from data sources. They're like any other C# class, but LINQ defines attributes that tell it how to use the class.

The [Table] attribute marks the class as an entity class and has an optional Name property that can be used to give the name of a table, which defaults to the class name. That's why you name the class Contact rather than Person.Contact.

```
[Table(Name = "Person.Contact")]
public class Contact
```

Next you'd have to change the typed table definition to

```
Table<Contact> contacts = db.GetTable<Contact>();
```

To be consistent the [Column] attribute marks a field as one that will hold data from a table. You can declare fields in an entity class that don't map to table columns, and LINQ will just ignore them, but those decorated with the [Column] attribute must be of types compatible with the table columns they map to. (Note that since SQL Server table and column names aren't case sensitive, the default names do not have to be identical in case to the names used in the database.)

You create a *data context.*

```
// Create data context
DataContext db = new DataContext(connString);
```

A data context does what an ADO.NET connection does, but it also does things that a data provider handles. It not only manages the connection to a data source but also translates LINQ requests (expressed in SQO) into SQL, passes the SQL to the database server, and creates objects from the result set.

You create a *typed table.*

```
// Create typed table
Table<Contact> contacts = db.GetTable<Contact>();
```

A typed table is a collection (of type System.Data.Linq.Table<T>) whose elements are of a specific type. The GetTable method of the DataContext class tells the data context to access the results and indicates where to put them. Here, you get all the rows (but only three columns) from the Person.Contact table, and the data context creates an object for each row in the contacts typed table.

You declare a C# 2012 *implicitly typed local variable,* contactDetails, of type var.

```
// Query database
var contactDetails =
```

An implicitly typed local variable is just what its name implies. When C# sees the var type, it infers the type of the local variable based on the type of the expression in the initializer to the right of the = sign.

You initialize the local variable with a *query expression.*

```
from c in contacts
where c.Title == "Mr."
orderby c.FirstName
select c;
```

A query expression is composed of a from clause and a *query body.* You use the WHERE condition in the query body here. The from clause declares an iteration variable, c, to be used to iterate over the result of the expression, contacts (that is, over the typed table you earlier created and loaded). In each iteration, it will select the rows that meet the WHERE clause (here, the title must be "Mr.").

Finally, you loop through the custs collection and display each customer.

```
// Display contact details
foreach (var c in contactDetails)
{
    txtLinqtoSql.AppendText(c.Title);
    txtLinqtoSql.AppendText("\t");
    txtLinqtoSql.AppendText(c.FirstName);
    txtLinqtoSql.AppendText("\t");
    txtLinqtoSql.AppendText(c.LastName);
    txtLinqtoSql.AppendText("\n");
```

```
}
```

Despite the new C# 2008 features and terminology, this will still feel familiar. Once you get the hang of it, it's an appealing alternative for coding queries. You basically code a query expression instead of SQL to populate a collection that you can iterate through with a foreach statement. However, you provide a connection string but don't explicitly open or close a connection. Further, no command, data reader, or indexer is required. You don't even need the System.Data or System.Data.SqlClient namespace to access SQL Server.

Pretty cool, isn't it?

Using LINQ to XML

LINQ to XML provides an in-memory XML programming API that integrates XML querying capabilities into C# 2012 to take advantage of the LINQ framework and add query extensions specific to XML. LINQ to XML provides the query and transformation power of XQuery and XPath integrated into .NET.

From another perspective, you can also think of LINQ to XML as a full-featured XML API comparable to a modernized, redesigned SystemXml API plus a few key features from XPath and XSLT. LINQ to XML provides facilities to edit XML documents and element trees in memory, as well as streaming facilities. Figure 18-8 shows a sample XML document.

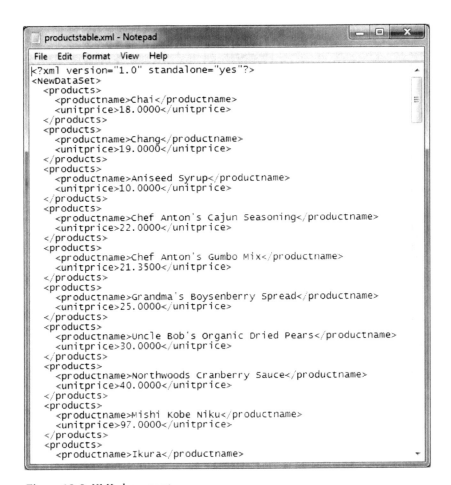

Figure 18-8. XML document

Try It: Coding a Simple LINQ to XML Query

In this exercise, you'll use LINQ to XML to retrieve element values from an XML document.

1. Navigate to Solution Explorer, right-click the Linq project, and select Windows Form. In the opened Add New Item dialog, make sure Windows Form is selected, and then rename Form1.cs to LinqToXml. Click Add.

2. Select the LinqToXml form by clicking the form's title bar, and set the Size property's Width to 377 and Height to 356.

3. Drag a TextBox control onto the form, and position it at toward the center of the form. Select this TextBox, navigate to the Properties window, and set the following properties:

- Set the Name property to txtLinqToXml.

- Set the Multiline property to True.

- Set the ScrollBars property to Vertical.

- For the Size property, set Width to 340 and Height to 298.

4. Now your LinqToXml form in the Design view should look like Figure 18-9.

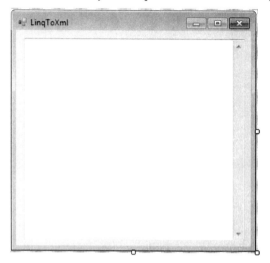

Figure 18-9. The Design view of the LinqToXml form

5. Open the newly added form LinqToXml.cs in code view. Add the code shown in Listing 18-3 in LinqToXml.cs.

Listing 18-3. LinqToXml.cs

```
using System.Xml.Linq;
//Load the productstable.xml in memory
XElement doc = XElement.Load(@"C:\VidyaVrat\C#2012 and SQL
2012\Chapter18\Code\Linq\productstable.xml");

//Query xml doc
var products = from prodname in doc.Descendants("products")
               select prodname.Value;

//Display details
foreach (var prodname in products)
{
    txtLinqToXml.AppendText("Product's Detail= ");
    txtLinqToXml.AppendText(prodname);
    txtLinqToXml.AppendText("\n");
}
```

▪ **Note** We have specified the productstable.xml file, which is located in a specific location on our machine; you can use another XML file path based on your machine and XML file availability. The productstable.xml file is also available with the source code for this chapter.

---

6. Now, to set the LinqToSql form as the start-up form, open Program.cs in the code editor, and modify the

    ```
    Application.Run(new LinqToSql());
    ```

    to appear as:

    ```
    Application.Run(new LinqToXml());.
    ```

    Build solution, and then run the program by pressing Ctrl+F5; you should see the results shown in Figure 18-10.

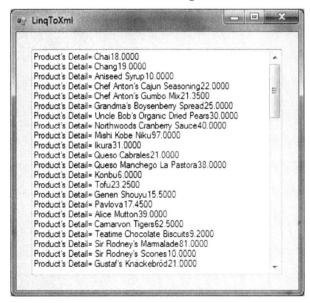

Figure 18-10. Retrieving product details with LINQ to XML

How It Works

You specify the following statement using XElement of System.Linq.Xml to load the XML doc in memory.

```
XElement doc = XElement.Load(@"C:\VidyaVrat\C#2012 and SQL
2012\Chapter18\Code\Linq\productstable.xml ");
```

You also write the following statement to query the XML doc, where the Descendents method will return the values of the descendant elements for the specified element of the XML document.

```
var products = from prodname in doc.Descendants("products") select prodname.Value;
```

Summary

In this chapter, we covered the essentials of using LINQ for simple queries. I introduced you to the three flavors of LINQ, mainly LINQ to Objects, LINQ to SQL, and LINQ to XML. In the next chapter, I will cover the ADO.NET Entity Framework.

CHAPTER 19

Using the ADO.NET Entity Framework

Many database developers thought that database APIs were mature enough with the release of ADO.NET 2.0 and LINQ, but these data access APIs continued to evolve. Data access APIs are reasonably straightforward to use, and they let you simulate the same kinds of data structures and relationships that exist in relational databases.

However, you don't interact with data in data sets or data tables in the same way you do with data in database tables. The differences between the relational model of data and the object-oriented model of programming are considerable, and ADO.NET 2.0 and LINQ do relatively little to reduce impedance between the two models.

With the release of .NET Framework 4.5 and Visual Studio 2011, a new version of ADO.NET Entity Framework 5.0 was introduced. This chapter will introduce you to the ADO.NET Entity Framework 5.0 data model, also known as the Entity Data Model (EDM).

EDM is Microsoft's way of implementing object-relational mapping (ORM). ORM is a way of processing and mapping relational data into a collection of objects, called *entities*. You will learn more about it, including the advantages of this approach, in this chapter.

In this chapter, I'll cover the following:

- Understanding ADO.NET Entity Framework 5.0

- Understanding the Entity Data Model

- Working with the Entity Data Model

Understanding ADO.NET Entity Framework 5.0

The vision behind ADO.NET Entity Framework (EF) 5.0 is to extend the level of abstraction for database programming and completely remove the impedance mismatch between data models and development languages that programmers use to write database-oriented software applications.

ADO.NET EF 5.0 allows developers to focus on data through an object model instead of through the traditional logical/relational data model, helping abstract the logical data schema into a conceptual model, a mapping layer, and a logical layer to allow interaction with that model through a new data provider called EntityClient.

In this chapter, I will review the purpose of each of these layers.

ADO.NET EF 5.0 allows developers to write less data access code, reduces maintenance, and abstracts the structure of the data into a more business-friendly manner. It can also help reduce the number of compile-time errors since it generates strongly typed classes from the conceptual model.

ADO.NET EF 5.0 generates a conceptual model that developers can write code against using a new data provider called EntityClient, as mentioned previously. EntityClient follows a model similar to familiar ADO.NET objects, using `EntityConnection` and `EntityCommand` objects to return an `EntityDataReader`.

Understanding the Entity Data Model

The core of ADO.NET EF 3.5 is in its Entity Data Model. ADO.NET EF 3.5 supports a logical store model that represents the relational schema from a database. A relational database often stores data in a different format from what the application can use. This typically forces developers to retrieve the data in the same structure as that contained in the database. Developers then often feed the data into business entities that are more suited for handling business rules. ADO.NET EF 5.0 bridges this gap between data models using mapping layers. There are three layers active in ADO.NET EF 5.0's model.

- Conceptual layer

- Mapping layer

- Logical layer

These three layers allow data to be mapped from a relational database to a more object-oriented business model. ADO.NET EF 3.5 defines these layers using XML files. These XML files provide a level of abstraction so developers can program against the OO conceptual model instead of the traditional relational data model.

The conceptual model is defined in an XML file using Conceptual Schema Definition Language (CSDL). CSDL defines the entities and the relationships as the application's business layer knows them. The logical model, which represents the database schema, is defined in an XML file using Store Schema Definition Language (SSDL). The mapping layer, which is defined using Mapping Schema Language (MSL), maps the other two layers. This mapping is what allows developers to code against the conceptual model and have those instructions mapped into the logical model.

Working with the Entity Data Model

Most applications running today cannot exist without having a database at the back end. The application and the database are highly dependent on each other; that is, they are tightly coupled, and so it becomes so obvious that any change made either in the application or in the database will have a huge impact on the other end; tight coupling is always two-way, and altering one side will require changes to be in sync with the other side. If changes are not reflected properly, the application will not function in the desired manner, and the system will break down.

Let's take a look at tight coupling by considering the following code segment, which you used in Chapter 13 as part of Listing 13-3:

```
// Create connection
SqlConnection conn = new SqlConnection(@"
                    server = .\sql2012;
                    integrated security = true;
                    database = AdventureWorks");

// Create command
string sql = @"select Name,ProductNumber
            from Production.Product";
SqlCommand cmd = new SqlCommand(sql, conn);
txtReader.AppendText("Command created and connected.\n\n");
```

```
try
{
    // Open connection
    conn.Open();

    // Execute query via ExecuteReader
    SqlDataReader rdr = cmd.ExecuteReader();
}
```

Assume you have deployed the preceding code into production along with the database, which has the column names as specified in the select query. Later, the database administrator (DBA) decides to change the column names in all the tables to implement new database policies: the DBA modifies the Production.Product table and changes the Name column to ProductName and the ProductNumber column to ProductSerialNumber.

After these database changes are made, the only way to prevent the application from breaking is by modifying all the code segments in the source code that refer to the Name and ProductName columns, rebuilding, retesting, and deploying the whole application again. So, the modified code segment in the preceding code will appear as follows:

```
// Create command
string sql = @"select ProductName, ProductSerialNumber
               from Production.Product";
```

Though on the surface it seems not so difficult to make such changes, if you factor in the possibility that there might be many database-related code segments that require modification of the column names according to the new column naming scheme, this can end up being a tedious and difficult approach to upgrade an application so it can work with the modified database.

With ADO.NET EF 5.0's Entity Data Model, Microsoft has made entity-relationship modeling executable. Microsoft achieved this by a combination of XML schema files and ADO.NET EF 5.0 APIs. The schema files are used to define a conceptual layer to expose the data store's schema (for example, the schema for a SQL Server 2012 database) and to create a map between the two. ADO.NET EF 5.0 allows you to write your programs against classes that are generated from the conceptual schema. The EDM then takes care of all of the translations as you extract data from the database by allowing you to interact with that relational database in an object-oriented way.

The EDM makes it possible for the client application and the database schema to evolve independently in a loosely coupled fashion without affecting or breaking each other.

The EDM of ADO.NET 5.0 Entity Framework provides a conceptual view of the database schema that is used by the application. This conceptual view is described as an XML mapping file in the application. The XML mapping file maps the entity properties and associated relationships to the database tables.

This mapping is the magic wand that abstracts the application from the changes made to the relational database schema. So, rather than modifying all the database-oriented code segments in an application to accommodate changes made in the database schema, you just need to modify the XML mapping file in such a way that it reflects all the changes made to the database schema. In other words, the solution offered by ADO.NET 5.0 EDM is to modify the XML mapping file to reflect the schema change without changing any source code.

Try It: Creating an Entity Data Model

In this exercise, you will see how to create an EDM.

1. Create a new Windows Forms Application project named Chapter19. When Solution Explorer opens, save the solution.

2. Rename the Chapter19 project to EntityFramework.

3. Right-click the project and select Add ➤ New Item; from the provided Visual Studio templates, choose ADO.NET Entity Data Model, and name it AWCurrencyModel.edmx; your screen should look like Figure 19-1. Click Add.

Figure 19-1. Adding an ADO.NET Entity Data Model

4. The Entity Data Model Wizard will start, with the Choose Model Contents screen appearing first. Select the "Generate from database" option, as shown in Figure 19-2. Click Next.

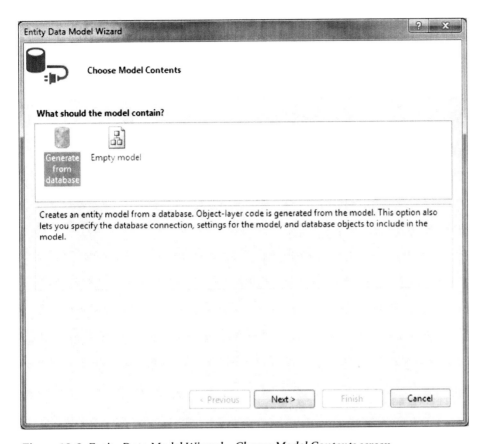

Figure 19-2. Entity Data Model Wizard—Choose Model Contents screen

5. The Choose Your Data Connection screen appears next, as shown in Figure 19-3. Click the New Connection button.

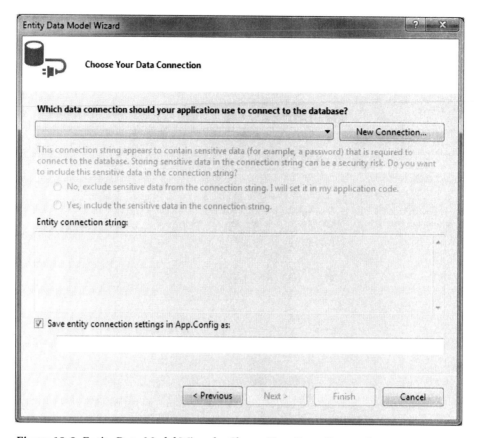

Figure 19-3. Entity Data Model Wizard—Choose Your Data Connection screen

6. The Choose Data Source dialog box appears. Select Microsoft SQL Server from the "Data source" list, as shown in Figure 19-4. Click Continue.

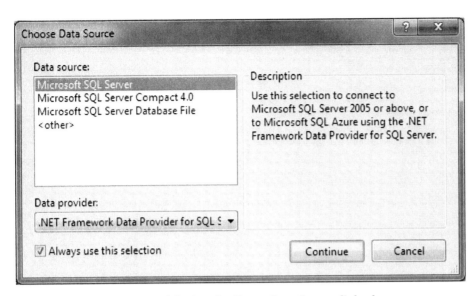

Figure 19-4. Entity Data Model Wizard—Choose Data Source dialog box

7. Next, the Connection Properties dialog box appears. Enter .\SQL2012 in the
   "Server name" list box and ensure that the Use Windows Authentication radio
   button is selected. From the list box provided below the "Select or enter a
   database name" radio button, select Northwind. Your dialog box should look
   like Figure 19-5. Click the Test Connection button.

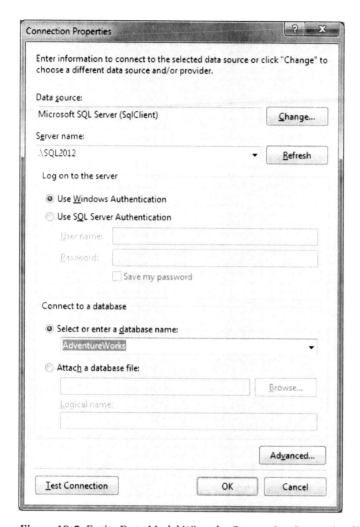

Figure 19-5. Entity Data Model Wizard—Connection Properties dialog box

8. A message box should flash showing the message "Test connection succeeded." Click OK. Now click OK in the Connection Properties dialog box.

9. The Choose Your Data Connection window appears, again displaying all the settings you've made so far. Ensure the check box "Save entity connection settings in App.config as" is selected and has AWCurrencyEntities as a value entered in it, as shown in Figure 19-6. Click Next.

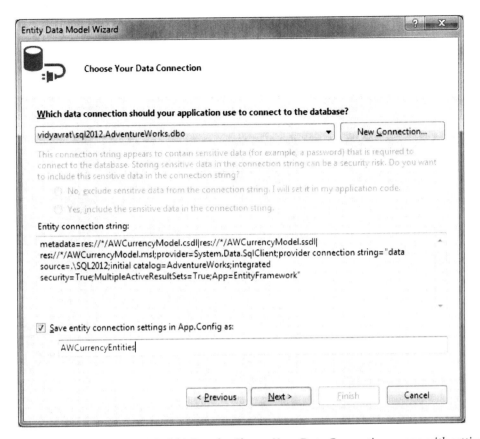

Figure 19-6. Entity Data Model Wizard—Choose Your Data Connection screen with settings displayed

10. The Choose Your Database Objects screen now appears. Expand the Tables node. If any of the table or tables are selected, remove all the check marks except for the ones beside the Sales.Currency table. Also, remove the check marks from the Views and Stored Procedures node. The screen will look like Figure 19-7. Click Finish.

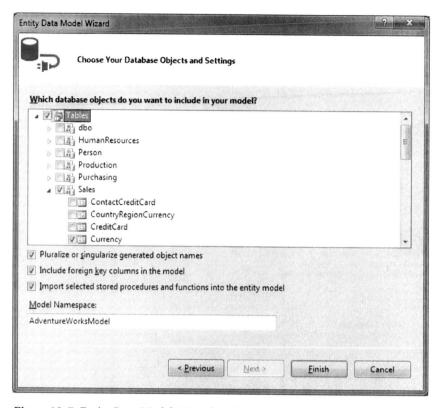

Figure 19-7. Entity Data Model Wizard—Choose Your Database Objects screen

11. Navigate to Solution Explorer, and you will see that a new
     AWCurrencyModel.edmx object has been added to the project, as shown in
     Figure 19-8.

Figure 19-8. Solution Explorer displaying the generated Entity Data Model

12. Double-click `AWCurrencyModel.edmx` to view the generated Entity Data Model in the Design view. It should look like Figure 19-9.

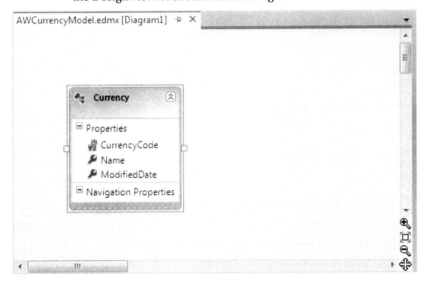

Figure 19-9. Entity Data Model in the Design view

13. The generated Entity Data Model also has an XML mapping associated with it especially for its `EntityContainer` and `EntitySets`. To view the XML mapping, navigate to Solution Explorer, right-click `AWCurrencyModel.edmx`, and choose the Open With option. From the dialog box that appears, select XML (Text)

Editor, and click OK. Notice the highlighted text in the mapping shown in Figure 19-10.

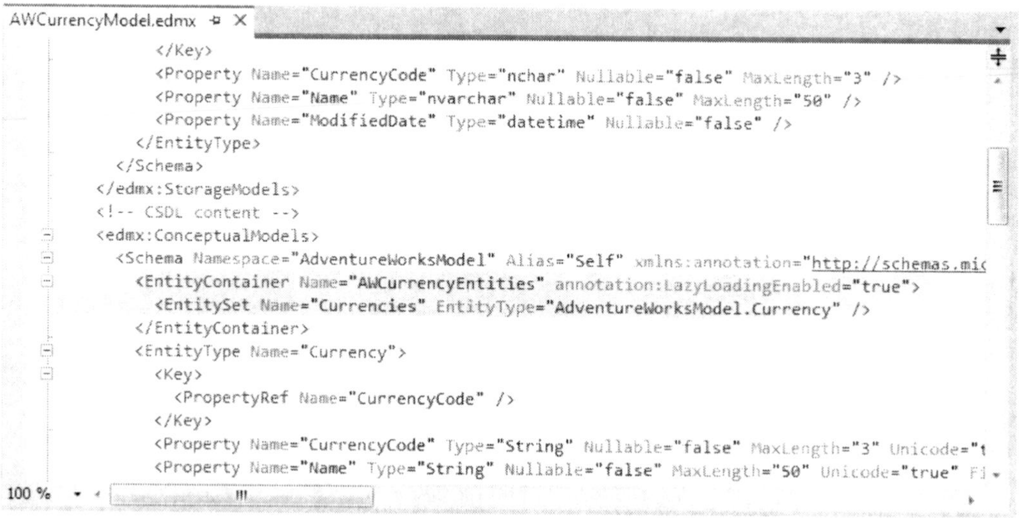

```
AWCurrencyModel.edmx  ⊕  ✕
            </Key>
            <Property Name="CurrencyCode" Type="nchar" Nullable="false" MaxLength="3" />
            <Property Name="Name" Type="nvarchar" Nullable="false" MaxLength="50" />
            <Property Name="ModifiedDate" Type="datetime" Nullable="false" />
          </EntityType>
        </Schema>
      </edmx:StorageModels>
      <!-- CSDL content -->
      <edmx:ConceptualModels>
        <Schema Namespace="AdventureWorksModel" Alias="Self" xmlns:annotation="http://schemas.mic
          <EntityContainer Name="AWCurrencyEntities" annotation:LazyLoadingEnabled="true">
            <EntitySet Name="Currencies" EntityType="AdventureWorksModel.Currency" />
          </EntityContainer>
          <EntityType Name="Currency">
            <Key>
              <PropertyRef Name="CurrencyCode" />
            </Key>
            <Property Name="CurrencyCode" Type="String" Nullable="false" MaxLength="3" Unicode="t
            <Property Name="Name" Type="String" Nullable="false" MaxLength="50" Unicode="true" Fi
100 %   ▾  ◂         III                           ▸
```

Figure 19-10. XML mapping associated with the Entity Data Model

14. Switch to Solution Explorer, and rename Form1 to PublishCurrency.cs.

15. Drag a TextBox control to the form, and position it toward the center of the form. Select this TextBox control, navigate to the Properties window, and set the following properties:

   • Set the Name property to txtCurrency.

   • For the Location property, set X to 12 and Y to 12.

   • Set the Multiline property to True.

   • Set the ScrollBars property to Vertical.

   • For the Size property, set Width to 518 and Height to 247.

   • Leave the Text property blank.

16. Now your PublishCurrency form in the Design view should like Figure 19-11.

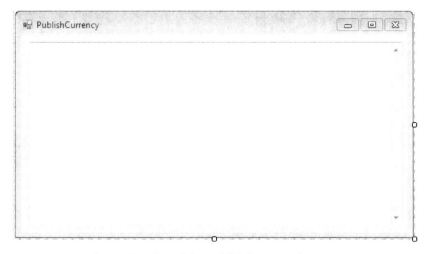

Figure 19-11. The Design view of the PublishCurrency form

17. Double-click the empty surface of the form, and it will open the code editor window, showing the PublishCurrency_Load event. Place the code listed in Listing 19-1 into the load event code template.

Listing 19-1. Using the Entity Data Model

```
AWCurrencyEntities currContext = new AWCurrencyEntities();

foreach (var cr in currContext.Currencies)
{
    txtCurrency .AppendText(cr.ModifiedDate.ToString());

    txtCurrency.AppendText("\t\t");
    txtCurrency.AppendText(cr.CurrencyCode.ToString());

    txtCurrency.AppendText("\t\t");
    txtCurrency.AppendText(cr.Name.ToString());
    txtCurrency.AppendText("\t");
    txtCurrency.AppendText("\n");
}
```

18. Build the solution, and run the project. When the PublishCurrency form appears, you will see all the currencies listed in the TextBox. The screen shown in Figure 19-12 should display.

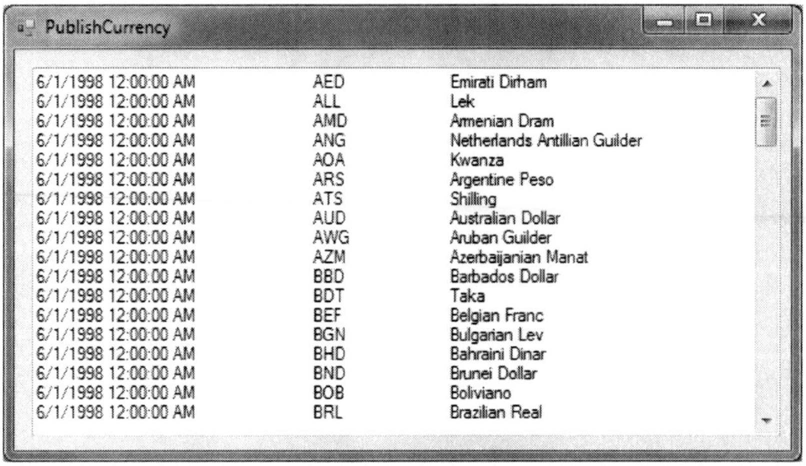

Figure 19-12. Displaying the PublishCurrency form

How It Works

Because you are working with an Entity Data Model, you do not need to deal with `SqlConnection`, `SqlCommand`, and so forth. Here you create an object referencing the `EntityContainer` named `AWCurrencyEntities`, which refers to the entire connection string that is stored in the `App.config` file.

`AWCurrencyEntities currContext = new AWCurrencyEntities();`

After specifying the object to `EntityContainer`, it's time to loop through the object set that is composed of `EntityContainer.EntitySet`, thus including the name of the `EntityContainer` object, which represents the `EntityContainer`, suffixed with `EntitySet`.

■ **Note** The `EntityContainer` element is named after the database schema, and all "entity sets" that should be logically grouped together are contained within an `EntityContainer` element. An `EntitySet` represents the corresponding table in the database. You can explore the names of your `EntityModel` objects under the `ConceptualModel` element of the `.edmx` file, as shown in Figure 19-10.

```
foreach (var cr in currContext.Currencies)
{
    txtCurrency .AppendText(cr.ModifiedDate.ToString());

    txtCurrency.AppendText("\t\t");
    txtCurrency.AppendText(cr.CurrencyCode.ToString());

    txtCurrency.AppendText("\t\t");
    txtCurrency.AppendText(cr.Name.ToString());
```

```
                  txtCurrency.AppendText("\t");
                  txtCurrency.AppendText("\n");
          }
```

As you can see, the `EntityContainer` object exposes the columns names through IntelliSense. Or, if you put a . (dot), you will see all the fields of the Sales.Currency table, which is simpler than doing the DataReader's `rdr[0], rdr[1]` technique, as you experimented with in the previous chapter. In other words, the Entity Framework has "mapped" each record from the Sales.Currency table into an object. The properties have the same names as the columns of the table, but working with an object fits the object-oriented coding style.

Try It: Schema Abstraction Using an Entity Data Model

In the previous exercise, you created an Entity Data Model named AWCurrencyModel (because this is the name of your `.edmx` file); in this exercise, you will see how this Entity Data Model will help developers achieve schema abstraction and modify the database without touching the data access code throughout the project or in the data access layer (DAL). That is, the developer can simply remove the table reference from the model and then add it back. The columns would be realigned, and the code could then be updated to reference the corresponding properties.

1. Start SQL Server Management Studio, expand the Databases node, expand the AdventureWorks database node, and then expand the Tables node. In the list of tables, expand the Sales.Currency node and then expand the `Columns` folder.

2. Select the Name column, right-click, and select the Rename option. Rename the Name column to CurrencyName.

3. Select the ModifiedDate column, right-click, and select the Rename option. Rename the ModifiedDate column to ModifiedCurrencyDate.

4. So, basically, we added the Currency term in these two columns. Now exit from SQL Server Management Studio by selecting File ➤ Exit.

5. As you can imagine, our PublishCurrency form and the database have a column name mismatch, so we will now view the exception that the application will report because of this recent column name change. To do so, we will add a TRY…CATCH block to report the issue. Modify the PublishCurrency.cs code to look like Listing 19-2.

Listing 19-2. Adding TRY…CATCH to PublishCurrency.cs to Show Exception Details

```
try
{       AWCurrencyEntities currContext = new AWCurrencyEntities();

            foreach (var cr in currContext.Currencies)
            {
                txtCurrency .AppendText(cr.ModifiedDate.ToString());

                txtCurrency.AppendText("\t\t");
                txtCurrency.AppendText(cr.CurrencyCode.ToString());

                txtCurrency.AppendText("\t\t");
```

```
                        txtCurrency.AppendText(cr.Name.ToString());
                        txtCurrency.AppendText("\t");
                        txtCurrency.AppendText("\n");
        }
    }

    catch(Exception ex)
    {
                MessageBox.Show(ex.Message + ex.StackTrace +
                    ex.InnerException);
    }
```

6. Now, build and run PublishCurrency by pressing Ctrl+F5. The
    PublishCurrency detail form should load and raise an exception window with
    the following message: "An error occurred while executing the command
    definition. See the inner exception for details."

7. If you look at InnerException, you will see a message that indicates the cause
    of this exception; it's because you have just renamed the Name and
    ModifiedDate columns of the Sales.Currency table. The exception details
    should look like Figure 19-13.

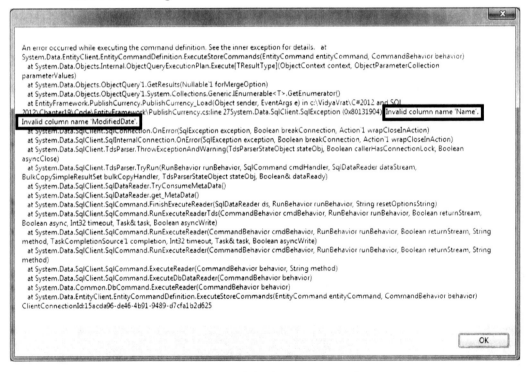

Figure 19-13. Exception details to reflect invalid column name(s) after recent renaming

8. Click OK to close the exception window, and close the opened form, which will be empty because the data did not load due to an exception occurring.

9. Now you will see the advantage of entity data modeling. Assume the same issue occurred in the code you wrote in previous chapters; the only solution is to modify the column name in each and every SQL statement that maps to the table we modified. In a real-world scenario, this will not be possible, because database schema updates changes are invisible and so the Entity Data Model comes to rescue.

   To fix this application, you have to modify the XML mapping file created by the Entity Data Model, namely, the `AWCurrencyModel.edmx` file you created earlier in the chapter. To view the XML mapping, navigate to Solution Explorer, right-click`AWCurrencyModel.edmx`, and choose the Open With option. From the provided dialog box, select XML(Text) Editor, and click OK. You will see the XML mapping, as shown previously in Figure 19-10.

Note In the opened XML mapping file, navigate to the `<!-- SSDL content -->` section and modify the name in the `<Property Name="Name" Type="nvarchar" Nullable="false" MaxLength="50" />` XML tag to `CurrencyName`; the tag should appear as `<Property Name="CurrencyName" Type="nvarchar" Nullable="false" MaxLength="50" />` after the modification.

Note The logical model, which represents the database schema, is defined in an XML file using SSDL. This is why you need to modify the column names to map with the database schema.

---

10. Also, modify the `<Property Name="ModifiedDate" Type="datetime" Nullable="false" />` XML tag to `ModifiedCurrencyDate` `<Property Name="ModifiedCurrencyDate" Type="datetime" Nullable="false" />` XML tag to appear as `<Property Name="ModifiedCurrencyDate" Type="datetime" Nullable="false" />`. The modified SSDL content section with the `CurrencyName` and `ModifiedCurrencyDate` values will look like Figure 19-14.

```
AWCurrencyModel.edmx*  ₊ X
    <?xml version="1.0" encoding="utf-8"?>
  <edmx:Edmx Version="2.0" xmlns:edmx="http://schemas.microsoft.com/ado/2008/10/edmx">
    <!-- EF Runtime content -->
    <edmx:Runtime>
      <!-- SSDL content -->
      <edmx:StorageModels>
        <Schema Namespace="AdventureWorksModel.Store" Alias="Self" Provider="System.Data.SqlCli
          <EntityContainer Name="AdventureWorksModelStoreContainer">
            <EntitySet Name="Currency" EntityType="AdventureWorksModel.Store.Currency" store:Ty
          </EntityContainer>
          <EntityType Name="Currency">
            <Key>
              <PropertyRef Name="CurrencyCode" />
            </Key>
            <Property Name="CurrencyCode" Type="nchar" Nullable="false" MaxLength="3" />
            <Property Name="CurrencyName" Type="nvarchar" Nullable="false" MaxLength="50" />
            <Property Name="ModifiedCurrencyDate" Type="datetime" Nullable="false" />
          </EntityType>
        </Schema>
      </edmx:StorageModels>
        <!-- CCD1    content    -->
100 %   ▼  ◄                         ║                              ►
```

Figure 19-14. Modifying the SSDL content section

11. Now look for the `<!-- C-S mapping content -->` section and modify the
`<ScalarProperty Name="Name" ColumnName="Name" />` tag to be
`<ScalarProperty Name="Name" ColumnName="CurrencyName" />`.•

■ **Note** The conceptual model is defined in an XML file using CSDL. CSDL defines the entities and the
relationships as the application's business layer knows them. This is why you need to modify the column names to
be readable and easy to find by the entity.

---

12. Next, modify the `<ScalarProperty Name="ModifiedDate"`
`ColumnName="ModifiedDate" />` tag to appear as `<ScalarProperty`
`Name="ModifiedDate" ColumnName="ModifiedCurrencyDate" />`. The modified
C-S mapping content section with the CurrencyName and ModifiedCurrencyDate
values will look like Figure 19-15.

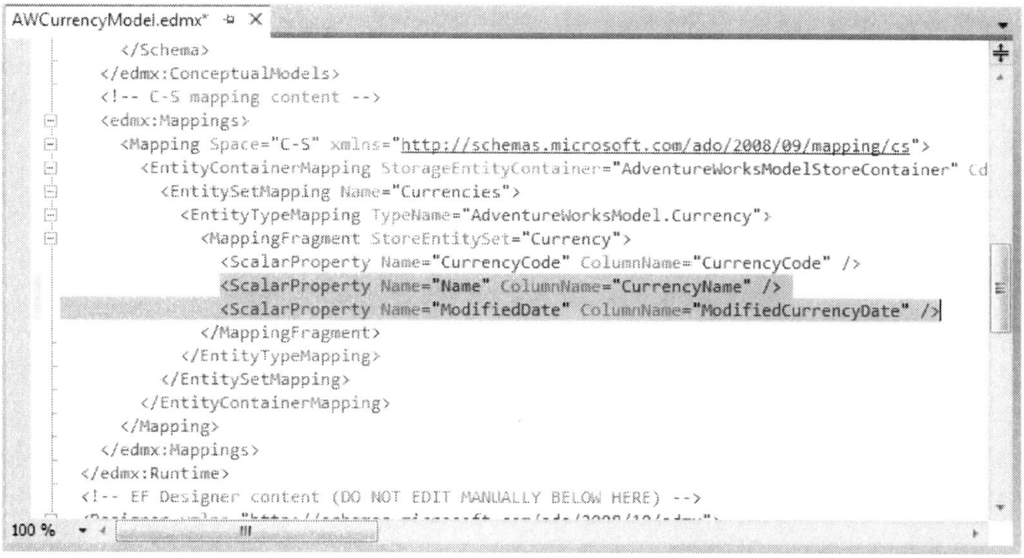

Figure 19-15. *Modifying the C-S mapping content section*

13. Now save and build the Chapter19 solution, and run the application. When the PublishCurrency form is open this should populate the TextBox with the ModifiedDate, Name, and CurrencyCode values, as shown earlier in Figure 19-12.

14. Switch back to the PublishCurrency.cs code with the foreach loop, as shown in Listing 19-2. You should still see the same column names being shown in the TextBox with the EntityContainer as cr.ModifiedDate and cr.Name, even though you have modified the column names in the AdventureWorks database's Sales.Currency table. But by taking advantage of the schema abstraction feature of the Entity Data Model, you only have to specify the updated column names in the XML mapping file under the SSDL content and C-S mapping content sections.

Summary

In this chapter, you looked at ADO.NET 5.0 Entity Data Model feature.

You also learned how schema abstraction works and how it will help you to achieve loose coupling between a database and the data access code or data access layer. In the next chapter, you will learn how to use SQL CLR objects.

CHAPTER 20

Using the CLR in SQL Server

For many years, writing business logic has been technology- and software-specific, especially in terms of databases. For example, if you wanted to create a stored procedure or other database object that required complex SQL code, the only way was to code the T-SQL logic in a database and write the calling code in a programming language like C#, as shown in previous chapters where we created a stored procedure using T-SQL in SQL Server and then wrote the calling code in C#.

This approach is still very popular, but there is an easier way that allows C# programmers to take control and code all the database-oriented objects such as stored procedures, functions, and triggers in the .NET language of their choice such as C# unlike done previously using T-SQL.

In this chapter, I'll cover the following:

- Introducing SQL CLR

- Choosing between T-SQL and SQL CLR

- Enabling SQL CLR integration

- Creating a SQL CLR stored procedure

- Deploying a SQL CLR stored procedure into SQL Server

- Executing the SQL CLR stored procedure

Introducing SQL CLR

The SQL Common Language Runtime (CLR) is a tiny version of .NET CLR that is integrated into SQL Server 2005 and newer. SQL CLR offers a choice to developers when it comes to dealing with complex business logic in conjunction with a database, especially when T-SQL makes it less than a pleasure to work with.

SQL CLR is a smaller version of .NET CLR, which mainly serves the purpose of a runtime execution engine by providing support for memory management and code execution of deployed .NET SQL CLR assemblies. An *assembly* is a .NET term that refers to a DLL or EXE file that consists of *metadata* (data about data) and a *manifest* (data about assemblies).

The following types of objects can be created with SQL CLR integration:

- Stored procedures

- User-defined aggregates

- Triggers

- User-defined types

Choosing Between T-SQL and SQL CLR

When you have two choices to implement the same functionality, one can be more advantageous than the other based on your scenario and requirements. Here are a few important points that will help you decide which to choose in what situation, T-SQL or SQL CLR:

- T-SQL is best used to perform declarative, set-based operations (select, insert, update, and delete).

- T-SQL works within a database connection, whereas SQL CLR must obtain a connection.

- T-SQL also has a procedural capability. In other words, it can perform procedural operations such as WHILE, and so on, but when it comes to feature-rich or more complex logic, T-SQL is not the best choice. In such a scenario, SQL CLR with C# allows the programmer to have better control over functionality.

- T-SQL is interpreted, whereas SQL CLR is compiled. Hence, interpreted code is slower than compiled procedural code.

- Before SQL CLR code can be executed, it requires the CLR to be loaded by the SQL Server, whereas T-SQL does not incur any such overhead.

- When any T-SQL code executes, it shares the same stack frame in memory, whereas every SQLCLR code requires its own stack frame and therefore results in larger memory allocation but better concurrent performance.

- T-SQL is composed of libraries full of data-centric functions, and hence it is better suited to set-based operations. SQL CLR is better suited to recursive, mathematical, and string manipulations types of operations.

Enabling SQL CLR Integration

After creating a database object using C#, you must enable SQL CLR in SQL Server 2012 where you would like either to use it or to deploy it. By default, this feature is turned off (config_value is set to 0); to enable it (config_value is set to 1), follow these steps:

1. Open SQL Server 2012 Management Studio; connect using Windows or SQL Authentication based on your setup type.

2. Once connected, click the New Query button, which will open a query window. Enter the following text in the query window, and notice the value of the config_value column, as shown in Figure 20-1.

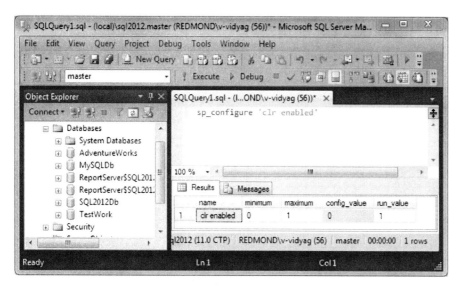

Figure 20-1. *Showing the default behavior (disabled) of SQL CLR*

3. Next, you need to enable SQL CLR, to do so; modify the code to look like Figure 20-2, and it will enable the SQL CLR integration.

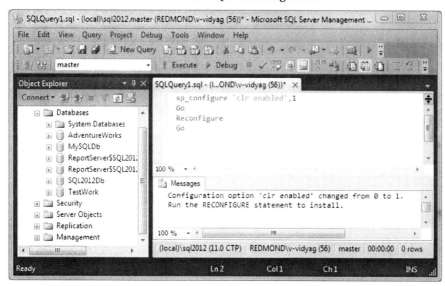

Figure 20-2. *Showing SQL CLR enabled*

Now your SQL Server is ready to execute the database objects that are built using the C# programming language, unlike T-SQL. You will do this later in this chapter.

Creating a SQL CLR Stored Procedure

Microsoft Visual Studio 2012 provides the project template and class files for various SQL Server objects such as stored procedures, triggers, functions, and so on, which you can code in C# as an assembly such as a dynamic link library (DLL).

Try It: Creating a SQL CLR Stored Procedure Using C#

In this exercise, you'll create a SQL stored procedure by adding a SQL CLR C# stored procedure item template into the SQL Server database project. The SQL CLR C# stored procedure you will create will help you insert currency data into the AdventureWorks.Sales.Currency table, as you did in Chapter 13 with Listing 13-4. But here you are using a different technique to accomplish the same task (currency insertion).

1. Create a new Windows Forms Application project named Chapter13. When Solution Explorer opens, save the solution, as shown in Figure 20-3.

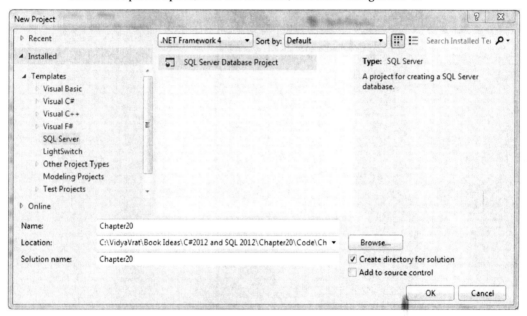

Figure 20-3. Showing the SQL Server Database Project template

2. This will load an empty project, that is, one without any .cs class file in it, as shown in Figure 20-4.

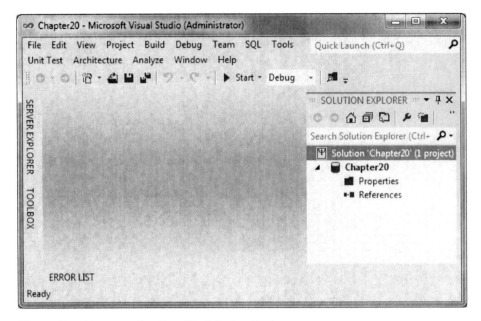

Figure 20-4. Empty project listed in Solution Explorer

3.   Right-click the Chapter20 project, choose Add ➤ New Item, and in the Add
     New Item dialog select SQL CLR Stored Procedure on the SQL CLR C# tab.
     Name it SQLCLRStoredProcedure.cs, as shown in Figure 20-5. Click Add.

Figure 20-5. *Adding a SQL CLR C# stored procedure as a new item to the project*

    4.   Your Visual Studio environment will now look like Figure 20-6.

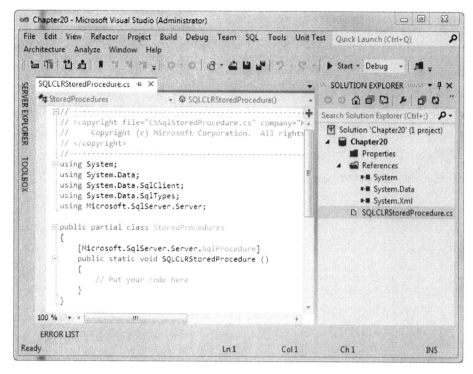

Figure 20-6. Showing Visual Studio after adding the SQL CLR C# stored procedure

5. Replace the code in the StoredProcedure class with the code in Listing 20-1.

Listing 20-1. SQLCLRStoredProcedure.cs

```csharp
[Microsoft.SqlServer.Server.SqlProcedure()]
public static void InsertCurrency_CS(SqlString currencyCode, SqlString currencyName)
{
    SqlConnection conn = null;

    try
    {
        conn = new SqlConnection(@"server = .\sql2012;integrated security = true;
            database = AdventureWorks");

        SqlCommand cmdInsertCurrency = new SqlCommand();
        cmdInsertCurrency.Connection = conn;

        SqlParameter parmCurrencyCode = new SqlParameter
                        ("@CCode", SqlDbType.NVarChar, 3);
        SqlParameter parmCurrencyName = new SqlParameter
                        ("@Name", SqlDbType.NVarChar, 50);
```

401

```
        parmCurrencyCode.Value = currencyCode;
        parmCurrencyName.Value = currencyName;

        cmdInsertCurrency.Parameters.Add(parmCurrencyCode);
        cmdInsertCurrency.Parameters.Add(parmCurrencyName);

        cmdInsertCurrency.CommandText =
            "INSERT Sales.Currency (CurrencyCode, CurrencyName, ModifiedCurrencyDate)" +
            " VALUES(@CCode, @Name, GetDate())";

        conn.Open();

        cmdInsertCurrency.ExecuteNonQuery();
    }



    catch (SqlException ex)
    {
        SqlContext.Pipe.Send("An error occured" + ex.Message + ex.StackTrace);
    }

    finally
    {
        conn.Close();
    }
}
```

6. Save the project, and build the solution. After a successful build, it will produce a Chapter20.dll file under the project's \bin\debug folder.

How It Works

Since this is a stored procedure coded in C#, it will be inserting currency data into the AdventureWorks.Sales.Currency table, which has three columns. Of those, you will be passing values for two as input parameters.

```
[Microsoft.SqlServer.Server.SqlProcedure()]
    public static void InsertCurrency_CS(SqlString currencyCode, SqlString currencyName)
```

The most important part of any database application is creating a connection and a command.

```
        SqlConnection conn = null;
        conn = new SqlConnection(@"server = .\sql2012;integrated security = true;
                            database = AdventureWorks");
        SqlCommand cmdInsertCurrency = new SqlCommand();
        cmdInsertCurrency.Connection = conn;
```

Once you have connection and command objects, you need to set the parameters that this stored procedure will be accepting.

```
SqlParameter parmCurrencyCode = new SqlParameter("@CCode", SqlDbType.NVarChar, 3);
        SqlParameter parmCurrencyName = new SqlParameter
                    ("@Name", SqlDbType.NVarChar, 50);

        parmCurrencyCode.Value = currencyCode;
        parmCurrencyName.Value = currencyName;

        cmdInsertCurrency.Parameters.Add(parmCurrencyCode);
        cmdInsertCurrency.Parameters.Add(parmCurrencyName);
```

After setting the parameters, you will set the INSERT statement, which will perform the actual task, but because you chose only two parameters for this Sales.Currency table, for the third column, which is a date column, you will pass the GetDate() function.

```
cmdInsertCurrency.CommandText ="INSERT Sales.Currency
                    (CurrencyCode, CurrencyName, ModifiedCurrencyDate)" +
                    " VALUES(@CCode, @Name, GetDate())";
```

Next, open the connection and execute the command.

```
        conn.Open();
        cmdInsertCurrency.ExecuteNonQuery();
```

The most important point to remember is that this code will actually be invoked from inside SQL Server Management Studio, so the exception handling catch block will need extra attention.

```
catch (SqlException ex)
{
    SqlContext.Pipe.Send("An error occured" + ex.Message + ex.StackTrace);
}
```

The SqlContext class allows you to invoke function to show errors in SQL Server's Error window.

Deploying a SQL CLR Stored Procedure into SQL Server

Once an assembly of a SQL CLR C# type for a particular type of database object is created, it needs to be deployed in SQL Server. Once deployed, SQL Server uses it like any other T-SQL database object.

Try It: Deploying SQL CLR C# Stored Procedure in SQL Server

In this exercise, you'll deploy the created assembly into the SQL2012Db database, and upon execution, this will insert currency into the AdventureWorks.Sales.Currency table.

1. Open SQL Server 2012 Management Studio, and connect to the SQL Server.

2. Select the SQL2012 database (if you don't have this database, you can use any database of your choice), and click New Query, which will open a new blank query window.

3. In the opened query window, insert the code in Listing 20-2.

Listing 20-2. *Deploying the Assembly into SQL Server*

```
Create Assembly SQLCLR_StoredProcedure
From
--change this path to reflect your database assebmly location
'C:\VidyaVrat\C#2012 and SQL 2012\Chapter20\Code\Chapter20\bin\Debug\Chapter20.dll'
WITH PERMISSION_SET = UNSAFE
GO

CREATE PROCEDURE dbo.InsertCurrency_CS
(
  @currCode nvarchar(3),
  @currName nvarchar(50)
)
AS EXTERNAL NAME SQLCLR_StoredProcedure.StoredProcedures.InsertCurrency_CS;
```

4.   Once code is added, click Execute or press F5. This should execute the
     command successfully. Then go to the Object Browser, select SQL2012DB,
     right-click, and choose Refresh. This will show the objects under
     Programmability and Assemblies in the Object Browser, as shown in
     Figure 20-7.

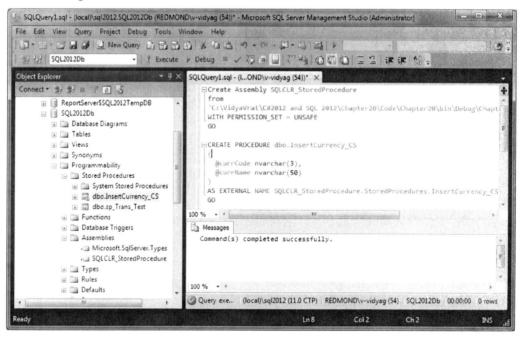

Figure 20-7. *Deploying assemblies and showing objects in Object Browser in SQL Server*

How It Works

This deployment process is a two-step process. First, you have to register an assembly (which you created in C#) with your own name in SQL Server.

```
Create Assembly SQLCLR_StoredProcedure
from
'C:\VidyaVrat\C#2012 and SQL 2012\Chapter20\Code\Chapter20\bin\Debug\Chapter20.dll'
WITH PERMISSION_SET = UNSAFE
GO
```

This PERMISSION_SET property allows the user to execute assemblies with specific code access permissions. UNSAFE enables this assembly to have unrestricted access within SQL Server.

Second, you have to create the stored procedure, which will basically invoke the stored procedure you have created from the C# assembly.

```
CREATE PROCEDURE dbo.InsertCurrency_CS
(
  @currCode nvarchar(3),
  @currName nvarchar(50)
)
AS EXTERNAL NAME SQLCLR_StoredProcedure.StoredProcedures.InsertCurrency_CS;
GO
```

The name used in CREATE PROCEDURE is the name (InsertCurrency_CS) you gave to the function in C# class (refer to Listing 20-1). Next you set the input parameters that are being passed to the C# function (refer Listing 20-1).

The external name is actually in the syntax of <SQL registered assembly>.<CS class name>.<CS function name>, so it turns out to be as follows:

```
SQLCLR_StoredProcedure.StoredProcedures.InsertCurrency_CS
```

Refer to Listings 20-1 and 20-2 for the class name, assembly name, and so on, which are in use here.

Executing the SQL CLR Stored Procedure

After deploying the assembly and creating a stored procedure, you are ready to execute this procedure from SQL 2012 and insert currency into the AdventureWorks.Sales.Currency table.

Try It: Executing the SQL CLR Stored Procedure

In this exercise, you will execute the InsertCurrency_CS stored procedure.

1. Open SQL Server Management Studio (if not already open), select SQL2012db and click the New Query button.

2. In the query window, add the code shown in Listing 20-3 to execute the procedure and add a currency.

Listing 20-3. Executing Stored Procedure to Insert Currency

```
Exec dbo.InsertCurrency_CS 'ABC','United States of America'
```

> **Note** You have to specify a unique value for the currency code. For example, I used ABC, because I know there is no such currency for United States. But If you try to enter USD or a duplicate value, you will receive a System error. If you add a duplicate value to the Sales.Currency table for the CurrencyCode column, you will get an exception, as shown in Figure 20-8.

Figure 20-8. Showing argument exception in the event of a duplicate entry

How It Works

As shown in the C# code in Listing 20-1, the insert statement accepts two input parameters, and the GetDate() method for the ModifiedCurrencyDate column will be automatically passed on each execution.

```
cmdInsertCurrency.CommandText ="INSERT Sales.Currency
(CurrencyCode, CurrencyName, ModifiedCurrencyDate)" +
  " VALUES(@CCode, @Name, GetDate())";
```

Hence, the stored procedure execution statement will look like Listing 20-3, which is passing values for both the input parameters, CurrencyCode and CurrencyName.

```
Exec dbo.InsertCurrency_CS 'ABC','United States of America'
```

Summary

In this chapter, I covered the essentials of SQL CLR integration, its advantages, and the type of objects you can create as a developer. You also learned about choosing SQL CLR over T-SQL, and vice versa. Finally, you created a SQL CLR C# stored procedure using hard-coded C# logic and keywords like try catch as a C# assembly. Then you deployed it and executed it to insert a currency. Pretty cool!

Index

CPSIA information can be obtained at www.ICGtesting.com
Printed in the USA
LVOW110744101112

306747LV00005B/23/P